248 Mentoring Webster

W9-COF-080

Praise for
With Purpose

"Here's a thought-provoking and uplifting view of working and learning in the second half of life by one of the world's true experts."

—ROBERT B. REICH, former U.S. Secretary of Labor

"Bringing together powerful stories, sage advice, and important insights, this book reveals a generation poised for its encore, ready to usher in a new era of individual and social renewal."

—MARK FREEDMAN, CEO, Civic Ventures, and author
of *Encore: Finding Work That Matters in the Second Half of Life*

"*With Purpose* is a call to change. It will show you how to use your talents to create a better life for yourself and for the people and causes that inspire you."

—ROBERT N. BUTLER, MD, founding director of
the National Institutes on Aging and Pulitzer
Prize–winning author of *Why Survive? Being Old
in America* and *The Longevity Revolution*

With Purpose

Ken Dychtwald, Ph.D.

and Daniel J. Kadlec

With Purpose

Going from Success to Significance in Work and Life

Collins

With Purpose

Going From Success to Significance in Work + Life

First Canadian edition

Published by Collins, an imprint of HarperCollins Publishers Ltd

Grateful acknowledgment is made to HarperCollins for permission to reprint material from *A Return to Love* by Marianne Williamson. © 1996 by Marianne Williamson. Published by HarperCollins Publishers. *If I Had My Life to Do Over*, a poem by Erma Bombeck, reprinted with permission from the Aaron M. Priest Literary Agency, 2008. Charts "Most Important Factors in Post-Retirement Work" and "Most Appealing Jobs in Post-Retirement" courtesy of Civic Ventures. "Sources of Happiness" data and chart courtesy of SRBI.

HarperCollins books may be purchased for educational, business, or sales promotional use through our Special Markets Department.

HarperCollins Publishers Ltd
2 Bloor Street East, 20th Floor
Toronto, Ontario, Canada
M4W 1A8

www.harpercollins.ca

Library and Archives Canada Cataloguing in Publication information is available

ISBN 978-1-55468-487-8

Printed and bound in the United States
RRD 9 8 7 6 5 4 3 2 1

Designed by Ashley Halsey

To Maddy, Casey, and Zak Dychtwald
I burst with love for each/all of you.
And from Dan:
To Kim, Lexie, Kyle, and Danielle
Nothing is possible without you.

Contents

ACKNOWLEDGMENTS

I would like to deeply thank the following very special people:

Dan Kadlec, for your extraordinary talents as a thinker, visionary, writer, storyteller, and collaborator.

Maddy Kent Dychtwald, for your unflickering radiance, limitless nourishment, and timeless beauty.

Casey Dychtwald, for your electrifying vibrancy and infectious enthusiasm.

Zak Dychtwald, for your deep thoughts and wizard wit.

Seymour and Pearl Dychtwald, for loving, supporting, and encouraging me—every day of my life.

Alan Dychtwald, my wonderful brother, confidant and lifelong best friend.

Sally and Ray Fusco, for nourishing me with respect and affection (and for the timely infusions of magical biscotti).

Richard, Linda, David, Michelle and Joel Kent, my terrific extended family.

Jane Friedman, for immediately seeing the "purpose" of this book and for lighting my fuse to write it.

Mary Ellen O'Neill, for being a truly Zen editor and for your grace, humor, wisdom, and sunshining thoughtfulness.

Elyse Pellman, for your willingness to walk, run, jump, and even fly when needed as my business partner and my dear friend.

David Baxter, for continually providing sound insight, terrific ideas, and fresh thinking to everything that I pursue.

Robyn Hamilton, for your transcendent kindness and unrivaled ability to orchestrate order from near chaos.

Kathleen Dowling, for your tireless and timely research efforts and uncanny ability to understand what is needed before the need is clear.

My wonderful friends, Kenny and Sandie Dorman, Jayme and Gayle Canton, Danny, Nancy, Justin and Liza Katz, Elyse and Stuart Pellman, Chip Baird, Don and Catherine Mankin, Brent and Katherine Knudsen, Luke Van Meter, Neil Steinberg, Dave, Robin and Grace Zaboski, Mark and Cynthia Goldstein, Ben and Maya Rappaport, Gordon and Nancy Wheeler, Michael and Dulce Murphy, Dan and Lisa Veto, Sarah Werling, Diam Barde, Tom Hunter, Tim McMahon, and Paul Davidson, for caring about me (and letting me care about you) and for putting up with me in spite of my ongoing battles with windmills.

The Esalen family, for showing me how to get color from my black-and-white set.

And all of the members of past, present, and future Age Wave teams, the most imaginative, passionate, creative, playful, and enjoyable work team imaginable.

INTRODUCTION

I first became interested in the study of aging, maturity, and retirement more or less by accident. I was twenty-three, living and teaching at the Esalen Institute in Big Sur, California, completing my doctorate and working on my first book, *Bodymind*. I was asked by Dr. Gay Luce, who was working on creating an innovative new human potential training program, if I'd be interested in partnering with her.

This was in 1973, years before the wellness movement, before the holistic health movement, before Pilates or peak performance, even before yoga had really caught on.

I decided to move to Berkeley to join Dr. Luce in crafting this program. It was going to be a year-long comprehensive curriculum, very different from the weekend workshops and two-hour lectures that were becoming popular. Before it even got off the ground, it struck Gay that in our youth-focused culture, nobody was using any of these innovative therapeutic techniques with the elderly. She changed direction and she asked if I'd be open to joining her. As a young man in my early twenties, the idea of working with the elderly didn't initially hold much charm for me. I liked being with people my own age and also doing programs for people in their thirties and forties. I told Gay I would get the project started and then move on.

But I got hooked—and have been hooked for thirty-five years. Once I was in the project, I became absolutely fascinated with older people. I realized that if you could see past the way they dressed, the wrinkles and gray hair, these were often towering figures, seasoned men and women who had a vast perspective on life. Many had a kind of home-grown wisdom that intrigued me.

With funding from the National Institutes of Health, our Berkeley-based Sage Project became the nation's first preventive health research program focusing exclusively on older adults. Our subjects, who ranged in age from sixty to ninety, were divided into groups of twelve and met twice each week in four-hour sessions over the course of a year. During these meetings, participants were introduced to yoga, meditation, aerobics, stress management, biofeedback, proper nutrition, art, movement and dream therapy, and were encouraged to share their thoughts, feelings, and progress with other group members in an open, "team-like" atmosphere.

Our project became extremely successful. Before I knew it, I was being invited all over the world to speak about a "new image of aging." Soon I began to be interested not only in the elderly, but also in the journey of aging itself. I was curious about how we get to be the people we become, about the choices we make along the way that make us either healthy, vibrant, and engaged, or unhealthy, impoverished, and disconnected.

Through my research and travels, I would meet people in their seventies who were poor but hadn't always been so, and they could describe the bad moves that had left them impoverished. I would meet older people who were terribly lonely, and it was clear that along the way, they had not made new friends or tried new activities that would have brought them into a new world of relationships. It became increasingly obvious to me that to a great extent, we ourselves make the decisions, consciously or not, that lead us to who we'll become in our later years.

When we go on vacation, we usually do a lot of prep work. We plan out where we're going to be, what kind of clothes we'll need, what kind of currency we should bring along. Yet for some reason, we don't do this same kind of thinking about the second half of our lives. We just assume that if we keep barreling away in the direction we're going, everything will wind up okay. And sometimes it does—but often it doesn't.

Way back in 1982, I served as adviser to a two-year project launched by the U.S. Congress's Office of Technology Assessment that focused on how America would be transformed by the aging of our population in the early twenty-first century. The twenty of us on the panel would study all sorts of provocative essays and white papers, and then assemble in Washington every few months to debate and try to make sense of it all.

This was when I was struck by the demographic piece of the puzzle. That was when I first saw the "age wave" coming. I realized that because of increasing longevity and declining fertility, but most importantly because of the aging of the baby boom, America would be undergoing a radical transformation by the beginning of the 21st century, as these 78 million people began moving into their fifties and sixties.

It occurred to me that we had shaped our world in every way around the form and fit of who we had always been—which was *young*. In the decades to come, I saw that we were going to have a world in which the typefaces would be too small, where doorknobs would have to be replaced by door levers, where the length of time it takes for the traffic lights to change would be too quick and the auditory range on our telephones and televisions would be out of sync with aging ears.

I thought, How will housing and community design be impacted? Is our health-care system prepared for the coming pandemics of chronic disease? What's going to happen to the pharmaceutical industry? How will foods and beverages be changed to accommodate aging taste palates and bodies with different nutrient requirements? How would the aging nations of the Americas, Europe, and Asia continue to be economically productive with so many dependent older citizens being supported by shrinking numbers of young workers? Could our political system restrain the demands that tens of millions of elder boomers would place on the social and economic infrastructure? Would our democracy become a gerontocracy? And, what about people who will want to reinvent their careers? What will become of retirement? Who might we each become—thanks to increasing longevity? And, who's going to pay for all of this? All these ideas started flooding my mind, and that flood hasn't stopped—not for one day in all of these years.

It struck me that all of life was going to have to be re-charted: "old age" would be moved back and there would be a new middle zone of life, which I began calling *middlescence*. People said, "Hey, you can't just make up a stage of life!"

But this isn't the first time this has been done. For example, the idea of adolescence didn't exist until relatively recently. At the beginning of the twentieth century, people would go from being children to being adults virtually overnight; there was nothing in between. Then, as we began instituting child labor laws and creating a fuller high school experience, adulthood was postponed. A sociologist named Stanley Hall identified this emerging new stage of life and called it adolescence. When the boomers came along in the 1950s, we did it again, further postponing adulthood by creating another new stage of life called "young adulthood."

Today, as people begin reaching their fiftieth birthdays, they are no longer turning the corner to old age as they had done in my grandparents' time. Instead, it is becoming a time of continued vitality with an appetite for new beginnings and personal reinvention. So we're not simply living longer, we've invented a new life stage—with more to come. People tend to assume that living longer simply means *being old* longer. I'm convinced that our entire concept of how we live our lives is shifting. This is an entirely new landscape that we've never charted before.

Years ago, an older friend shared an interesting pair of memories. When he was a boy, his grandfather passed away at the age of sixty-two. At the funeral, people talked about how he had led such a long and rich life. Years later, as fate would have it, the man's son (my friend's father) died at exactly the same age—but at *his* funeral everybody said, "It's so sad ... he died so young!"

In a single generation, sixty-two went from "such a long life" to "he died so young!"

Consumed by the massive scale of this challenge and worried by the absence of preparation, I decided to focus all my attention on a Paul Revere–like call that "the aging are coming, the aging are coming." And, there was an opportunity, I perceived, to join the tools of the nonprofit sector with those of business and media for social good. In 1986, in partnership with my wife, Maddy Kent Dychtwald, I founded Age Wave as a research, consulting, and communications firm. Our corporate mission was to help companies and governments develop products and services for the multiplying numbers of mature adults. The very demographic changes we were proclaiming became wind in our sails. Over the years, Age Wave has worked with more than half of the Fortune 500 companies while continuing to counsel not-for-profit organizations and governments.

From all these experiences, book and film projects, and challenging research and consulting assignments, I am convinced that life's prolonged second half will provide an opportunity for people to chart a new course. We'll have the time and resources to reverse past failures or build on past victories, perhaps changing careers, taking a sabbatical, returning to school, or rolling up our sleeves and redirecting our minds and hearts to changing the world.

Historically we have lived what I call the *linear life plan*: first you learn; then you have a period of intense work, for three or four decades; and then, if you're fortunate enough to have a bit of longevity, you have a period of time to rest and relax a bit before you die. Learn, work, rest, die—so more longevity simply means stretching out the "rest" part a bit longer.

But that's not what people are doing anymore. Instead, people are going back to school, or quitting their jobs and starting whole new careers. Finding themselves widowed or divorced at sixty, they're thinking, maybe it's not too late to fall in love again. Or they've come through a battle with cancer and think, "Hey, rather than assuming I'm in the bottom inning, maybe there's still time for me to rebuild my health and have a fantastic new life in front of me."

Instead of assuming that outdated linear life plan, we're starting to think in terms of a *cyclic* life plan. It is becoming a story not of the rise and fall of an individual, but of continual rebirth and reinvention.

For example, remember the "midlife crisis"? The idea was that life is like a climb up Mount Everest. When you hit year fifty you reach the summit, look around and see this fantastic view—and that's the highest point you'll ever reach. From there on, you're descending with every passing day: your view will grow more dim, your expanse more contracted, and you'll gradually move to the sidelines.

I don't think that's what anybody wants anymore. I think people are saying, "Hey, I'm forty-five—maybe I have another good forty-five years ahead of me!" Or, "I'm sixty and still feel pretty great; maybe it's time to reignite my engine and begin the greatest work of my life."

My company, Age Wave recently conducted a massive study that found about 75 percent of boomers would like to work in retirement.

When we asked what kind of work arrangement they'd like, they said, "Maybe I'd like to start my own business, be my own boss." Many want to work at something that will stoke their fires again. They want more schedule flexibility and a better balance between work and leisure. Fully 60 percent said they'd like to begin a whole new career. When my parents were in their late fifties, they weren't thinking about new careers—they were happy just to be getting close to the finish line.

All the studies now show that money is *not* the main reason people want to remain engaged longer. Money is typically the second or third reason, but the main reasons are *mental stimulation* and *the feeling of making a contribution*.

Most people now seek a version of maturity that's still turned on, one where we're socially connected and our mind is engaged, where we're continuing to be productive and useful. Too often, our twentieth-century version of maturity left out the crucial element of *purpose*. For many of us, hanging up our cleats and "retiring" just won't be enough. We want to keep our minds stimulated and maybe continue earning an income—but we also want to be involved in something that feels meaningful, that has purpose, that allows us to feel lit up and turned on.

For a lot of people, this "encore" can become the most liberating and energizing time of their lives. Rather than being a second choice, I often hear people say, "Why didn't I do this sooner? I feel so much better doing this!"

In the decades ahead, I believe there will continue to be extraordinary breakthroughs in medicine and the sciences that could very well elevate life expectancy by another five, ten, or twenty years. As a result, living to ninety or 100 will become commonplace. The eighty-year-old *philan-thropreneur*, the ninety-year-old newlywed, the 100-year-old explorer who goes up into space, these will be the new and extraordinary stories of the decades to come.

I also recognize that this age wave will make it increasingly challenging for governments and employers to fund the multiplying numbers of pensioners and retirees, and therefore the responsibility for creating a secure and long life will fall largely on our own shoulders. We'll see a seismic shift from entitlement to financial self-reliance. This is going to be tough news for some people, but the earlier we come to grips with it, the better.

This longer life span is not ours simply so we can keep being a twenty-year-old for another seventy years. It's to allow us to grow up and give back. Adulthood and maturity is a time not only to cultivate knowledge and wisdom but also to replant your life and re-fertilize the soil, to give back of your knowledge and wisdom, your experiences and life lessons, to your family and to your community. In the decades ahead, we'll have the potential to realize our full intellectual, social, and political influence, not as youth, but as elders. If we can step outside the modern tendency toward self-centeredness and wield this power with wisdom and generosity, we could rise to our greatest height and make a remarkable success of history's first multiethnic, multiracial, and multigenerational melting pot.

To live the coming decades of our lives *with purpose* or *without* is a *choice*. And the choice is ours.

KD, San Francisco, California, October 2008

With
Purpose

Chapter 1

ARE YOU USING YOUR LIFE— OR IS YOUR LIFE USING YOU?

There are two ways of exerting one's strength:
one is pushing down and the other is pulling up.

—BOOKER T. WASHINGTON

A few years ago I was winding down work on my last major book, *The Power Years: A User's Guide to the Rest of Your Life*, when a series of peculiar events, which I'll describe, overtook me. These events changed the way I look at the world and ultimately led to the book you now hold in your hands. But this book is not about me—it's about you. It's about why your worldview may be changing, how you can better understand the shift and find purpose in everything you do. It's about how you can finally set aside, or at least temper, your focus on personal gain in order to identify with a different kind of success—one that centers on meaning and satisfaction. It's about doing something significant with the rest of your life, something that will help others and at the same time fill a void you may not even be fully aware of. For many years I wasn't fully aware of my void. But I knew something wasn't right. So let me start by explaining what changed that.

The Power Years, which I coauthored with Daniel J. Kadlec, was a new kind of project for me. I've made a career out of studying the lifestyles, needs, and aspirations—and the related spending and savings patterns of baby boomers. For three and a half decades, I've been writing and speaking both about the lifestyle of maturity and about boomer habits and consulting with global companies eager to capture the attention of this highly influential and wealthy generation. In *The Power Years* we wanted to fast-forward to gaze into the future. So we set out to examine what boomer lifestyles might look like in the traditional retirement years, which were approaching fast. In the end, we attempted to put forth a groundbreaking vision for what people might become in their fifties and beyond. The message was fairly simple: later life is evolving into an extraordinary period of good health and extended opportunity for people to do whatever they want to do. So what would they do? I loved exploring the future of relationships, leisure, learning, and work, and making sense of how people are going to pay for it all. But for me, the heart and soul of that book was the final chapter, which was called "Leaving a Legacy."

It is my heartfelt belief that living a longer life, as we certainly will in an age of advanced medicine and unprecedented information about healthy living, isn't simply a matter of playing longer or working longer—but of reaching a place where you have gathered enough life experiences and perhaps the financial freedom to dedicate the decades of life still before you to doing good things for your family, community, country, and the world. What use could you put your skills to that might give someone else, whether you know them or not, an otherwise missed opportunity to better their life? This was the parting challenge that we presented in our new way of looking at a reinvented retirement.

Not many years ago, when people reached their fifty-fifth birthday they were pretty close to the end of their days. They were concerned mostly with putting their affairs in order and maybe trying to have a little fun before their last sunset. But someone who reaches that age now can look forward to twenty, or thirty, or even forty more years of life. What might be the most satisfying way to spend all of that time?

We concluded that leaving a legacy—not necessarily the financial kind; but doing something memorable to lift others—would emerge as a retirement revolution. Today there are hundreds of millions of men and women around the world approaching a period of life when they'll have unprecedented amounts of discretionary time and are looking for a new challenge. Maybe they haven't achieved what they thought they might in their career and are now looking for someplace totally new to invest their energy. Maybe it's the opposite: they have achieved more than they set out to do and now find at age fifty-one or fifty-seven or sixty-three that they want a fresh purpose for getting up in the morning.

In my travels and conversations I don't often hear anymore about people in their fifties or older focused on making another $1 million. Certainly, greed, deceit, and ambition haven't vanished from the globe. Corporate scandals, glass ceilings for women and minorities, identity theft, Internet fraud, and other forms of lying, cheating, and stealing are as prevalent as ever. And a lot of us are still rightly concerned with making a decent, honest living and finishing the job of raising happy and prepared children. You may not be financially secure at this point in life. Yet what I increasingly hear are people talking about what's next; about what's in store in the next stage of life. They wonder how they might get past their routines and do something that makes their heart sing, that reminds them of their humanity and gives them a chance to reboot from the hard-driving work and family pursuits that have preoccupied them for decades.

Life can certainly be draining, whether you are managing a career and paying the bills or seeing to your kids' health, education, and moral grounding—or, as is increasingly the case in modern societies, doing both. Past a certain age, though, you can loosen up on the reins and let yourself be led down unknown trails. This can be an exciting and liberating time as you begin to think about your life not as a mission accomplished—but as a time for finding a new purpose that will give your life meaning and just might become your most joyous and nourishing time on earth.

This view, I believe, is multiplying in the minds and hearts of people around the world, and not just adults on the crest of retirement, but students and young children as well. People of all ages are warming to the notion of giving something back and in their generosity discovering intrinsic rewards and possibly a whole new purpose to their life. What might it mean for the world and all its problems if an international army of volunteers would emerge, each individual determined to fix just one small—or large—problem?

Humankind's quest for a meaningful life is hardly new. Aristotle wrote volumes on the subject. Service to others has long been the backbone of the world's oldest and largest religions, from Judaism to Christianity to Buddhism to Islamism. Yet in the modern world, with a pop culture that has become increasingly awash with superficial concerns, introspective questions as to what amounts to a good and decent life are rarely pondered outside places of worship or some random philosophy class at a university. That is, however, beginning to change. In the United States alone there are now more than a million registered charities—double the

number in 2000. There are probably another million unregistered charitable organizations. Registered nonprofits constitute one of the fastest
growing sectors of the economy. This movement is global. From nothing,
in fewer than ten years some 400,000 charities have sprung up in Russia;
300,000 in China; 500,000 in India. The movement is especially strong
in the U.K., which has a blossoming "Third Sector."

Former president Bill Clinton, in his book *Giving*, argues that this
global outpouring is the result of three factors: the fall of communism
and rise of democracies, which has created more opportunity for citizen
activism; the development of global trade and information technology,
which has provided the means for people to give both time and money;
and the build out of the Internet, which has enabled ordinary people to
find each other and coalesce around shared interests or causes.

Those are certainly valid observations. But in my view the primary
force at work today lies in millions of people the world over reaching an
age and a time in life when they'll have the opportunity to consider a
higher purpose—and still have enough good years in front of them to act
on their conclusions. No previous generation has had this opportunity;
none had the experience of watching their parents and grandparents live
so long and waste decades of extra years thinking that each day might
be their last. Today we understand that longevity isn't a fluke; our lives
will continue to stretch out, probably much longer—maybe very much
longer, than you imagine.

Springing forth is a collective sense of purpose, a realization that individuals can do something worthwhile with the resources and extra time
they're being given on Earth. The world has never been in greater need of
kindness and selfless contribution. Hurt in its many forms retains an iron
grip on the world—from simple crime and disease to poverty and illiteracy to the many problems associated with terrorism and the environment.

The combination of global need and an emerging army of educated, motivated, purpose-seeking volunteers with their own ideas on how to fix things is a potent mix. Their ultimate force is to be determined, but I believe that we are on the verge of a golden age of giving—and change.

Currents Converge

I'm often taken by the wisdom and depth of thinking of Hindus, whose spiritual leaders have long championed things like service to others and leading a life of meaning. Among their more interesting rites and customs is a celebration they call Maha Kumbh Mela, which means grand pitcher festival. Every twelve years some seventy million Hindu pilgrims meet near Allahabad, India, for six weeks, where they dip, millions at a time, into the water where three different rivers converge—the Ganges, the Yamuna and, in lore, the Saraswati, which years ago went dry.

Hindu mythology holds that gods and demons once fought a war over the nectar of immortality and spilled some from a pitcher into the confluence of those three rivers. By bathing in them, according to Hindu custom, they heal their souls and may become free from the desire for material things, which leads to spiritual purity.

The massive gathering results in a temporary city of 50,000 tents, and the movement of millions of people into the waters at once is so gigantic that it is visible from outer space. But this ritual is more than just a spectacle of humanity. It's an enormous public profession that there are more important things in life than personal gain. Hindus believe that the world population is one large family, and there at the nexus of three great rivers, every dozen years they celebrate the simple holiness of doing good things for others.

That the festival takes place at the meeting point of three rivers is no accident. These waters flowing from the Himalayas have long sustained life in the region and are a symbol of great power—in this case, at least to Hindus, the power to become better human beings. Why do I mention this ancient rite? First and foremost, it speaks to mankind's innate desire to lead good and decent lives, which must include some higher purpose.

But I also like the image of three powerful currents meeting in one place, generating enough wattage to foment large-scale change. We are today at just such a confluence, not of three rivers but of three social currents that are coming together for the first time. As the Hindus believe in the magical convergence of the Ganges, Yamuna, and Saraswati, so I believe in the magic of these merging trends:

1. *Retirement is being retired.* As I've said, people today are living longer and are healthier than ever, and they want more than a daily golf game or round of pinochle to occupy their time. Today's retirees feel youthful and vital; they want to stay engaged and relevant. For some, that means staying at work longer. But for many others it means working at giving away their money in ways that make them feel good, or giving away their time, skills, and energy to further a cause near to their heart. The days of accepting a gold watch and disappearing into a meaningless leisure-filled sunset for twenty or thirty years are coming to an end. New generations of maturing men and women are coming to view their unprecedented longevity as a time to play, certainly, but also to share not just what they've earned but also what they've learned. Millions of people are now wondering what the most satisfying balance between leisure and legacy might be.

2. *Boomers are maturing.* This large generation is by no means going it alone in the field of giving back. But boomers are now migrating through their "mature" years, and they will put their unique stamp on

philanthropy as retirees—and rehirees. This generation is now entering the sweet spot in life, where their careers are becoming less important, their child-rearing obligations are receding, and they still have the energy and the desire to be engaged and productive. We are on the cusp of the largest class of retirees in history—a staggering legion of well-schooled and accomplished individuals who, if they stay true to form, will leave their mark on this period of life as they have on every other period that preceded it. Will boomers volunteer and otherwise give back in waves large enough to change the world? Only time will tell. But this generation has itched to make its mark on a global scale since the first Vietnam War protest.

Despite their me-first reputation, boomers are a deceptively generous lot. A 2005 study by Craver, Mathews, Smith and Co. and The Prime Group found that boomers gave an average of $1,361 annually to charities and political causes—compared to $1,138 for older Americans, including the so-called greatest generation. Boomers are also the most likely cohort to volunteer, and they compare favorably with older generations when they were at this same stage of life. It is now estimated that the number of older volunteers will increase by 50 percent as boomers reach maturity. Typically, people who volunteer during their working years double their hours of service after retiring. So when boomers really do step back and ponder what's next they may finally have the cumulative impact longed for in the classic 1970s anthem by Ten Years After: "I'd Love to Change the World."

3. *The world of giving has a revolutionary new face.* The rich tradition of giving something back dates to prehistoric times and was first given form around 500 BC with Greek writer Aeschylus's *Prometheus Bound.* According to Greek mythology, Prometheus stole fire from the gods and

out of goodness gave it to humans. In so doing, Prometheus incurred the wrath of his less egalitarian superior, Zeus, who then bound him to a mountain for centuries. But Prometheus regarded the sacrifice as well worth the result. The act of selfless giving has inspired countless stories since, cementing philanthropy as a worthy endeavor in the human psyche.

Yet the social purpose of philanthropy has, like the institution of retirement, undergone profound change over the millennia and is today at another tipping point. Those who give their money or their time have become frustrated; despite billions of dollars given each year to eradicate poverty, illiteracy, and other blights it sometimes feels as if relatively little gets accomplished.

Big-money philanthropy increasingly is driven by the new-age rich, who earned their money as hard-driving entrepreneurs—not as the heirs of old-line wealth. Titans like Larry Ellison at the software firm Oracle, Oprah Winfrey, Phil Knight at Nike, and Bill and Melinda Gates at the Gates Foundation are relatively young and bring an entrepreneurial zeal to the world of charity. There are many others, and they span the globe and include titans such as Hong Kong's Li Ka-shing, who has pledged to leave one-third of his $32 billion fortune to charity; Anil Agarwal, who has committed $1 billion toward creating a new university in India; Malaysia's Leonard Linggi Tun Jugah, who puts his donations into preserving the culture of the Ibans, an indigenous group on Borneo; and Yang Huiyan, China's richest person, and her father, Yeung Kwok Keung, who donated $32 million to charities in a single year.

Venture philanthropy is one of the top trends in British charity too, according to trackers at www.philanthropyuk.org, a relatively new and comprehensive clearinghouse of advice, information, and news on the

U.K.'s Third Sector. "Changes in amount and source of wealth are giving rise to a new type of donor," the Web site reports. "One who is younger, typically (but not necessarily) self-made and socially conscious. The new philanthropists want to be engaged in their giving, using their business experience and expertise to support the charity more closely. They also are willing to invest a significant amount of capital—including funding core costs—and take significant risks to test innovative ideas. Importantly, because they are private individuals, they are able to take risks that government and many foundations, who are accountable to other stakeholders, simply cannot."

Across the globe, a new generation of givers wants solutions, not Band-Aids, and they demand measurable results. Millions of common people—everyday philanthropists, or Everymanthropists—are striking out on their own in a downsized version of what titans are doing. They are using their smarts and energy to fund and launch personalized non-profits dedicated to causes that speak to their souls. Everymanthropists want results as well, and most want nothing to do with emptying bed pans and cold calling potential donors. They want to give back a talent, share what they've learned, and see the impact they make. Traditional volunteer opportunities do not cater to them. So they are crafting their own, a phenomenon that I will return to often throughout this book.

Success to Significance

The potential of a retirement revolution, where millions and millions of long-lived accomplished men and women offer their skills and time to the world, is nothing short of staggering. Yet not nearly enough is being done to harness this vast resource. In study after study people past forty-five indicate their willingness to give of their time—but don't follow through because they don't know how to get started. We squander a valuable asset by not finding ways to tap into this desire. "We in the government always think about the aging of boomers in terms of their departure from the world of work and contribution—to being recipients of entitlements," confesses Robert Reich, the former U.S. Labor Secretary. "We don't have it as part of our equation that they might be contributors, that they might be givers. Can we imagine an army of ten million or fifty million retirees contributing their skills, time, and energy to transform the world? That would be something."

So these were some of the many thoughts filling my head as we wound down our work on the book I mentioned and prepared for its launch in September 2005. At the same time, though, I was ramping up to full pre-publication mode, planning the book publicity tour and dreaming about how well the book might sell. Could it be the great book of my career? Might it lead to fame and fortune? (Hey, I said I was dreaming!) Anyway, it was at this moment that Katrina hit the Gulf Coast, and I, like many Americans, sat helpless in front of the TV for many hours, spellbound by the destruction and ruined lives before me. I was stirred by the incredible devastation being brought down on the city and dismayed by our nation's slow response.

How could we be living in the twenty-first century with all our advanced technology and just watch as the days unfolded and these good people struggled without relief? I still had the "Leaving a Legacy" chapter in my head and began to reflect: how did I, Ken Dychtwald, want to be known when my days ended? What would be my legacy?

I decided rather quickly to donate all future earnings from the book to help rebuild New Orleans. This was no PR stunt. I didn't talk about it with anyone but my family. I wanted my teenage daughter and son to know that I stood for something bigger than a nice house near the San

Francisco Bay with a pool and a view. I wanted them to measure me not by what I said and wrote, but by what I did. So I went to an acquaintance of mine, Jonathan Reckford, the executive director of Habitat for Humanity. Habitat is a fabulous organization that builds shelter for the needy across the globe, and I intended to make this group my primary beneficiary. After telling Reckford about my financial pledge, he shared with me a simple, yet eye-popping observation: "Ken, I see and hear a lot of people your age [late fifties] going through what you're going through."

"What do you mean?" I asked.

"You know, you've got that gnawing feeling."

"What gnawing feeling?"

"You're trying to make the transition—from *success to significance*."

There was a long pause. I've enjoyed my accomplishments in my life. I haven't done everything I've dreamed of. But I've done a lot. I have an enormous amount to be thankful for, and at this stage in my life it's beginning to matter less to me how much more money I make or how influential I am in my field. What's becoming far more interesting to me is finding fun, interesting, helpful, and personally rewarding ways to give something back. Sometimes you hear a clever phrase and it sticks with you for a while, and then dissipates. But "success to significance" has stayed with me as a powerful, lasting call to action.

I immediately began to insert this idea about what people might do with the second half of their lives into my speeches around the world and noticed a common response: people would cock their head, raise their eyebrows, and smile ever so slightly—as if a light in their brain just went on. When you speak to 10,000 people a month, as I usually do, and a line in your speech bombs—you know it. This line definitely wasn't bombing; it was striking a nerve. This idea went right through people's barriers, their business at hand, their BlackBerrys, their newspapers, their worries and hassles. It seemed to stir them.

When people approach me after my presentations I like to ask them what part interested them most. These days, nearly everyone says something along these lines: "You know, that concept of going from success to significance rocked my world." Well—just a few more words on this story—let me tell you what further rocked *my* world:

I've never been part of a more impressive speaking roster than one at a private conference titled "Imagining the Future," which was held at Pebble Beach in 2006 for the very top executives at media conglomerate News Corp. I was one of four keynote speakers. The others were Bill Clinton, Tony Blair, and Bono, the rock star. Others on the program included Shimon Peres, Al Gore, John McCain, Malcolm Gladwell, and Vinod Khasla. Session topics ranged from international terrorism to global warming to the role of the media in the Internet era. So here I was speaking in a room full of hard-nosed media executives and bona fide dignitaries and stars, and when I inserted the idea of moving from success to significance, I saw it again—those same tilted heads and smiles.

After the speech, Jane Friedman, then the CEO of publisher Harper-Collins (a News Corp. division) and who's been called the most powerful woman in publishing, grabbed me by the arm and said she thought the timing was perfect for a book on the subject. "The idea of making the transition from success to significance," she said, "is the most powerful thing I've heard here." And the rest, as they say, is history.

How Will You Use Your Life?

So now let me ask: when is the last time you did something significant, did something for someone else or the greater good and didn't expect a thing in return? Most of us can identify with modest good deeds, mostly for family. We willingly give our time and counsel and often our money so that those closest to us can gain whatever edge we may be able to offer in ways big or small. Helping this way is among the most basic of human instincts. But when goodwill and purpose extend beyond family, their healing power is both a wonder to behold and, in large enough numbers, a potential elixir for many of society's worst ills.

As a young man years ago, I experienced my first jolt about the importance of leading a life of purpose. I was on a book tour through Denmark in 1977. I was only twenty-seven years old and had just published my first book, *BodyMind*, which achieved unexpected sales success in Denmark, where it was a national best seller for more than a year. So I was something of a young phenom in that far-off country and had been invited to give a series of lectures on holistic health and self-actualization. Shortly after arriving in Copenhagen I got a call from the offices of Denmark's renowned octogenarian geriatrician, Dr. Esther Mueller, who was a highly respected physician and philosopher in her home country.

This was all new stuff for me. My book was in the window of bookstores throughout the city. Newspapers were covering my lectures. On top of that, an esteemed doctor and scholar had asked me to lunch. Wow. My life was really taking off. I loved it. I was flying.

Then, with a single question, Dr. Mueller brought me back to planet Earth. At lunch, we exchanged the usual small talk. Soon enough our conversation turned to professional concerns and issues. She wanted to know about my insights and research on preventive health, aging, and human potential. I was interested in her views on health care and medicine in Europe. Things were going well, and then out of nowhere—here's the jolt—she hit me with a guilt bomb. "Ken, you're obviously smart and ambitious," she started. "You have a keen interest in what will become a hugely important field as the global population ages. You have a hit book and can command a fair amount of attention through your lectures. What I want to know is this: how do you intend to use your life?"

I wasn't sure what she meant and asked, "You mean in terms of what I'm going to make of my career?"

"No."

"Do you mean in terms of the books I may write?"

"No."

I thought something was lost in translation. What did she mean?

"Ken, how will you *use* your life?" she repeated.

Remember, I was just twenty-seven. My mind was stuck in concerns over my emerging career, celebrity, and hopes for a family one day. How would I use my life? I was going to make some money and have a couple of kids, I said to myself. Yet I knew she was getting at something deep, and at that time the meaning of her question didn't sink in. I fumbled for an answer and ended up telling her that I wasn't sure; I'd have to see where my career took me. We finished our lunch and then parted ways, and I couldn't help but feel that I'd betrayed shallowness in my approach to life and that it had disheartened her. Her question—how will you use your life?—haunted me for many years.

With time I came to understand Dr. Mueller's point. I had one life to live. There might be fifty years of it or eighty or a hundred. But it's one life and it can have a higher purpose. In fact, it must have a higher purpose in order to be a life truly worth living. Only now, as I complete my sixth decade of life, do I fully grasp what Dr. Mueller was saying to me back in Copenhagen: How might I pursue my interests and career—and utilize whatever abilities I had—in a way that helped others and might redefine success for me, not in terms of how much money I make or how many books I sell, but by the way I bring meaning and purpose to everything I do and the impact I have on others? That question looms before me still. And so I will ask you—how will you use your life? It's never too late to begin to figure out the answer.

Roll Up Your Sleeves

Significant acts are all around us, from ordinary people mentoring a child at school to Warren Buffett pledging $31 billion to the Bill and Melinda Gates Foundation, a charitable enterprise with the not-so-modest goal of wiping out disease around the world. The Gates Foundation is on the leading wave of new-style charities headed by "philanthropreneurs," who seek not just to alleviate pain and suffering in the world but also to make certifiable progress in destroying the root causes, and who roll up their sleeves and get involved. This movement is just now taking wing and promises to finally make a dent globally in problems like poor health, poverty, and illiteracy. It's the new thing in giving—generosity combined with personal involvement and linked to businesslike management and performance measures. You can be part of it too.

Seeking a meaningful life is part of what makes us human. It's why volunteers drive ambulances and fight fires, why donors give blood and pledge their organs, why moms and dads coach Little League and serve on community boards, why professionals mentor those learning their trade or craft, why you may work at the soup kitchen or raise money for your place of worship. Happily, there is no imperative to be rich, or even religious, before stepping up to a life of purpose.

I have had a long relationship with Habitat for Humanity. Years ago I had the good fortune to work on a build with President Jimmy Carter, whose greatest work has come after his presidency and has been mostly centered on giving back to the global community. Carter has become the face of Habitat since his first involvement in 1984. He raises funds and awareness and once a year takes part in the Jimmy Carter Work Project "blitz build." In 2006, for example, Carter and two thousand volunteers built 101 homes in impoverished Lonavala, India. Why did I get started with this group? Helping people rebuild their lives after a natural disaster, or simply build a life after being born to disadvantage, just feels good inside.

Too many people think they have to be wealthy to make a difference. When I first began to explore the transition from a focus on personal gain and career success to a focus on becoming significant—the kind of person who does good things for others and lifts them up in some way—I encountered plenty of resistance. Isn't that something you do after you've worked forty years and provided for your family and have saved enough money to give it away or can afford to quit work for pay and become a volunteer?

A good friend of mine, Jay Ogilvy, who has a Ph.D. and is a philosopher and author, and who has long given of himself in the nonprofit world, put it to me this way: "Ken, you know I'd like to make the reverse transition—from significance to success!" Jay may not be rich, but the idea that he isn't already a huge success is flat-out ridiculous. His success is measured in his happy family, high academic standing, and obvious sense of self-fulfillment. Through his work he's been lifting people up for most of his adult life. Lots of ordinary people are doing it too. ReDonna Rodgers, a runaway at age fourteen, fought her way through college and while still a young woman launched a nonprofit in Milwaukee, Wisconsin, that teaches urban youth basic business skills. Paige Ellison in Anniston, Alabama, took $20,000 from the sale of her home to start a nonprofit that builds temporary but secure playgrounds and day care centers at disaster sites so that "kids could go about the business of being kids" while their parents got back on their feet.

Let's dispense right away with any thought that only the rich make a difference. Sure, it's easy for Bill Gates with his extraordinary wealth to write a check to the University of Manitoba to start an AIDS prevention program in India. But it's just as easy for folks with ordinary income to read to a child at school one hour a week. And here's the thing—it's just as potent, when we act en masse. "Let's not just praise billionaires," Colin Powell once said. Let's praise anybody who lifts a finger or donates a dime, because small deeds and small amounts matter. As it turns out, the very rich are not even the most generous. Giving does increase with income—up to a point. But one study found that households with an annual income of $100,000 to $200,000 gave less proportionately than those with an income of $50,000 or less.

I'll look more closely at the ripple effect of giving in chapter 8, where you'll learn about the modern pay-it-forward movement and meet an extraordinary family that lost one of its own in the Columbine High School shooting. This family now travels the world teaching students about the beauty and art of chain reaction kindness through a program known as Rachel's Challenge. So when I talk about moving from success to signifi-

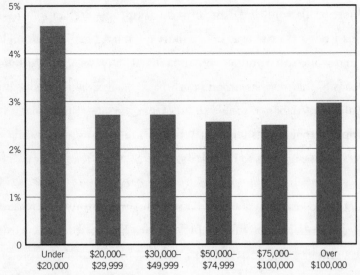

Average Annual Donation as a Percent of Total Income

Source: 2000 Social Capital Community Benchmark Survey

cance I'm talking to everyone. I'm talking to you. Being significant isn't only about moving mountains; it can also be about moving handfuls of dirt. Anyone can do it. To quote Mother Teresa: "We realize that what we are accomplishing is a drop in the ocean. But if this drop were not in the ocean, it would be missed."

All thought explicitly to TM

Purpose in Your Daily Routine

There is probably nothing more important to your daily well-being as having a sense of purpose about everything you do. It's an attitude, and you can adopt it—and find it in the simplest routines. This may sound trite. But I assure you that it is possible to contribute something to the world and feel better about yourself through the most basic everyday acts. For example, you can:

Eat with purpose. I'm not kidding. You can make a difference simply by thinking about the food you put in your mouth. At a recent high school commencement, the actor Sam Waterston implored graduates to go out into the world and put their mark on it. But even if you have not yet discovered your special gifts, he told them, just be smart about what you eat. Waterston, a longtime activist for preserving the oceans, told the kids they could make a difference that would be felt around the globe simply by avoiding seafood that is overharvested—like certain halibut and cod, shark and chilean sea bass. Stick with farmed mussels, clams, oysters, and char, and mackerel and striped bass, which are more abundant. Farmed salmon may be cheaper than wild Alaskan salmon, but the farming takes a far greater toll on the environment because of pollutants and the great amount of wild fish that farmed salmon are fed. Eating responsibly, Waterston said, can literally save the oceans. How's that for purpose in a daily routine? For a pocket guide on ocean-friendly dining, go to www.blueocean.org or www.oceana.org. And don't stop at the shoreline. Why not get smart about everything you consume? Go to www.erasemyfootprint.com to learn how you can offset all of your carbon-producing activities.

Read with purpose. We all know that *Hamlet*, the brilliant story of an indecisive prince, teaches us much about a purposeful life and the universal struggle to separate good from evil. But Shakespeare isn't the only writer with a message. Choose novels and movies and lectures and art exhibits and columnists that make you think and will challenge your assumptions and open your mind to new possibilities. That is where self-discovery, tolerance, and new passions may be found.

Travel with purpose. I have a phrase that I use when traveling: get off the map. Just once during every trip I take I like to venture a little farther than the tour guide or trip planner had scheduled. I sometimes have to push myself; temporarily leave my comfort zone. But getting off the map leads to unexpected, joyful learning experiences—like a perfect cup of chocolate coffee in Torino or a personal tour through a small French vintner's cellars in Burgundy. Such unique and unsanitized experiences expose me to things I don't know and understand and help me define my place in the world. They are also a heck of a lot of fun.

Decorate your home with purpose. Most of us already do this. You hang up family pictures and post a good report card on the refrigerator. Don't underestimate the value of this expression of love. Everyone, and kids especially, need to be reminded of how much they are loved. But you can go further, especially if you have children at home. Let them decorate their room however they like. Heck, let them decorate the family room too. Frame a picture they took or one of their paintings and display it. If your kids are still young, let them write on the walls in their room. This feeds their creativity and reinforces your faith in them and helps them grow confident. You'll have plenty of time to wipe away their marks when they've gone. But they will never wipe away the positive marks you left on them.

Tip with purpose. You cannot believe the importance of an extra dollar or two for many people who work in a services field—cabdrivers, parking attendants, the person who brings you groceries or cleans your home, and of course the waitress at the diner. Some years ago I made a point of *over*tipping everyone in my life for a short period just to see how it feels. I was repaid swiftly with smiles and sincere gratitude—and I never had to wait for my car at the lot again! I soon found that I was not only helping people who have a little less in life but feeling better about myself as well, and this good feeling was influencing my other daily activities. I smiled more and often felt greater energy at work—all because of a small deed.

OK, you get the idea. You can bring responsible and generous behavior to just about everything you do, and turn simple things into significant moments that enhance your life. This is the essence of purpose, and it isn't all that hard to find. Try thinking about how you can bring more purpose to your life the next time you're walking the dog or running on the treadmill. You'll find that such reflection is far more invigorating than obsessing over a gray hair or perhaps your neighbor's new BMW.

Giving Back Equals Economic Gain

The notion of shifting your priorities from success to significance has immensely positive implications for the world. While dour economists and fatalistic policymakers have been wringing their hands over the coming retirement storm of boomers, I've been contemplating a more optimistic model. Might this massive generation, which has repeatedly reshaped society since birth, reorder the world one more time—with glowing results?

The worrywarts certainly have troubling evidence to cite. As I've previously written about in *Age Wave*, *Age Power* and *Workforce Crisis*, aging populations across the globe threaten to stretch our resources as folks quit work, stop paying taxes, and suck up pension assets and health care budgets. In the United States, one in four citizens will be sixty or older by 2030. In Japan, South Korea, Italy, Spain, and Germany at least 40 percent of the populations will be sixty or older by 2050. The oldest living human being (in Japan) just turned 112. Even China (with its one-child policy) has a fast-approaching demographic problem—one in three will be sixty by midcentury. So aging is a global event—and one that is normally referred to as "a problem."

But my own research tells another story, one of extended healthy living, employment, continued involvement, and ongoing personal growth and contribution that could make boomers in their later years net givers to society—not the fiscal drain that is widely supposed. In recent years, governments have begun to get serious about promoting productive aging—getting some kind of return on the accumulated wisdom and skills of people entering their retirement years. So far, the discussion has centered on how to keep people past sixty in the workforce, for two reasons—their retirement threatens to cause a "brain drain" that leaves companies groping for skilled labor and management, and most people that age are physically and mentally able to work much longer. Today's average sixty-five-year-old man has the same 2 percent chance of dying within a year as did the average fifty-nine-year-old man in 1970, notes John Shoven, director of the Stanford Institute for Economic Policy Research. Says he: "If you have a low chance of dying, you're not old."

Shoven believes the starting of pension benefits should be measured backward from how long a person is expected to live, not forward from how long they've been alive. By his calculations, counting back from the expected end of life would lead to reasonably delayed benefits that boost the labor force by 10 percent by 2050 and add 10 percent a year to the national output. If those who retire are encouraged to volunteer it could add another 5 percent to the gross domestic product (GDP)—and this is his point: such contribution from retirement-age people would pay for a lot of the government's promises. "Seasoned men and women," said David Walker, U.S. comptroller general, "are the most underutilized asset in America." Indeed, in the world.

"We're moving in the right direction, fitfully," says Marc Freedman, founder of Civic Ventures, a nonprofit focused on productive-aging issues. "But we haven't begun to see the kind of creative energy put into productive aging as we saw during the last fifty years go into leisure for the aging. We need our leaders to step up and create a new cultural paradigm. We need a new vision for what success looks like in the second half of life."

Purpose Has Entered the Mainstream

Countless studies have shown that as we mature, our fascination with the superficial naturally ebbs. Many of us are now discovering deeper feelings and seeking information and advice on how we can contribute something important in the time we have left. Slowly, the media is latching on to this shift in the public consciousness, breathing life into the giving-back phenomenon. The search for purpose is becoming part of pop culture—not just high society. Clinton's *Giving* was an instant best seller. Rick Warren's *The Purpose Driven Life* has sold thirty million copies worldwide. The *Wall Street Journal* began a weekly giving-back feature. *Time* magazine started a column called "Power of One," which reports on ordinary individuals making a difference.

Meanwhile, reality TV is morphing into charity TV. Call it "philanthrotainment." In *Extreme Makeover: Home Edition,* good people who are struggling get their house remodeled for free. In *NASCAR Angels,* professional racers soup up the jalopies of financially strapped good Samaritans. Such shows are even more popular in England, where they offer the likes of *Fortune: Million Pound Giveaway,* where a panel of rich folks decides who to give money to after a series of sixty-second pitches, and *The Secret Millionaire,* where wealthy benefactors go undercover in poor neighborhoods for ten days to find worthy recipients. When the most highly rated TV program in America, *American Idol,* in 2007 decided to give something back through a telethonlike two-hour program, it raised $76 million and a similar amount in an encore telethon a year later.

In the past few years, financial firms have begun trying to hook new clients with an appeal to higher purpose. None have been more focused on this than mutual fund company American Century, which in its commercials asks: "What exactly is success? Is there a difference between making it big and making a big difference? Maybe wealth can be measured two ways—financially, and how we live our lives as human beings." In another ad the firm states: "a successful life can be measured in two ways: by what you've gained and what you give back."

Luminaries like Bill Gates, who at a relatively young age turned his attention away from the business of Microsoft to become a full-on philanthropist and focus on his foundation's work, Warren Buffett, who is not only giving away his fortune but also setting an aggressive timetable for when it must be spent, and Bono, the rock star-turned-statesman, have made giving extremely cool and are helping to set a new moral tone for thinking people around the world. "Philanthropy is one of the greatest pleasures I have," Gates says. Adds Bono: "When the powerful go to work for the powerless, amazing things happen." He's called putting every child in the world in a classroom "the moon shot of our generation" and has said, "I'm not asking you to put another man on the moon; I'm asking you to put humanity back on this Earth."

Bono works so tirelessly for his causes that it's strained relations with his U2 band mates. But his commitment has paid huge dividends and testifies to the power of a single individual. "He's a kind of one-man state who fills his treasury with the global currency of fame," the *New York Times* wrote. With that currency Bono has helped convince the developed world to forgive Third World debts—where nations are now spending their windfall on medicine and education. He's almost single-handedly steered the debate on how to help poverty-ravaged Africa. The *Times* calls him "the most politically effective figure in the recent history of popular culture."

OK, that's Bono. He's a superstar on a global stage. But think of the impact you could have in your community if you gave a fraction of his effort. Those who get involved almost invariably say giving back provides genuine rewards. For example, it's a great way to stay engaged and relevant. "Retirement is a totally false concept," says Gerald Chertanian, a dot-com millionaire who quit his for-profit ways and started the Boston-based nonprofit Year Up, which counsels urban youth on business basics. "It's about finding the next challenge."

Speaking in the months after 9/11, President Bush called for a commitment of at least two years from every American "to the service of your neighbors and your nation." Five years later, the most stirring part of Bush's state of the union speech came near the end, when he noted that "the greatest strength we have is the heroic kindness, courage, and self-sacrifice of the American people." At that instant, the spotlight shone on three individuals who achieved inspirational significance by doing for others.

In the balcony that night were basketball star Dikembe Mutombo, who grew up in Africa and returned to build a hospital in his old home-town; Julie Aigner-Clark, founder of Baby Einstein Co., who after selling her company to the Walt Disney Company began producing child safety videos for the National Center for Missing and Exploited Children and called it "the most important thing that I have ever done"; and Wesley Autrey, who jumped onto the tracks at a Harlem train station and res-cued a man who had fallen. Said Autrey: "We have to show each other some love."

There's nothing unusual about a president calling on citizens to serve. But President Bush actually did it often and, building on initiatives begun by former President Clinton (Americorps.gov) and adding a few of his own, has helped set up a vast volunteer infrastructure through his USA Freedom Corps.(www.usafreedomcorps.gov), a White House office that he organized in 2002 to promote service and volunteerism around the world. The office keeps an exhaustive database of some four million volunteer opportunities at www.volunteer.gov, promotes emergency pre-paredness volunteerism at www.citizencorps.gov and international volun-teerism at volunteersforprosperity.gov.

Just months from the end of his administration, Bush reiterated his call for all Americans to spend at least 4,000 hours—two years—"to serve our nation through acts of compassion." Two years during a life-time is a lot, he conceded. "But the truth of the matter is, citizens who do give realize that they become enriched just like those folks that they're helping."

We—Not Me

Yes, you can change the world. It may even be your calling at this new stage in your life. Finding the right mix of earning, saving, spending, and giving isn't easy. You'll have to experiment. And don't be discouraged if what you try at first doesn't quite fit. There is a lot of trial and error in this endeavor, as with most pursuits in life. Heck, even Match.com gives you six months for one fee, realizing that a good fit takes time to find. You'll have to stay with it. But in the right situation, giving of yourself could very well provide your path to a life with purpose.

Try to clear out some of life's trifles that might be clogging your agenda and make service a part of your life—be it an hour a day, a week, or a month. This trail has been blazed; you have role models. President Clinton may be the quintessential example of a young retiree reinventing himself and finding meaning through his efforts to make the world a better place. He is now focused on his work for the Clinton Global Initiative, an annual international superforum where he brings together those who have resources to contribute and those who could benefit from their contributions. "I wanted to use my time, experience, and contacts to help in saving lives, solving problems, and empowering more people to achieve their goals," Clinton says in *Giving*. He speaks for many of us. The meaning and purpose of civic responsibility is being rediscovered.

As you emerge from your householder phase, a long period where you have been overwhelmed with duties to your employer and family and probably consumed with material gain, you will rediscover that doing more meaningful things with your time and helping others is the way to bring your life into balance and achieve a higher state of existence. Modern psychology teaches that ultimate fulfillment is about exploring oneself; success in that vein is self-awareness. You've hit the jackpot if you become comfortable with who you are. But I believe there is more to fulfillment. We are not islands. We live together, and when you die you leave a legacy for good or ill. At this stage in your life you've got to think in bigger terms—about your moral commitment to leave the world a better place than you found it. Only in going beyond self-awareness—to legacy and giving back—is true fulfillment possible.

Chapter 2

What You Think
You Know about Success—
and How You're Wrong

*I get up every morning determined to both
change the world and to have one hell of a good time.
Sometimes, this makes planning the day difficult.*

—E. B. White

When I was a young man and had barely begun what would become a huge part of my life's work—the psychology of aging—I had the great fortune to be invited to Berkeley, California, to partner with Dr. Gay Luce in an innovative research program that came to be known as the Sage Project. Our goal was to examine how the bodies and minds of men and women past the age of sixty might be refreshed so that they could continue to contribute to society or, at least, remain sufficiently engaged to enjoy their later life. This was long before yoga and meditation became popular. Indeed, it was the first major late-life preventative health care study in North America. The Sage Project helped lay the foundation for the work of Andrew Weil and Dean Ornish and others in the field of self-healing.

More than thirty years later I still recall most of the names and faces of our initial fifteen volunteers, who met with us two times a week for several hours over a twelve-month span. We regularly assigned homework to our subjects—journal writing or certain physical exercises including yoga and the Chinese movement meditation tai chi—and then tried to assess which had been most helpful in turning back the aging clock. It was exciting work. There were no formulas. This was new research. We could let our instincts lead the way. Working with older men and women in the areas of personal growth and preventative health wasn't done back then, at least not on a noticeable scale.

Before long we could see that we were engaged in something special. If life is a learning process where each day we uncover one more meaningful tidbit and hope eventually to come to a full understanding of who we are and what our purpose is, then just imagine the advantage of old age. In this view, through time and experience we can become truly knowledgeable. Now, imagine being able to coax decades of wisdom from the elderly and then to apply it to your life today. It was during the Sage Project that I came to believe (and still do) that we can all be wise beyond our years if we simply take the time to listen to people who are in their twilight years and have climbed the proverbial mountain. I was awestruck by my elderly subjects' ability to reflect honestly on their good and bad experiences, and speak coherently about what they had learned from them.

Yet a disturbing theme emerged in our research, and that theme is the whole point of the story I'm now telling. In one assignment our fifteen initial subjects were asked to chart the highs and lows of their life on a single sheet of graph paper. It was up to them to decide what that meant. There were no required inputs such as income, career advancement, marriage, children, or social status. We simply wanted to know when and for how long they felt good about themselves. We asked our sages to draw a line across the center of a page, section it off by half decades, and then map a line above and below for all the years of their life, much as you might chart a stock price, monthly rainfall, or spotted owl sightings. Above the line were periods when the sages enjoyed their life; below the line were periods when life didn't measure up to their expectations. They could draw way above the center line or way below it as a measure of how strongly they felt about a particular high or low point.

We had no idea what to expect and, frankly, worried that most of our sages would paint the rosiest possible picture of their life; by engaging in a little revisionist history they might end up drawing a chart that had them living consistently above the line. But that is not what we got. On the day of reckoning, when our group met to discuss the charts, we gathered in a circle on comfy pillows on the floor with a breathtaking view of the San Francisco Bay. Perhaps it was the relaxed setting that led to their candor. But we had no trouble pulling sincere and thoughtful comments from our subjects.

The first to speak was Herb, who was eighty-one. Herb was a lively sort. He had been married for many years and was successful in his line of work. He seemed content; certainly he was not unhappy. To our spectacular surprise, though, his chart was mostly below the center line and rose above it only sporadically. By his own judgment, he had lived vast parts of his life below what I'll now call the success line. Sure, there were great moments, he told us. Those generally centered on his career and children—having them and then watching them do well. But overall he felt his life had been a colossal disappointment. He hadn't loved his job, though he'd stayed with it for decades. His long marriage was OK, but he felt he had let his true love get away when he was a young man.

Until this exercise, Herb had never faced the critical decisions he'd made in his life. But here they were summarized, clear as day, in a chart that he had produced using his own criteria for what it meant to lead a successful life. Needless to say, Herb was not pleased. His life had been wasted in many ways, he realized, and it was too late to do anything about it. He wished the insights he had gleaned from the mapping exercise were visible to him when he was younger. He would have taken more risks and focused on more meaningful pursuits, he told us, rather than have led his safe, largely routine, and relatively unsatisfying life.

This was a supremely poignant moment. Herb wasn't in tears. At some level, he knew he had played it safe and done mostly what was expected of him—not what he might have preferred to do. Herb was OK. But I was fast becoming a mess. This wasn't fiction. Herb was a real person and here he was owning up to a lifetime of insignificance and regret. Herb said that if he had it to do over he would have focused far more on the people who mattered to him. He would have switched careers at an early age. He would have taken more risks and pursued his passions. He would have spent more time helping others. Our discussion was a cathartic moment for Herb, and it reminds me of the Argentinean poet Jorge Luis Borges, who in his classic *Instants* laments a lifetime of safe choices. "If I were able to live my life anew," Borges wrote, "I would try to commit more errors . . . not try to be so perfect . . . relax more . . . I would run more risks, take more vacations . . . I was one of those who never went anywhere without a thermometer, a hot-water bottle, an umbrella, and a parachute; If I could live again . . . I would contemplate more dawns, and play more with children . . . But already you see, I am 85, and I know that I am dying."

One by one, each of the elders in the Sage Project shared their life chart and their deepest thoughts, and like Herb, expressed tremendous remorse over time wasted on things that did not bring joy and purpose to their life. One sage, Vivian, displayed a largely flat line across the page. She said there were entire decades in her life that she barely remembered because nothing special had taken place. Among the last to speak was a man named Worden McDonald. This was the father of famed singer Joe McDonald of Country Joe and the Fish. At Woodstock, Country Joe was the poster child of youthful rebellion after he led the Woodstock masses in the famous cheer that began "Gimme an F." Well, Pop McDonald was equally colorful. His chart contained many highs—but it had even more lows.

"Unbroken happiness is a bore," wrote the seventeenth-century French playwright Molière. "It should have ups and downs." Worden McDonald and I might agree—but only if there were significantly more ups, which does not appear to be the general experience. On average, these sages in their eighth or ninth decade of life reported that around one-third of their waking time on earth had been spent above the success line. Low points outnumbered high points two to one. Each of them had known joy and fulfillment; they just hadn't known how to make the moments last.

The sages' peak moments revealed a pattern. They tended to cluster around three types of success— rich personal relationships; accomplishment or personal growth of almost any kind; and activities that transcended their own self-indulgences and made them feel their life had meaning. I didn't have an inkling of what I'd tripped on back then. But all the latest research on happiness falls right in line with those rough findings of thirty-plus years ago.

A particularly noteworthy outcome was the abject disappointment the sages registered with respect to the great amounts of time they had spent going through life on autopilot, doing what was expected—as so many of us do almost without thought. I learned that when you do things because other people think it's the right thing to do you inevitably end up disappointed. Don't be driven by external goals and objectives. "Peace comes from within," noted Siddhartha Gautama, the founder of Buddhism, some 2,500 years ago. "Do not seek it without." Some part of you ought to be constantly looking ahead—to when you'll be looking back at the decisions you made along the way.

When you were a kid your aunts and uncles and grandparents used to comment how it seemed like just yesterday they were your age. The sages made the same comments, and what struck me was that this wasn't just some cute thing that old people say. This was the truth. Life is a blink. It's a fast ride. You have to make every moment count. I have tried to live my life with that in mind. When I turn eighty-eight or ninety-two I'm sure I'll have regrets. But those regrets won't include spending too little time with my family, or pursuing a career that I didn't feel passionate about, or focusing so much on me that I failed to see the needs of others. These are things that have a purpose. At the end of the day, these are the things that count.

Success Redefined

So the concept of success needs an overhaul for the next phase of your life. Maybe it shouldn't be about money and advancement; maybe it should be about personal growth, contribution to the greater good, warm relationships, genuine happiness, and finding purpose in everything you do. Maybe it should be about self-fulfillment or honorably overcoming a handicap or hardship, or about generosity of spirit. "The cynical and indifferent know not what they miss," said John McCain while running for office in 2008. "For their mistake is an impediment not only to our progress as a civilization but to their happiness as individuals."

I often think of the glossy photos of moguls and celebrities that regularly grace the covers of magazines. These men and women are promoted as the very definitions of success—captains of industry, fashion trendsetters, daring newsmakers. They live in large houses and drive—nay, are driven—around town in their Bentleys. Yet I have my own take on this picture of success. I landed on the cover of *Inc.* magazine in 1989 and at the time regarded it as a badge of honor, my ticket to an exclusive and desirable club of highly successful individuals. When your mug shows up on a magazine cover a funny thing happens: other cover boys and girls invariably seek you out. So I began to befriend other "success" stories, and it turns out that more than a few of them had been divorced several times; more than a few of them had kids in drug rehab; and more than a few of them hadn't talked to their living parents for more than a decade. Some of them seemed to have mortal enemies around every bend. Were they really successful?

Unfortunately, we've created a society where we too often define people as successful even though we don't like them, even though they may be horrendous human beings, even though they haven't done anything that we truly admire. Sure, these so-called successes may have created the next widget and made their stockholders billions of dollars. Maybe they have the latest hairstyle, buns of steel, and a fancy car. But the rest of their life might be a wreck. We have allowed the notion of success to become inextricably tied to material gain and outward appearances, and this definition is a sham and will not serve you well in the years ahead.

It's time to rewrite the rules of success. You are entering a time of life when your innate longing to share what you've learned may be just beginning to flower. Success at this time of life will be very different for different people. Aristotle equated success to happiness and wrote that "all men desire happiness, but each man has a different idea of it." Plato struggled with the concept as well. His view was that life's finish line—true happiness—is a moving target. You never actually get there. At different ages you have different ideals, and you think if you could just have what someone else has you'd be happy. But when you get there you find you're then operating from a higher base and with a higher standard for what would make you feel successful.

As a child you felt successful if you scored good grades, got along with your friends, and made Mom and Dad happy. As a teen, success was about excelling in a sport or artistic endeavor, going to the prom with a "dream" date or getting into a good college. As a young adult, success was about getting a job, pleasing your boss, starting and raising your family, keeping a tidy home, and optimizing your earning power. It's at this time of life when you generally begin to define success by position, wealth, or fame. In fact, one dictionary definition of success is "impressive achievement, especially the attainment of fame, wealth, or power." We are practically bred to embrace that model; it can be difficult to break free from it. The reality, though, is that you must decide for yourself what defines success in this next stage of life. If you rate yourself against someone else's definition, you will never know the kind of success that I'm talking about.

I submit that true success is probably a little like pornography: it's difficult to define—but, in the immortal words of Supreme Court Justice Potter Stewart, "I know it when I see it." Perhaps you cannot see it yet. But be certain of this: success in your life going forward will center on purpose. It is critical that you find your purpose and pursue it with the same ambition and energy that has led you to material or social success the last few decades.

It's time to get going. As a generation, we have a lot of ground to make up and we're in some danger of being lapped by those who are much younger than we are. Success of the type I am writing about is already being experienced on a massive scale by schoolchildren who regularly hold a car wash or bake sale to raise relief funds after a natural disaster. When she was just five years old, Katherine Commale of Hopewell, Pennsylvania, used an old pizza box and her dolls to build a simple diorama of an African family at sleep in their hut. Using a small plastic bug and a piece of fabric, she developed a short skit showing how a mosquito net could save the lives of poor villagers by guarding them from malaria as they sleep. Katherine and her mother still take the skit to area churches every Christmas and raise thousands of dollars to buy mosquito nets, which they send overseas.

This kind of success is built around purpose and empathy—and action—and it's being incorporated into many younger people's lives as a matter of course and education. Giving back isn't just something you have to wait to do after age fifty or sixty. More than three million college students in the United States volunteer each year. That's nearly a third of the university population, and this cohort's volunteer rate is growing faster than any other. Some sixteen million teens in the United States participate in some kind of formal volunteer work and contribute more than 1.3 billion hours of service, according to the Corporation for National & Community Service, a federal agency that promotes volunteerism. That's an amazing 55 percent volunteer rate. Much of this is arranged through schools, but only 5 percent of teens say they volunteer because it is a school requirement. Many students were stirred to action by the events of 9/11 and Hurricane Katrina and have flocked to rebuilding programs. But others were already taking an interest in mentoring younger students.

In recent years, more high schools have begun to introduce a service obligation as part of their curriculum, and the hottest trend these days in college spring breaks is a vacation that may include tilling the fields in a poor farm community or tutoring migrant workers. Through an organization like Teach For America (www.teachforamerica.org) many thousands of newly minted college graduates sign on for a two-year stint to teach in poor rural or urban neighborhoods in an effort to spread educational equality. Campus Compact (www.compact.org), a coalition of 1,100 public and private universities, is another student-focused organization that has taken wing. Through it, some twenty million young people have volunteered in thousands of communities around the world. They tutor at-risk youth, help build homes in poor neighborhoods and care for the sick and hungry. They lobby government for change. Some start their own nonprofit and target causes that for one reason or another are special to them. Sure, these young people may not attract as much attention as Paris Hilton. Shame on us!

Many student groups are becoming active in the search for global peace, thanks in part to philanthropist Kathryn Wasserman Davis's Projects for Peace program (www.kwd100projectsforpeace.org), which grants a hundred student-led grassroots peace initiatives $10,000 each in annual funding. The idea is to bring new thinking to the global peace process. Ursula Devine and Joseph Campo at the University of Oklahoma are using their grant to produce a documentary film that explores the life of ordinary people in the world's five most peaceful nations, as ranked by the Global Peace Index (Norway, New Zealand, Denmark, Ireland, and Japan)—hoping to learn and illustrate what helpful practices might be transferable to other cultures. Fallon Chipidza, a student at Hamilton College in Clinton, New York,, is using her grant to build a self-sustaining chicken farm at St. Theresa's preschool and orphanage in Zimbabwe. She hopes the chicken business will generate enough ongoing revenue to pay for the children's school fees. Eric Harshfield and Ana Jemec, students at the University of Virginia, are using their grant to build a sustainable water filtration system using abundant local resources in poor sections of South Africa.

These programs and these kids are an inspiration. Many of them are taking advantage of a major life shift—graduating from college, or from high school—and using that moment as a stopping point to consider what good they might bring into the world before they press on with their daily affairs. Can you approximate, or even best, their example by using retirement or disability or the death of a spouse or becoming an empty nester or mailing in the last mortgage payment as the stopping point in which you redefine success and consider your potential to live a life of purpose?

Davis is herself an inspiration. A world-class philanthropist, political figure and international dignitary for much of her life, only on the eve of her one hundredth birthday did she hatch the Projects for Peace program, which may end up as her signature and most enduring legacy. The project, in just its third year, is an invitation to undergraduates to design grassroots projects that they develop over the summer. Those judged most promising and practical get funded. The idea is to encourage today's youth to create ideas for building peace. "I want to use my one hundredth birthday to help young people launch some immediate initiatives—things that they can do during the summer—that will bring new thinking to the prospects of peace in the world," she said upon committing $1 million to the effort in February 2007. She regarded the students' peace projects that summer as so inspiring that she has continued to fund the program.

Davis is outspoken and surprisingly spry, in defiance of her age. An avid painter who likes to finish her pieces in less than three hours, she laughs while admitting to leaving the wrinkles out of her self portrait. She loves athletics and swims with dolphins, rides on the back of a motorcycle, and has hobnobbed with presidents and other heads of state. Friends describe her glowingly as "an international curiosity," "utterly fearless," and "one of the planet's true treasures." They say she was bold at an early age, not wanting to attend Wellesley College because it was a family tradition (but ultimately relenting) and "picking up" her husband, the internationalist and onetime U.S. ambassador to Switzerland, Shelby Davis, by making the first advance on him while traveling by train from Geneva to Paris.

Davis has a doctorate in international affairs and honed her interests in global issues and activism as a young child, when she traveled with her parents extensively and at the age of four marched with her mother during the suffragette movement. Later in life, she helped found a group that promoted greater communication between the U.S. and Russia in hopes of lessening the likelihood of nuclear war. She has devoted much of her life to improving American understanding of world culture and politics, with Russia and eastern Europe as a central focus. For many years, she lectured before educational and civic groups on India, Russia, China, and Switzerland.

Throughout her life, Davis has been a major supporter of arts, education, science, and environmental conservation. But global peace initiatives have always held her highest interest. "There will always be conflict," she says. "It's human nature. But love, kindness, and support are part of human nature too." One of her goals at this late stage of life is to foster ideas that will wipe out armed conflict as a means of settling state disputes, just as duels to settle personal disputes are no longer tolerated.

That's a tall order, one that she hopes her student funding will play a role in filling. Yet even if the program ultimately proves ineffective in this regard, Davis's example is a shining light to all of us to do something for others for as long as we may breathe. "We don't always know what tomorrow holds," Davis says. "So let's take advantage of today and be as useful as we can be." A phrase she uses often sums up her view of life neatly. There are three basic stages, she says: "Learn, earn, return."

Dying to Make a Difference

That's the way Randy Pausch saw things when he learned he had invasive pancreatic cancer and less than a year to live. He stopped and reconsidered everything and in a matter of months was able to reach millions of people around the world with his inspiring message of hope, patience, and no regrets. You may already know the Randy Pausch story. He was a popular and energetic lecturer at Carnegie Mellon University who shared his vision of a life worth leading with four hundred teary-eyed students in what became his last campus lecture, which he delivered in the fall of 2007. The great irony of Pausch's lecture was that it was scheduled as part of a "last lecture" series in which professors would pretend this was their final time at the dais and impart their most significant lessons. For Pausch, a young man with small children, it was no mere exercise.

In a gutsy presentation he waxed on for a mind-boggling hour-plus of wit, charm, and humor, and invaluable life lessons. The circumstances and the freewheeling manner in which he spoke lent a gravitas to his wisdom. Loyalty is a two-way street, he said. Never give up. Accept help, and give it. Tell the truth. Apologize when you screw up. Focus on others, not yourself. Don't bail. Don't complain, work harder. Shut up and listen. Be good at something because it makes you valuable. Work hard. Be patient and you'll find the best in everybody. Dream. Be prepared.

Pausch spiced his lecture with personal anecdotes and offered his words with the ease and calm of one who had found his place, found his version of success in the wisdom he was imparting—wisdom made all that much more dear because he would not be there to repeat it. There is something sacred about a dying person taking the time to make an impact on those around him. He had nothing to gain. So you knew it was coming from the heart; you know it was the truth and that it was priceless. The earnestness of his words—and his obvious sense of purpose—is what made them special. "As you get older, you may find that enabling the dreams of others is even more fun" than realizing your own, he said.

This lecture, designed for just four hundred students (cmu.edu/uls/journeys/), ended up riveting the world as a viral video on the Internet, where it was viewed tens of millions of times. It was later turned into a book. In one brief and shining moment of significance, Professor Pausch reached more people than he had in a career on campus. Pausch never lacked for purpose. Indeed, he seemed to find more of it with each passing day and, ultimately, came to view success not just as a full and rich life, not just as a life worth leading, and not just as a life of helping others—but also as a life that would serve as an enduring example for all. He seized on his life change and used it as a stepping-stone to personal greatness.

You Only Think You're Happy

There is an avalanche of new research in the areas of success and happiness. Perhaps the leading light in this field is Martin Seligman, a University of Pennsylvania research psychologist, who in the last few years has coaxed his profession into going beyond the mere study of what makes people depressed and leads to their neuroses to a more uplifting place—to the study of what makes our heart sing and what might be done to improve our level of satisfaction. In his book, *Authentic Happiness*, he boils down true happiness to three components: pleasure (things that feel good), involvement (being immersed in things like family, work, and hobbies), and meaning (using personal strengths to serve a larger end).

Of the three, Seligman says, pleasure (the one most closely linked to material gain) is the least consequential, a finding that has been reaffirmed in numerous follow-up studies. For example, Edward Diener, a psychologist at the University of Illinois, and another leading light in the study of happiness, interviewed members of the *Forbes* 400, the richest Americans, and found that they were only marginally happier than the population as a whole. Those with wealth often feel the most envy and stress, Diener concluded. Sociologists call this type of jealousy "reference anxiety." But you will know it for what it is—keeping up with the Joneses. People don't usually ask, "Do I have enough to meet my needs?" They ask instead, "Is my house nicer than my neighbor's?"

Money and happiness really do not go hand in hand—at least not in the manner you would expect. Canadian researcher Elizabeth Dunn found in a series of studies that how much money you have is inconsequential to your happiness, but how you spend what you have is critical. In her study she looked at workers who received bonuses of varying sizes and discovered that those who spent at least a third of their bonus on others were measurably happier than those who spent all of the money on themselves—no matter how much bonus money they had been given.

In polls taken by the National Opinion Research Center, about one-third of Americans say they are "very happy," and that rate has been fairly constant for decades. Yet over the same time frame wealth in the United States has increased dramatically, and by the way so has the incidence of clinical depression, which is as much as ten times more common than it was two generations ago. One out of every five women in America is on antidepressants, and each year six million more begin taking them. The World Health Organization predicts that by 2020 depression will be second only to heart disease in terms of the global burden of illness. Greater wealth hasn't made us happier; it may even have contributed to greater amounts of stress.

The World Database of Happiness presents one of the most interesting examinations into whether or not money buys happiness. This database is an ongoing register of scientific research on the subjective en-joyment of life. It brings together findings that are scattered throughout many studies and provides a basis for synthetic work. Overall life satis-faction is assessed by means of numerous surveys in general population samples worldwide including data from 1995 up to and including 2005. The scores are based on responses to a question about satisfaction with life and perceptions of personal well-being, the answers to which were rated on a numerical scale ranging from dissatisfied to satisfied. Rating scales ranged from 0 to 10.

As you can see from the following list, when you place each coun-try's GDP per capita (in current U.S. dollars), there is only marginal correlation between how much money people make and how happy they feel. For example, Guatemalans have the same happiness score as Canadians, although their income is only one-eighth as much. What does tend to reliably correlate with happiness is the quality of relation-ships with family and friends and a personal sense of belonging to one's community.

HAPPINESS AND MONEY?

Country	Happiness Score	GDP
1. Denmark	8.2	$ 37,400
2. Colombia	8.1	$ 6,700
3. Switzerland	8.1	$ 41,100
4. Austria	8.0	$ 38,400
5. Iceland	7.8	$ 38,800
6. Australia	7.7	$ 36,300
7. Finland	7.7	$ 35,300
8. Sweden	7.7	$ 36,500
9. Canada	7.6	$ 38,400

10.	Guatemala	7.6	$ 4,700
11.	Ireland	7.6	$ 43,100
12.	Luxembourg	7.6	$ 80,500
13.	Mexico	7.6	$ 12,800
14.	Norway	7.6	$ 53,000
15.	Netherlands	7.5	$ 38,500
16.	Malta	7.5	$ 22,900
17.	United States	7.4	$ 45,800
18.	Belgium	7.3	$ 35,300
19.	El Salvador	7.2	$ 5,800
20.	New Zealand	7.2	$ 26,400
21.	Germany	7.2	$ 34,200
22.	United Kingdom	7.1	$ 35,100
23.	Honduras	7.1	$ 4,100
24.	Kuwait	7.0	$ 39,300
25.	Saudi Arabia	7.0	$ 23,200
26.	Cyprus	6.9	$ 27,400
27.	Italy	6.9	$ 30,400
28.	Spain	6.9	$ 30,100
29.	Argentina	6.8	$ 13,300
30.	Brazil	6.8	$ 9,700
31.	Dominican Republic	6.8	$ 7,000
32.	Singapore	6.8	$ 49,700
33.	Venezuela	6.8	$ 12,200
34.	Chile	6.7	$ 13,900
35.	Israel	6.7	$ 25,800
36.	Slovenia	6.7	$ 27,200
37.	Uruguay	6.7	$ 11,600
38.	Indonesia	6.6	$ 3,700

39.	France	6.5	$ 33,200
40.	Czech Republic	6.4	$ 24,200
41.	Greece	6.4	$ 29,200
42.	Nigeria	6.4	$ 2,000
43.	Philippines	6.4	$ 3,400
44.	China	6.3	$ 5,300
45.	India	6.2	$ 2,700
46.	Japan	6.2	$ 33,600
47.	Taiwan	6.2	$ 30,100
48.	Uzbekistan	6.2	$ 2,300
49.	Kyrgyzstan	6.1	$ 2,000
50.	Vietnam	6.1	$ 2,600
51.	Iran	6.0	$ 10,600
52.	Peru	6.0	$ 7,800
53.	Portugal	6.0	$ 21,700
54.	Croatia	5.9	$ 15,500
55.	Poland	5.9	$ 16,300
56.	Bolivia	5.8	$ 4,000
57.	Korea, South	5.8	$ 24,800
58.	Bangladesh	5.7	$ 1,300
59.	Senegal	5.7	$ 1,700
60.	Hungary	5.6	$ 19,000
61.	Morocco	5.6	$ 4,100
62.	Montenegro	5.5	$ 3,800
63.	Slovakia	5.5	$ 20,300
64.	South Africa	5.5	$ 9,800
65.	Lebanon	5.3	$ 11,300
66.	Algeria	5.2	$ 6,500
67.	Jordan	5.2	$ 4,900
68.	Kenya	5.2	$ 1,700

69.	Turkey	5.2	$ 12,900
70.	Bosnia and		
	Herzegovina	5.1	$ 7,000
71.	Estonia	5.1	$ 21,100
72.	Serbia	5.1	$ 10,400
73.	Uganda	5.1	$ 900
74.	Romania	5.0	$ 11,400
75.	Azerbaijan	4.9	$ 7,700
76.	Macedonia	4.9	$ 8,500
77.	Mali	4.9	$ 1,000
78.	Egypt	4.8	$ 5,500
79.	Ghana	4.8	$ 1,400
80.	Iraq	4.7	$ 3,600
81.	Latvia	4.7	$ 17,400
82.	Lithuania	4.6	$ 17,700
83.	Albania	4.4	$ 6,300
84.	Angola	4.4	$ 5,600
85.	Russia	4.4	$ 14,700
86.	Pakistan	4.3	$ 2,600
87.	Bulgaria	4.2	$ 11,300
88.	Georgia	4.1	$ 4,700
89.	Belarus	4.0	$ 10,900
90.	Armenia	3.7	$ 4,900
91.	Ukraine	3.6	$ 6,900
92.	Moldova	3.5	$ 2,900
93.	Zimbabwe	3.3	$ 200
94.	Tanzania	3.2	$ 1,300

Despite this evidence most people still judge success in superficial terms.

* * *

Bigger Is Better. The late U.S. senator Everett Dirksen once noted that "a billion here, a billion there, and pretty soon you're talking real money." It wasn't his intent to glorify the more-is-better model of success. But that is the lesson you might walk away with after reading those words, and it is precisely the kind of thinking that dominates free societies in the world today. Yet, as we've seen with the recent collapse of numerous financial markets, this model is seriously flawed.

Consider this puzzle: in surveys, the impoverished people of Calcutta, India, living in crude shacks and with little access to clean water, register about even with Americans on the happiness scale—and well ahead of the Chinese, South Koreans, and Japanese. Meanwhile, relatively poor Puerto Ricans and Colombians, according to surveys, appear to be among the happiest people on the globe. It may well be, as Edith Wharton said, that "if only we'd stop trying to be happy we'd have a pretty good time." How else can we explain the life satisfaction of people of such modest means? Cultural differences explain some of this conundrum. Asians, for example, seem to value understatement and are least likely to show off or express contentment, while Americans appear to expect so much that they are easily disappointed.

But underlying these thought-provoking results is the simple fact that more is not necessarily better when it comes to enjoying life and feeling satisfied. More may be more, but it is never enough. We're caught up in the myth that by achieving and going up the ladder and having more stuff we'll feel full inside. Yet it isn't so. Certainly, money can make a difference for people who have none. Studies by Ruut Veenhoven, a sociologist at Erasmus University in Rotterdam, show that the extremely poor—those earning less than $10,000 a year—may be rendered unhappy by the relentless stress of poverty. Yet his work shows that after a poor person's income exceeds that level there is no further correlation between money and happiness. After a certain level of income, typically enough to meet basic expenses, money ceases to be a factor. I'm not saying we should all live in tents under the freeway or go back to a natural life and give away all material possessions. It's great to work hard, achieve material success, and feel good about it. But that is not how you reach the Promised Land.

The Success Mirage. Another popular notion of success is that you've hit your mark when you measure up to other people's ideals. Again, this notion is firmly planted in our psyche but represents a hollow version of happiness, one that is certain to disappoint in the end.

You may have parents or grandparents who grew up in the shadow of the Depression. Life was terribly hard then. People owned relatively few things. They were frugal. They didn't splurge. The name of the game was just getting by, and to a large extent success was measured from the outside in. What few nice things you did own you might display, and those became symbols of achievement. There wasn't a lot of self-reflection during this period. The feeling was that if you could afford a car, a house, or some jewelry you deserved it. There was a sense of pride and accomplishment that came from showing these things to others.

Things are different today. Most adults own a house or condo. Who doesn't own a car—maybe even two? Global prosperity has heaped material things upon us in abundance. Heck, even if you can't afford a summerhouse, a Jaguar, or private jet, for relatively little you can time-share such things and give the impression of material success beyond your means.

But here's the thing. Increasingly, as people reach their forty-fifth or fiftieth birthday they start to think about success from the other side—not from the outside looking in but from the inside out. It's not about the material things I can show the world, but about how I feel about the work I do; it's about the relationships I have and the love I share.

Not long ago I was watching Larry King interview the rock-and-roll legend Eric Clapton on TV. At one point King began to carry on about how Clapton, in his heyday, was hailed as a guitar god—the best ever. It must have been an incredible high and extremely gratifying to be so highly regarded, King noted to Clapton. In journalist circles this kind of flattery is known as lobbing a softball. It gives the person being interviewed an easy thing to talk about. But Clapton wouldn't swing at it. His response was impressively self-reflective.

No, the rock legend said, that was not such a great period in his life. Even though others saw him as on top of his game he was not able to play the way he wanted to play, make the sounds he wanted to make. Sure, he had lived up to other's expectations of success. But from the inside looking out, he had disappointed himself. He was not yet what he wanted to be, and that was an urgent matter to him—no matter what his fans thought.

One last thought on this kind of success. Some years ago I was helping Jimmy Carter gather his thoughts for his book *The Virtues of Aging*, and at one point I said to him, "President Carter, I have a crazy question for you. I'm about the age now that you were when you were president. Have you come to any new perspectives about what matters in life, now that you're older?" His answer was to the point: "Earlier in my life I thought the things that mattered were the things that you could see, like your car, your house, your wealth, your property, your office. But as I've grown older I've become convinced that the things that matter most are the things that you can't see—the love you share with others, your inner purpose, your comfort with who you are."

President Carter's words sent chills up my spine. It may make perfect sense to dance to society's beat for the first fifty years of your life. You have physical and material needs, and to get them a certain amount of conforming and practical thinking is required. But in this next stage of life things are different. You have the opportunity to reflect on what really matters and move your measuring stick for success—from the outside looking in, to the inside out.

Beyond Maslow

There's a third version of success in today's world, one that comes far closer to hitting the significance mark but that falls short nevertheless. This version is what psychologists call self-actualization. Let me dive into this theory a little deeper because, in the end, the point I want to make is that in terms of finding your purpose, self-actualization may fall nearly as short as "bigger is better" and the "success" mirage.

You're probably familiar with Dr. Benjamin Spock, who in 1946 wrote one of the best-selling books of all time, *Baby and Child Care,* and in it presented views on child rearing that have rarely been questioned and that have guided parenting throughout much of the world for six decades. Spock was a cultural force with few equals. But psychologist Abraham Maslow, a contemporary of Spock's, was most certainly one of them. Maslow's pioneering work in the area of human behavior has dominated global thinking about happiness and fulfillment since the 1950s. You can't help but have run across his name in any study of modern psychology. But even if you know the name you likely do not appreciate the impact that Maslow has had on your life.

It was originally in 1943 that Maslow first proposed his hierarchy of human needs, a tome on psychological development and human potential that during the following decades revolutionized the field of psychology. Maslow's idea was that there are five levels of psychological well-being.

The lowest rung must be fulfilled before you can move up a rung, and the higher you climb the happier you are. Each level is more challenging and complex, and you can't get to the next one without mastering the level below it.

Maslow's theories have come to form the foundation of policy in virtually every key institution in our lives—education, government, employment, media, and even, in some respects, religious instruction. It was his view that gave birth to the modern human potential movement and self-help revolution of the 1960s and even shaped a large portion of our culture, language, and music from that era.

Maslow believed that at the very basic level of human fulfillment are *physical* needs like the need for water, oxygen, protein, sugar, and salt. Without those, you can't put much thought into higher needs. So they must be satisfied before you can develop further. The next rung is the quest for *security* in your life. You become increasingly interested in finding safe circumstances and stability. You develop a need for structure and limits. Think about it. If you live somewhere where crime is rampant and you're always worried about your possessions and your personal welfare, how much time will you have for seeking more advanced needs?

The third rung of fulfillment is *love and belonging*, which usually begins in the teenage years as you begin to feel the need for friends, a sweetheart, affectionate relationships in general, even a sense of community. From there you advance to *esteem*, and here you seek self-respect, including such feelings as confidence, competence, achievement, mastery, independence, and freedom. Finally, you advance to the top of the pyramid—*self-actualization*, which is truly knowing yourself. The idea is that if you've lived long enough and had enough chance to reflect, enough learning, and enough development in your life, then you become truly in touch with yourself, familiar with yourself, and achieve a level of integrity and connection and alignment with who you truly are.

And that's it. Maslow's view, which still dominates thinking in the free world, argues that we should all aim our rockets at the ultimate prize of being self-actualized; the reason you went to college and then to work and developed your relationships has been to feel a sense of deep comfort with who you are and your feelings and your aspirations.

Well, at the risk of seeming disrespectful to a man whose work I greatly admire (and whose ideas have certainly shaped my own journey), I think Maslow didn't go far enough. It's fine to transcend physical needs and move up through health, friendship, and self-esteem to self-aware-ness and understanding. Yet that model largely aggrandizes a self-focused mind-set and lifestyle. It might be fine if you're going to live fifty or sixty years and need almost all of that time to reach a final awareness of who you are. But longevity has changed the game. More is demanded of us if we're going to live into our nineties.

I've come to believe there are elements of psychological development where you go beyond self-awareness and are primed and driven to leave a legacy by sharing your skills, wisdom, and resources with those who are less fortunate. Seen from this perspective *interdependence* might be a higher level of aspiration than *independence*. So I would add a sixth rung to the top of Maslow's hierarchy, and call it *legacy*. At this level, rather than retreat and retire, you go beyond self-actualization to a state of rich *engagement* where you take the best of who you are and the best of what you've cultivated over your life, and bring about meaningful involvement in activities and pursuits that light up the sky for others—as well as for yourself. It's about being involved with people and situations where you can make a difference and reap the satisfactions that derive from those kinds of self-transcendent connections.

Self-actualization is far too oriented toward self-satisfaction; engagement is about going beyond that to generosity and giving back—to living and leaving a legacy. It's about moving from success to significance, and I'm convinced that this idea resonates with people at a very deep level, even as it hints at a new model of psychological development in which the top of the pyramid is not me—but *we*.

German philosopher Erich Fromm said, "Giving is the highest expression of potency. In the very act of giving, I experience my strength, my wealth, my power. This experience of heightened vitality and potency fills me with joy. I experience myself as overflowing, spending, alive, hence, as joyous. Giving is more joyous than receiving, not because it is a deprivation, but because in the act of giving lies the expression of my aliveness."

Psychologist Erik Erikson, the father of adult development theories, echoes this reasoning. "I am what survives of me," he said. Others have weighed in as well: "The great use of life is to spend it for something that will outlast it," said the American philosopher and psychologist William James more than a hundred years ago.

Mold a Version of Success That Suits You

So what makes your heart sing? What does success mean to you? In a moment I'm going to give you a strategy to help you figure that out. But let's start with a simple quiz to measure just how happy you are. This isn't my quiz. It's the brainchild of professor Diener, who came up with it in 1980. It's brilliantly simple. It's been widely published, including in *Time* magazine, and it's been used all over the world. If you want a second opinion or something more complex there are any number of happiness quizzes on the Internet. There's one at www.iVillage.com that's pretty good. So is the one at psychologytoday.com. You can even take Diener's

test on the Web at www.time.com/time/2005/happiness/graphics/quiz
.html.

But there is no reason to rush to a computer. The quiz is so simple you
can do it in your head. Here it is:

Below are five statements that you may agree or disagree with. Using
a 1 to 7 scale, where 1 means strongly disagree, 4 is neutral, and
7 means strongly agree, indicate your agreement with each item by
placing an appropriate number on the line preceding that item. Be
reflective and honest, or the exercise will prove meaningless.

_6_ In most ways my life is close to my ideal

_4_ The conditions of my life are excellent

_6_ I am satisfied with my life

_5_ So far I have gotten the important things I want in life

_5_ If I could live my life over I would change almost nothing

_26_ Your life-satisfaction score (total of above)

Here's how you rate your life, and what it means:

—30 to 35. Good (and perhaps obvious) news: you love your life.
Things may not be perfect, but they are going well. This doesn't
mean you are complacent. In fact, growth and challenge in your life
might be part of what makes you so satisfied.

—25 to 29. Things are going well. This isn't a bad place at all. Life is
enjoyable, and things are just fine in the major domains of life—work
or school, family, leisure, and personal development.

—20 to 24. This is the range that most people in developed nations fall into. You are generally satisfied but have some areas where you very much want improvement. You may fall into this range because you are mostly satisfied with most of your life but see a need for modest improvement in all spheres, or because you are quite happy in most areas of your life but feel a need for dramatic improvement in just one or two places. You probably have that gnawing feeling I wrote about in chapter 1 and are ready to take action to feel better about yourself.

—15 to 19. You can see a need for modest improvement in just about all aspects of your life.

—14 and under. You are not happy. This may be the temporary effect of a death in the family, a divorce, a job loss—and things will get better with time. But if this state is chronic, big changes are in order.

———

To help understand your life-satisfaction score it is useful to understand the components that go into most people's view of happiness. One of the most important influences on happiness is social relationships. People who score high tend to have a family and friends that are close and supportive. Work or school, or performance in an important role such as homemaker or grandparent, is another critical area. When you enjoy your work, be it paid or unpaid, you tend to feel needed and productive, which adds meaning to your life.

Another important aspect of happiness is a sense of satisfaction with who you are. Some religious affiliation definitely contributes to feeling good. So does a good marriage, learning and growth, health, exercise, and adequate amounts of leisure time. But for many people, Diener concludes, "It is important to feel a connection to something larger than oneself."

I can't say it any clearer than that. The path to this fulfilling state of engagement often lies in the direction of doing something to try to make the world a better place. You don't even have to succeed. Just trying makes a difference. "There is no duty we so much underrate as the duty of being happy," said Robert Louis Stevenson. "By being happy, we sow anonymous benefits upon the world."

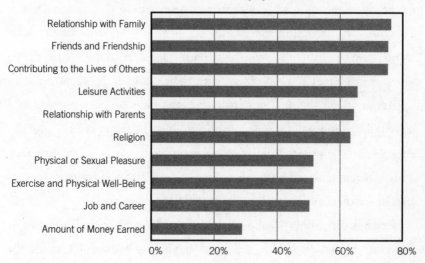

Sources of Happiness

One thing you may notice about Diener's quiz is that there is no mention of age. A lot of people consider *old* and *cranky* words that naturally fit together. But that's not the case. More people in their sixties and seventies report being happier than people in their forties, according to a survey spanning twenty-one countries conducted for bank HSBC. Laura Carstensen, director of the Stanford Center on Longevity, has researched happiness in people ages eighteen to a hundred, and she too has found that people get happier as they age. They may have reservations about the way they've spent large parts of their life, as was the case with my sages. But on a day-in, day-out basis, as you age the frequency with which you feel angry, sad, disgusted, envious, or contemptuous declines. When these feelings do occur they don't last as long. One survey by the Centers for Disease Control and Prevention found that people ages twenty to twenty-four are sad 3.5 days a month; people sixty-five to seventy-four are sad just 2.3 days a month.

Psychologists believe it is possible to raise your happiness quotient by taking specific steps. For starters, do things you enjoy more often. That might mean taking a walk, sleeping late, or calling your sister without a reason. Try becoming more involved in everything you do. In other words, don't mail it in. If you're coaching a Little League team get to know your players and help them with their weaknesses. Try to have an impact at work. Trying a new recipe? Don't take the easy way out and leave out an unusual spice. Go to the store and get the correct ingredients. Make the effort. Find ways to make your life more meaningful. This is often achieved through volunteer activities and other endeavors that help others and contribute to your personal growth.

Psychologist Sonja Lyubomirsky at the University of California—Riverside has studied what she calls "happiness boosters." One of the most effective is what she calls a "gratitude journal." Taking the time to write down what you are thankful for once a week can increase your overall life satisfaction in less than two months, she found. Counting your blessings may also improve physical health, raise your energy level, and relieve pain and fatigue. This is no joke. Happy people generate 50 percent more antibodies—a huge amount—in response to a flu vaccine, researchers have discovered. Studies have linked hopefulness, optimism, and contentment to less risk of cardiovascular disease, pulmonary disease, diabetes, hypertension, colds, and upper respiratory infections. According to a Dutch study of elderly patients, the happiest subjects had a 50 percent less chance of dying over nine years.

Laughter also makes a difference. In one study, ten volunteers gave blood before, during, and after viewing a one-hour comedy. The stress hormone cortisol was significantly lower at the end of the video. Another major happiness booster, Lyubomirsky found, was doing acts of altruism or kindness that may be as simple as calling a grandparent or praying for a friend. The more acts of kindness, the quicker and more lasting the boost.

Professor Seligman's research at the University of Pennsylvania found that the single most effective way to supercharge your happiness is to make a "gratitude visit." He suggests writing a testimonial thanking a teacher or workplace mentor or dear friend, and then visiting the person to read them the testimonial. People who do this just once are measurably happier a month later, Seligman says. He also says that lasting happiness requires you to find your core strengths and figure out how to deploy them. He defines core strengths as generosity, humor, gratitude, zest, and capacity for love. So one of the most effective happiness inducements you can concoct might be as simple as making someone laugh or painting your team colors on your face and going to the game with equally zestful friends.

Find Your Purpose

In my view, the whole point of living longer is to have time to discover your purpose and replant your wisdom. "Baby boomers have always been in the how-do-I-find-meaning business," observes Howard Husock, who directs the Manhattan Institute's Social Entrepreneurship Initiative and each year offers prize money to retirement-age men and women who are doing something novel or important to help others. Now, he says, with many boomers reaching fifty-five and sixty and sixty-five and expecting to live another twenty or thirty years "they have the luxury of being able to reflect on what meaning is, and having the time to act on it."

Yet serious reflection is more art than science. You may not know how to get started. So let me offer a few techniques for discovering your core strengths and what kind of giving, or significant experience, might be a good fit for you.

Write It Down. Start with a pen or pencil and a blank sheet of paper. There's nothing like reducing your thoughts to words on paper to help you focus. You're searching for a form of contribution that will bring meaning and excitement to the next phase of your life. So start by making a list of all the meaningful and exciting moments you can remember from your adult life. These may naturally center on family and work but may include extracurricular moments like playing in the tennis or softball league or with the local theater, or volunteering with the parks department or in a political campaign or mentoring a child or visiting regularly with an isolated elderly neighbor. As a starting point, a simple list of family, work, and "other" will do just fine.

Search your memory from age eighteen through today in each category. What were your great moments at home? Maybe one was the birth of your first child. What feelings did that evoke? Sharing? Responsibility? Commitment? Selflessness? Possibly another was a conversation with an aging grandmother. Why did it leave such an impression? Were you moved by her wisdom? Was it a sad moment? Why? Reflecting like this can give you clues to your core strengths.

Go through the same exercise at work. It's OK if "made a lot of money" finds its way onto your piece of paper. Income and the benefits that come with it may have been a critical part of your life. But try thinking harder about your work-related moments of meaning. Money may have been the result and the thing you can quickly identify. Yet think about what happened that led to the promotion or payday you have in mind. Odds are there was something inherently satisfying about the work, and that is what led to your material success. You may discover that it wasn't really the money that satisfied—but the joy of certain aspects of the job, like overcoming a challenge or learning something new or teaching something to a young colleague.

Now search your leisure hours. Think about what motivated your interests to begin with and what parts you've most enjoyed. Look also at your spiritual and social lives and your friendships. Sometimes how you pray and play tells as much about your true self as how you work and connect with family. What kind of people have you most enjoyed spending time with? What kinds of contacts have been most satisfying? What activities and events have you most enjoyed? If you were part of a team, what role did you play? Were you the captain, or did you prefer to be the scorekeeper? What skills and personality traits came alive during these endeavors? Did you take risks, did you venture into something new, did you master a skill that had previously intimidated you, or did you demonstrate courage or persistence?

You may be surprised to discover that the things that you've done that have made you feel most significant were the simple things that brought a smile to someone's face or improved their life in some small way. You may not even have recognized this joy at the time. Yet upon reflection you find that the service aspect is what lit your fire.

Search Your Youth. Now apply the same exercise to your earliest years. Take a minute to think back to your childhood. What did you dream about doing with your life? Write down everything you remember about those dreams and ask yourself how you may have kept them alive in your work, hobbies, or recreation. Although your joys may have evolved, many people find this exercise to be a powerful starting point for recovering their core strengths and passions. Remembering the first things you wanted to do with your life and the first things that made a lasting impression on you can provide invaluable insight, especially if you feel that your dreams have been obscured by the struggle to survive and raise a family over the past thirty years.

Study People You Admire. You do it all the time in other parts of your life. If you see someone who seems especially well put together or confident, you may take note of their clothes or hairstyle or how they speak. If someone beats you at tennis every week you may observe their serving technique or when and how often they come to the net. At work, you may take note of fellow workers who always seem to have the boss's ear and try to figure out what they're doing to get that recognition.

It's natural to study things that impress you and try to learn from them, and you can go about your search for new purpose the same way. Find role models and try to identify what makes them so special. Is it their honesty? How carefully they listen to others? How they respect old people or relate to young people? How they care for an aging parent or sick spouse? Do you admire their commitment to their religion or a community project? Write it all down, and after you've studied three to five role models find the traits that appear on your list most often. Look for ways to practice those traits in your life.

Craft a Vision Statement. Key to unlocking your strengths and vision for the next phase of life is making the effort to think things through. Once you've reflected on the meaningful points of your life, use them to mold a vision statement. Your vision statement doesn't need to be longer than one paragraph, and it should summarize what you are good at, where your core strengths and passions lie, and how you plan to fuse the two.

Here are two sample vision statements:

I am a terrific car salesman who values giving people a fair shake and matching them with a car and a loan that they can afford and which fits their needs. In my life I have seen colleagues take advantage of unsophisticated, low-income buyers by selling them junk vehicles and placing them in high-interest loans to maximize their own income. I will start or join a nonprofit that evaluates the purchase price of a used car on behalf of the working poor and arranges affordable, low-interest car loans for them.

I am a loving at-home mother with deep concerns about humankind's ability to manage the planet. I see that my children are learning almost nothing in school about the tenuous balance between human activity and the natural world and believe that only through education can we secure our long-term future. I will encourage my school system to integrate sustainable-living lessons into their core curriculums and use that experience to develop a program that can be adopted easily by schools everywhere.

By the way, these are real vision statements that have been put into practice by real people and with spectacular results. You'll meet Robert Chambers and Katie Ginsberg in the next few pages. Like their vision statements, yours should resonate with your core desires and fill you with excitement. If you pursue your honest-to-goodness passion you can find significance in your life that may or may not include a paycheck but will certainly fill you with purpose—and you just may have a blast in the process.

I'll close this chapter with another quote, this one from a person who knows a thing or two about material success. Financier George Roberts, part of the Wall Street powerhouse Kohlberg, Kravis & Roberts, has an estimated net worth of $2.5 billion. Says Roberts: "I'm often asked by people, especially younger people, 'What do you have to do to be successful?' And I assume they're asking not what you have to do to make money, but what do you have to do to be a successful individual. You've got to work hard, set goals, be prepared to be disappointed, keep a sense of humor, keep a perspective of what's really important, and lastly, help others that are less strong and less fortunate than yourself, because you will get back many, many, many fold what you have done for yourself."

Chapter 3

Dreams and Goals Aren't for Kids—They're for the Kid at Heart

Just because I'm old doesn't mean I don't have dreams.

—John Glenn

The comic Billy Crystal made us laugh years ago when, on *Saturday Night Live* and in other appearances, he would impersonate the actor Fernando Lamas as a talk-show host interviewing celebrities. "Dahling, yooouuuu look mahvelous," he would gush, and then famously conclude that "you know, dahling, it's better to look good than to feel good." Crystal's exquisite timing, his inflections, and his expressions made the lines hilarious. But there was a real joke buried in there too; it is, of course, much better to feel good than to look good. At some level, we all know that or Crystal's laugh lines would have bombed.

Robert Chambers and Katie Ginsberg, whose mission statements you read in the last chapter, looked better than they felt. They weren't unhappy, to be sure. In fact, life had been pretty good to them both. But they were cruising, and they knew it. They were on that life path known as autopilot, which the folks in my Sage Project so earnestly warned about. They were leading a good and successful life—from the outside looking in. But, like Eric Clapton unable to coax just the right tone from his guitar, they expected more of themselves. They did not feel success-ful—from the inside out.

"If you ever get a second chance in life for something, you've got to go all the way," Lance Armstrong, the heroic cyclist and cancer survivor has said. Well, Chambers, an ordinary car salesman nearing sixty, and Ginsberg, a stay-at-home mom nearing forty, did just that. At midlife they set a new goal and decided to pursue a new dream, and each was able to ignite a passion and discover meaning by building on the skills and wisdom they had acquired in their life. They found a bigger reason to be alive, and it changed everything for them.

Selling Cars with Purpose

Serving on the USS *Kitty Hawk* during the Vietnam War, Robert Chambers got his first good look at poverty while stationed in the Philippines—and it left him shaken. "We could read it in the papers and we could see some pictures," he recalls. "But really seeing kids begging, not having enough to eat; how skinny they were, how unhealthy they looked just left a deep impression on me." Those images stayed with Chambers over the many decades of his postmilitary life, when he earned his keep as a computer specialist for a phone company, then for a bank, then for an affiliate of Dartmouth College in Hanover, New Hampshire, and finally for his own firm serving several banks in New York City.

But when the stock market crashed in 1987, Chambers's small opera-tion was left in shambles. He shut it down and moved back to Hanover with modest savings and little income (but where he still owned some property) to contemplate what would come next. Could he afford to retire? Perhaps—but he'd have to phase into it with part-time work. That's when a friend convinced him to go into the car business.

As a car salesman, Chambers became reacquainted with other peoples' poverty in a visceral way. The lot where he worked served many low-income car buyers, which Chambers and other salesmen knew from experience tended to be unsophisticated about car values and loan rates. "I got sick of watching guys high-five behind glass walls" after they had bullied someone "who probably makes $10 an hour" into overpaying for a gas-guzzling jalopy, Chambers recalls.

Such buyers almost always assume they do not qualify for a new-car loan, which isn't the case. New fuel-efficient cars are often available to even low-income households through an attractive manufacturer-subsidized rate. Those are the kind of deals that Chambers tried to find for his clients. But he couldn't control the other salesmen, who led their low-income lambs to the slaughter—taking them directly to the oldest cars on the lot, which also happened to be the most profitable for the dealer.

Here's how used-car math typically works: the dealer takes an old car with 90,000 or so miles in a trade, paying, say, $1,000 for it. The dealer spends $500 to give the jalopy a face-lift, and then places it on the lot with a $5,000 sticker price. The sales staff is offered a $1,000 incentive to sell it. So that car, which is certain to start costing the new owner big money in repair bills within months, nets the salesman a hefty bonus and the dealer a profit of $2,500—double or even triple the profit on a new car that may sell for $25,000. Meanwhile, the unsophisticated buyer may have been put in a high-rate auto loan as well and stands a chance of defaulting on it and tarnishing his or her credit rating. That, in turn, has the effect of furthering this individual's downward financial spiral.

Seeing this happen time and again, Chambers recalled the faces of those poor Philippine children he saw as a sailor. Before his eyes, unscrupulous salesmen were preying on the working poor in his hometown. Not only were these problem-beset people buying even more problems—they were also certain to suffer additional economic pain when their car broke down and they were unable to get to work, missing out on a day's pay.

So Chambers took matters into his own hands. He decided he would quit the car lot and start a service that would negotiate fair car prices for the working poor, help them with their overall finances and see to it that they get fair loans. It was a leap of faith. In five years as a car salesman Chambers had learned plenty about wholesale and retail prices—and how to spot a lemon. But he was in over his head when it came to partnering with banks and offering financial counseling to the poor.

But Chambers charged ahead anyway, calling to mind the words of Ernest Hemmingway in *The Old Man and the Sea*: "Now is no time to think of what you do not have. Think of what you can do with what there is." Chambers talked a few banks into backing him and in 2001 launched Bonnie CLAC (Car Loans and Counseling; www.bonnieclac. org), a nonprofit dedicated to getting the working poor of New England into reliable vehicles and helping them shore up their credit rating.

Since launching his firm Chambers has underwritten more than $10 million in car loans, and his clients have each saved an average of $7,000 over the life of their loan. The banks are thrilled because Chambers's referrals collectively have a better-than-average repayment record. "It's a win-win," Chambers says. "I get people who come up and give me hugs, saying, 'I never thought I could get out of debt.' I believe that most individuals really do want to do well. It's just that the system has built a circle around them that they can't escape."

Chambers takes a comfortable annual salary ($72,000) for his do-good efforts. But that's a small reason for him to be in the game. "It's changing people's lives," he says of his loan and counseling service. By making reliable transportation affordable, he helps clients hold a job and also build their credit. If more folks can afford to get to work, more will, he reasons. That's how he's living with purpose and making a difference.

Teach about the World's Needs

Just out of college, Katie Ginsberg began a promising career on Madison Avenue, where she worked in account management and served clients, including Unilever and other packaged goods companies. She later helped build a family business in leather goods and supervised the marketing and design of several product lines. But with the birth of her third child, and her husband's legal and investment career on track, she decided to stay at home full-time and now treasures the years she spent as a homemaker.

Yet Ginsberg, forty, always knew that as her kids grew older she would want to do more with her life than spend countless hours at the mall or country club with her affluent friends and neighbors in the northern suburbs of New York City. She has the highest respect for mothers who build their lives around their children, husbands, schools, and communities. But it wasn't right for her. Just what was her calling? Once she started thinking about it, several years passed before she figured it out.

Ginsberg knew a few things, for sure. Going back into advertising was out of the question, and she didn't want to do anything that would require resuming her long daily commute into the city. She contemplated trading stocks full-time. But for her that seemed like an emotionally empty pursuit. Gradually, the daily headlines in the newspaper started her thinking about some of the world's massive problems. This was post-9/11 and post-Enron. Global warming was starting to stir a lot of discussion, and the gap between the rich and poor was widening.

"These problems seemed so massive," she says. "I just started really thinking about what it means to be a human being in the twenty-first century. What struck me was how our habits and perspectives are so skewed by our culture. You must be rich and successful. Being successful means you make a lot of money; that you are in the corporate world, or a doctor or a lawyer." This ingrained mind-set seemed so powerful in adults, she thought, that the only way to change it was to reach out to young students and try to get them to think differently on a daily basis.

She still wasn't sure what she might do. But she began tilting toward environmental concerns, which were reinforced by conditions and events in her own home. Her youngest son, Gregory, and to a lesser extent his sister, Madeline, were both extremely sensitive to sunlight. Gregory also had an allergic reaction to sunscreens. "He's usually painted like a white ghost with zinc oxide," Ginsberg says. It dawned on her that this skin condition might be at least partly the result of some ecological imbalances. "I looked around on my street and the streets in our town and took note of all the little signs on lawns that warned 'do not enter: pesticide application.' We were using a service too, to spray the trees and lawn at our house and I started thinking maybe this stuff isn't so great for my kids. That's what made me start thinking about environmental health issues."

Among friends, Ginsberg would bring up her concerns and get mostly disinterested nods. They thought she was turning into an insufferable tree hugger. "I was feeling very frustrated," Ginsberg says, and that's when she decided that, as a society, we need to start educating kids so that they grow up aware of environmental dangers—much as baby boomers grew up aware of the nuclear threat, in part owing to drills at school that instructed us on how to take cover.

The first thing she did was investigate her own school district to see what was being done to teach kids, not just about environmental issues, which are generally acknowledged, but also about full-scale sustainable living. "There are all these issues with the world—scarcity issues, resource issues, human-health issues," Ginsberg says. They are interconnected and ultimately must be viewed as one. Say, for example, you're a company manufacturing environmentally safe detergents but your suppliers are clear-cutting the rain forest to get ingredients; the whole effort is worse than pointless—it's counterproductive. Yet the well-intentioned manufacturer may not even know the adverse impact of his efforts.

Connecting the dots in this way, Ginsberg found, was a new concept in schools, and so she set her sights on educating school districts about how to integrate lessons on the economic and social impact of environmental problems and solutions into their core curriculums. There, she believed, lay the master solution.

Ginsberg's school district welcomed her involvement. So she began attending conferences and researching the issues. That was in 2002, and within a year she and a small group of individuals with backgrounds in education, corporate environmental affairs, and environmental law had launched the Children's Environmental Literacy Foundation (www.cel-foundation.org). Their stated mission: educate children about sustainable living practices by integrating the lessons into everyday subjects like math, English, and science.

How does it work? In choosing a book to study, an English teacher might choose *The Ecology of Commerce* by Paul Hawken or *The Future of Life* by Edward O. Wilson or *Collapse* by Jared Diamond. These are modern classics dealing with the vulnerabilities of the natural world and human societies. A math teacher might cite algebraic equations based on carbon emissions and what it takes to offset them. Students might learn, for example, that in the United States the average citizen uses up about fifty-five acres of Earth in their lifetime, a devastating burn rate—but one that can be neutralized by changing certain consumption habits. Somewhere in all of that sits a whopper of a math problem!

Ginsberg's organization is starting to get traction; the ideals that she champions are already being incorporated in about twenty-five school systems. She believes that through annual forums and classroom work her organization's programs have already reached some 15,000 students. But grant money is starting to roll in, which will help her expand, and after several years of working long hours for no pay she expects to begin taking an annual salary of $40,000 or so in the next year or two. Ironically, even though most grantors insist on low overhead they also insist on the presence of some paid staff at the charities they support. Paid staff is perhaps the best signal that a program is functioning and will be around for a while.

"I just feel grateful that this passion came to the surface," Ginsberg says. "It wasn't something that I was intentionally seeking. I just feel really lucky and fortunate. A lot of people have said to me 'I wish I had a passion like that. I wish I had something that I felt so dedicated to that I could identify a way to spend time and make a commitment like this.' I think you just reach a point in your life when you're old enough to have the perspective of looking back and starting to think about what kind of legacy you want to leave. Maybe this is the benefit of age."

What does Ginsberg get from her efforts? Like so many of the people I have interviewed, who have found a larger purpose for living and invested their time and energy into learning how to spark meaningful change, she believes she now possesses knowledge that is just too valuable to go unused. "What I get is knowing that I am making a difference to some kid, somewhere, and to some teachers' ability to bring these lessons into their students' lives. I feel like I'm making a difference for the future, and that's what keeps me going. If I didn't do this, knowing what I know, it would just be irresponsible."

OK. I have spilled a bit of ink on Robert Chambers and Katie Ginsberg. Why? After all, they aren't headline grabbers like Bono or Angelina Jolie or Bill Clinton or Warren Buffett, all of whom are contributing to meaningful change in the world through their celebrity and riches. While interesting and noteworthy, though, celebrity contributions are a trifle compared to the cumulative good that people of ordinary means can bring about. Robert Chambers and Katie Ginsberg are just such ordinary people—perhaps like you—and they show us that it's not too late to discover your calling; that you too can set new goals at any age and pursue new dreams and reach for something grand. "Far away there in the sunshine are my highest aspirations," wrote Louisa May Alcott. "I may not reach them. But I can look up and see their beauty, believe in them and try to follow where they lead."

New Goals for a New Life Stage

Prior to this stage of life your goals were all about meeting needs and doing well at work. Yet it is imperative to have new dreams and chase them in order to keep from being stagnant. You have a responsibility to keep yourself vital by thinking about what you want to be and by thinking about how you want to use your life. Remember, as Professor Shoven said: if you are not going to die soon, then you are not old. If you are not old, you have many years left and you must decide what to make of them.

This is a new challenge presented by our new longevity. Embrace it. People who have dreams and set goals are more likely to find achievement. Yet many folks never do set goals, either personal or professional,

Why people don't set goals --
live in TM web?

not while they are young and not even after they mature. Why don't
more people set goals? In general, psychologists point to seven reasons:

- They have not yet accepted personal responsibility for their lives.
  Many of us go through life doing as we are told—trying to live up
  to other peoples' expectations instead of creating our own.
- Fear of criticism. The world is full of doubters. When you set a
  goal that others see as lofty, they will surely try to bring you down
  and recite many reasons why you'll never reach your goal.
- Fear of failure. What if you don't reach your goal? Everyone will
  know, and you may feel foolish.
- They don't know how. Goal setting is not usually taught in school.
  If it doesn't come naturally, you may not know where to start.
- They don't understand the value of goals. Most people don't
  understand the correlation between having goals and achieving
  their dreams. They think just trying to keep moving forward is
  sufficient. But it usually is not. Setting a goal—and identifying
  checkpoints—allows you to monitor your progress and adjust your
  plans along the way.
- They may have achieved things early in life without setting goals.
  Early success and popularity have a way of making you complacent, which if you can't shake it will catch up with you.
- Fear of success. Believe or not, some people do not set aspirational
  goals because they do not want to stand out. They feel safe when
  they conform.

Maybe you're reluctant to set new goals at this age. Don't be. Try
to understand your feelings and correct your thinking. It's not too late.
It's never too late. In fact, in the context of living to eighty-five or one-

hundred-and-five—it's quite early in the game, and the fears and excuses I've described can be easily overcome through the wisdom and experience of maturity.

A whole new period of productivity and engagement is opening before you. In recent years I and others have tried to put a name on this period when you may be done focusing on your career but be far from resigned to playing golf or bridge every day. You will most likely stay active in your family and community, and possibly even engaged in some sort of paid work. No word or term for this new phase of life has quite captured the public consciousness. *Rehirement* had legs for a while. Jeri Sedlar's clever word *rewire* gets used here and there. Neil Young asserted, "I won't retire but I might retread." In *The Power Years*, we wrote about *freetirement* and *unretiring*.

Rehire. Rewire. Retread. Re—hmmm. As I said, none of these has really stuck, even though all of them get at the essential point that in the new life stage I'm describing you'll need to keep setting new goals and having big dreams. You will not retreat or withdraw, which is the literal meaning of *retire*. Instead, as you cross into maturity you'll likely want to reboot and reengage, and find ways to apply your skills and hard-won insights to new endeavors and to learn new skills and tackle old problems as you infuse purpose into the many years still before you.

Now, as you reach your sixties and beyond you may have reached the critical point of economic freedom; having saved in your 401(k) plan, paid down the mortgage, and watched your youngest child leave the nest. You'll be able to use your time however you choose, and hopefully you'll have the good health and longevity to possibly do something grand. You may write a book on a subject that fascinates you. You may turn your love of music into a new career organizing concerts that benefit a cause. You might study scripture and lead a congregation. Maybe you'll decide to mentor a child, manage a book drive, or raise money for a third world business that needs help getting off the ground.

To encompass this broad new vision for a full life after your primary career, the definition of retirement is changing radically—even though the term itself appears too sticky to shed. For better or worse, "active retirement" seems to be entering the lexicon to describe this new stage of life. But I prefer *middlescence*. Just as the new life stage of adolescence—the period between childhood and adulthood—emerged about a hundred years ago; middlescence—a period between adulthood and old age, say ages fifty to seventy-five—is surfacing today.

For six million years humans didn't live much past twenty-five or thirty years of age. But in the past two hundred years our life span has tripled. Extraordinary breakthroughs—in public health, penicillin and other antibiotics, early immunizations for polio and other diseases, modern surgical techniques, and new pharmaceutical compounds—mean that more and more of us wake up each day with the idea that we just might live to ninety or even a hundred. And here's the thing: the best is yet to come. The longevity revolution is not over; it may even be picking up steam.

Just 160 years ago the elderly were a tiny fraction of the world population. Back then, less than 5 percent of Americans and Europeans reached age sixty-five. The figure remained well below 10 percent as recently as 1930. Now, projections have the number of sixty-five-year-olds globally doubling by 2050, at which time there will be more people over age fifty than under age fifteen, and the average fifty-year-old will be able to expect to live another forty-plus years.

How far might this all go? One notable extremist, Dr. Aubrey de Grey, a computer scientist at Cambridge University in England, thinks we can extrapolate recent longevity gains far into the future. It may be possible for the human body to live several hundred years in an optimal environment, he believes.

This is an admittedly radical prediction. But it points up just how much progress is taking place before our eyes. There is right now a wide and stunning range of promising research in medicine, from stem-cell break-throughs to new pharmaceuticals to new hormone therapies and organ replacement and rejuvenation techniques. This work promises to lengthen your life for years beyond what you probably expect. Molecular biologist Cynthia Kenyon was able to double the life span of a worm by tweaking a single gene. She believes her work will eventually eradicate Alzheimer's and other age-related diseases. Scientists simply will not rest until they've found the fountain of youth, or at least the fountain of health.

People commonly living to ninety or more will represent a challeng-ing new frontier for mankind. We are explorers by nature, accustomed to harnessing our courage and resolve to cross a river, a continent, an ocean—the heavens—to discover new lands. Yet the longevity frontier poses a new kind of challenge. It's about exploring the space in your head and in your soul, not necessarily in just the world at large. What are you to make of your longevity bonus years? Do you tag them on at the end of life without changing what comes before? Why not dis-tribute this longevity bonus at intervals along the way? Does your life cycle remain unchanged—learn, earn, retire—with the last part, old age, simply lasting longer? Or is a more interesting model beginning to surface—learn, earn, return? In this model you may use the "return" years to have and pursue new dreams and set energizing new goals for how to give something back.

I've also talked about a new "cyclic" life, one where you distribute your longevity bonus throughout your adult life. You work longer but take extended sabbaticals along the way. You retire from one job, and then start a whole new career. Along the way you might take the time to go back to school, fall in love again with your spouse or someone new, discover new passions, and generally reinvent yourself over and over again. "Follow your bliss and doors will open where there were no doors before," said Joseph Campbell, the mythology expert. That is what your bonus years can be all about. With good health and more time you may enjoy a virtually ageless middlescence, where instead of learning, working, retiring in chronological order you move in and out of these life phases as it suits you.

The world hasn't yet wrapped its arms around this bold new life-cycle concept. Longevity is still portrayed as a demographic and economic force, and as a physical phenomenon. You hear about people living longer (weatherman Willard Scott became famous with his quaint vignettes of centenarians), how the graying population will destroy the pension system (which is at the heart of the debate over entitlements around the world), and how certain foods (organic) will let you live more healthfully or how vitamins will extend your youthfulness. Yet we fail to grasp that longevity is psychological and spiritual as well. It goes to the core of who you are because your bonus years cry out for an answer to questions like, where am I in the journey of my life? Am I near the end or only in the middle? How far have I traveled? How much farther do I have to go?

Historically, life has been like a climb up a mountain—on the way up every step is a struggle, but one that improves your skills and brings you closer to your zenith. It's exhilarating as you ascend the mountain and your hard work is rewarded with an ever widening view. But then you reach the top and there is nothing more to look forward to. That's what happens to a lot of people when they hit age sixty or so—they have reached their top and feel that they have achieved all they likely will. From there life is a long walk down the mountain; with every step the view contracts. Life's thrills are at an end. No matter how you sugarcoat it—"the golden years"—this kind of descent ultimately proves depressing because your achievement is behind you and you have nothing to look forward to. You are winding down.

Today, though, more and more folks are rejecting this model. They want to stay on top longer—or find new mountains to climb, and longevity lets you do it. Your bonus years aren't about being old for a longer time—they are about new achievement; second, third, and fourth acts; and making a difference in ways that you might never have imagined.

Four Views of Life

Amazing rebirths and transformations are quite common in nature. "A drop of water becomes vapor, which is invisible, yet vapor materializes into billowing clouds, and from clouds rain falls back to earth, forming river torrents and eventually merging back into the sea," writes Deepak Chopra in *Life after Death: The Burden of Proof.* "Has the drop of water died along the way? No, it undergoes a new expression at each stage . . . Any drop of water in my body could have been ocean, cloud, river or spring the day before." The potential for dramatic change exists throughout nature, and within you.

Life is like a flower that blooms once. Think of a spring garden filled with newly opened flowers. Perhaps they are impatiens or begonias, or some other annual that starts as a seed, sprouts, grows and in time bursts into spectacular color. Then, at season's end, the petals fell off and the stalk wilts and the plant shrivels never to bloom again. The flower goes to seed. While its seeds can be replanted, the plant itself has but one life, one bloom, and it musters all its energy to make that one bloom as spectacular as possible. Many people (maybe even most) view their time on Earth in a similar light. You are born. You grow. You learn. You get a career, and you struggle to achieve as much as you can—to reach full bloom. Then you retire and wither away. With just one crack at being spectacular, you give it your all. But by fifty or sixty you are whatever you're going to be;

you have reached your fullness and taken your shot, and you spend the rest of your days just fighting to keep the petals from falling off. The transformation from seed to flower—from birth to maturity—is breathtaking. But it occurs just once. With this model, there are no second chances.

Life is like a flower that blooms every year. There is a second type of flower that I find far more interesting—the perennial. These are ingenious and hardworking little creations that burst forth every year for many years, repeating the cycle of going from seed (bulb, to be more precise), to sprout, to flower, and at season's end back to bulb, where they lie patiently waiting for the next season. They're still flowers. They have roots and petals just like their cousins, the annuals. But they are constitutionally different. They don't really die; they hibernate. They come back again and again and again.

What's especially fascinating about perennials is that they never change. A pink tulip is a pink tulip—and will become a pink tulip again. It'll grow eighteen inches; have a green stem and green leaves, and six pink petals year after year. Perennials have staying power. They have the capacity to return many times. This isn't a bad model for life: do one thing well, take a break now and then, and come back and do it well all over again. You may enjoy re-creating the same flower, or successes, time and again, and taking some time off along the way to rest and gather yourself for the next season. This is a far better model for life than the flower that blooms but once. But it's also far from perfect.

Life is like a snake shedding its skin. A third metaphor that fascinates me is that of a snake shedding its skin. This is a somewhat bizarre occurrence, and yet it happens regularly in the reptile world. A snake basically rebirths itself every month or so by crawling out of its own skin—often right before a big event like mating or giving birth. A snake must literally reject its own skin in order to change and grow. When it does this, what emerges is a more beautiful, more mature version of itself. A snake has to fight and struggle to wriggle free of its old skin. It's an exhausting process that may take up to two weeks, during which time the snake becomes irritable and partially blind. If you ever see a snake shedding its skin— even a pet—take special care! It may be unusually aggressive. Yet this is all part of the snake's nature—it must periodically go through this odd ordeal to become something bigger and better than it was before.

This isn't a bad way to go through life either—intermittently struggling with who you are and making the big effort to shed parts that aren't working anymore, and ultimately emerge as a new and improved you. It represents a path of continued growth. If you're going through life this way, congratulations—you'll never be bored and you'll always be growing. But no matter how many times you get bigger and better—you'll always essentially be what you were, just a little more of it.

Life is like a caterpillar becoming a butterfly. Why settle for shedding your skin and becoming a little improved, when you can transform into something fundamentally different? This is what I believe the new middlescence is really all about; this is what moving from material success to a life of higher purpose really offers. You can be a simple earthbound caterpillar one day, working diligently at keeping house and striving for some security, and the next day blossom into a soaring butterfly that brings a touch of beauty into the lives of all who behold you. This isn't just blooming once and going to seed. This isn't just blooming over and over but never changing. This isn't shedding your skin and coming back better at what you already do. This is a spectacular metamorphosis into something different than what you've been before. There may not be anything more majestic than your potential for utter transformation in adulthood. Listen to the words of Marianne Williamson from *A Return to Love*:

> Our deepest fear is not that we are inadequate. Our deepest fear is that we are powerful beyond measure. It is our light, not our darkness that most frightens us. We ask ourselves: Who am I to be brilliant, gorgeous, talented, fabulous?
>
> Actually who are you not to be? You are a child of God. Your playing small does not serve the world. There is nothing enlightened about shrinking so that other people won't feel insecure around you.
>
> We are all meant to shine, as children do. And as we let our light shine, we unconsciously give other people permission to do the same. As we are liberated from our own fear, our presence automatically liberates others.

Over the decades of my career, I've always been fascinated by people who reinvent themselves in adulthood. You know, the mom who goes to law school at forty-five, the person who comes back from health problems to run a marathon at sixty, the couple that falls in love at eighty, the retiree who starts a whole new career after his retirement life stage begins to bore him. At the same time, we were raising our own children and reading them stories at night. We were struck by the fact that stories about personal reinvention in adulthood just weren't present in the popular childrens' books that we were reading to our kids—in which maturity was often portrayed as a time for crones and geezers.

In response, Maddy and I recently had the great fortune of teaming up with a remarkably talented former Disney animator Dave Zabosky (*Beauty and the Beast, Lion King, Aladdin*) and his magical seven-year-old daughter

Grace. Together we four created a wonderful illustrated children's book, *Gideon's Dream: A Tale of New Beginnings.* According to Maddy, "It's a story about a little grub caterpillar who slogs through his day just doing the same old, same old until one day he gets stuck on a leaf that starts falling to Earth. And he gets the experience of flying and it's totally exhilarating to him. Yet once he falls to Earth he can't figure out how to make it happen again. It gets to the point where the little grub begins to dream about it and think about it all the time—daydreaming, dreaming at night. So he goes off into the meadow all by himself and he builds a little place to live and he starts trying to figure out how to have his dream come true. And the next thing you know, he reinvents himself as a buttlerfly."

In this book we attempted to craft a hopeful story for the ages, a story for parents to read to their children, for children to be influenced by, and even for kids and grandparents to share together.

Let Your Inner Butterfly Loose

My daughter, Casey, and my son, Zak, are terrific young adults. At twenty-one, Casey is set to finish college and develop her own unique game plan and philosophy of life. She's learning to relate to all sorts of people, has wonderful close friends, and has been sorting out her hopes and dreams regarding her career. In her field of study, media and communications, her insights and budding talents dazzle me. She is emerging as a wise, charismatic, and powerful young woman. At eighteen, Zak has just left the nest to begin his college life. I look at the books on the shelf in his newly vacant bedroom and I'm amazed: *The Sun Also Rises, Siddhartha, The Iliad, Childhood's End,* to name a few. I enjoy watching him try to make sense of all that is going on in his life, like any teen—getting to know the opposite sex, contemplating a field of study. He, too, is already showing promising signs of thoughtfulness and leadership. Yet at their ages, there is so much that my kids don't yet know or understand—from politics and business to relationships and struggle and hardship. They're still young. Their inner butterflies are still taking shape.

I, on the other hand, have those extra forty years of ups and downs, problems and solutions, arguments won and lost, disappointments, successes, learning what works and what doesn't. My inner butterfly—the sum of my experiences and how they make me feel and behave—is just waiting to burst forth. Yours may be too. Your life experiences (and you've had literally thousands of them) give you the critical knowledge you need to reach your full potential in middlescence. There are so many valuable assets that come with age. You probably have more seasoned people skills. You can better separate what's important from what is not. You have perspective and technical skills. You have learned some things about patience and compassion. Your experiences make you the way you are and shape what you can yet be—namely, an influential force of one with the opportunity to make a difference by keying on what's important to you and doing something about it.

When you bloom as a young adult there's a beauty and innocence to it—but you are just beginning to discover who you are. When you bloom or go through a metamorphosis in middlescence there's an authority to it; you have knowledge and roots and perspective. Such wisdom is no small thing. Socrates found the notion of wisdom so perplexing that when asked to define it he simply shrugged and said he had never seen it—in himself or anyone else. Wisdom has been thought to be so rare that it typically is ascribed only to heroes in folklore like King Arthur or biblical figures like King Solomon or spiritual visionaries like Confucius, Buddha, Abraham, Mohammed, and Jesus Christ.

Yet scientific research over the last thirty years shows us that the wisdom we need to keep growing and making good decisions is within almost everyone's grasp, and that it is closely associated with the aging process. Indeed, German researchers in the mid-1980s working on something called the Berlin Wisdom Paradigm concluded that you are most likely to experience peak wisdom at age sixty, though it is possible to peak at almost any age up to year seventy-five. The Berlin Paradigm defined wisdom as "an expert knowledge system concerning the fundamental pragmatics of life." Wisdom in action, the Berlin group concluded, amounts to good judgment, shrewd advice, insight, keeping one's emotions in check and empathizing.

This research has had practical effects: leading companies like Boeing, Volkswagen, John Deere, Stanley Consultants, S.C. Johnson, L.L. Bean, CVS, and Home Depot now actively recruit and seek to retain a fifty-plus workforce. Older workers cost about 1 percent more to employ mainly because of the greater cost of their benefits, according to an AARP study. But employers have come to assign an even greater value to the knowledge, experience, perspective, and ability to mentor young workers that a seasoned employee may offer.

What does this mean for you? Well, for one thing your odds of finding a welcoming employer later in life are better than ever. Forward-thinking companies are beginning to understand the value of experience in a knowledge-based economy. But the main point is that your middlescent years are your wisest to date; right now is when you have the most to offer in any endeavor you tackle.

Monika Ardelt, a German sociologist, concluded that wisdom is built around the ability to understand human nature, perceive a situation clearly, and make good decisions despite competing interests and conflicting information. Wisdom also incorporates the ability to step out of oneself and understand multiple perspectives. All of these traits, researchers agree, become more prevalent as you progress up the age spectrum. Wise people learn and gain perspective from setbacks; they are able to view problems as puzzles to be solved—not as fate or punishment. Wisdom can arise in people of ordinary backgrounds, Ardelt found, as readily as it arises in those who have been highly educated.

Are you wise? Try this short quiz:

Answer each question like this: 1, strongly agree; 2, agree; 3, neutral; 4, disagree; and 5, strongly disagree:

2 In this complicated world, the only way I can know what's going on is to rely on trusted leaders and experts.

1 I am annoyed by unhappy people who feel sorry for themselves.

2 There are some people I know I would never like.

4 Things often go wrong for me by no fault of my own.

5 It is better not to know too much about things that can't be changed.

Now answer each of these questions like this: 1, not true of myself; 2, rarely true of myself; 3, about halfway true; 4, mostly true of myself; and 5, definitely true of myself.

4 I try to look at everybody's side of a disagreement before I make a decision.

2 When I'm upset with someone I usually try to put myself in his or her shoes.

4 When I am confused by a problem, the first thing I do is consider all the pieces of information.

2) Before criticizing someone I imagine how I would feel in their place.

4) If I see people in need I always try to help them in one way or another.

3) Your wisdom total.

There's a certain pattern to the "wisest" answers. If you figured it out and worry that you didn't answer each question completely honestly, you might want to take the more difficult, extended version online. It can be found at www.nytimes.com/ref/magazine/20070430_WISDOM. html?_r=1&oref=slogin. But if you're satisfied with your answers, simply add your scores and then divide by 10. Most people end up between 3 and 4. If you scored higher than 4 you are relatively wise; if you scored lower than 3 you are—well, let's just say that you may need a more considered point of view.

With age-related wisdom most of us come to understand that you are best served by turning your energy toward positive pursuits. Here's three steps that will help you focus on your new dreams:

Get rid of unnecessary baggage. Too much weight slows you down, both literally and metaphorically. You will never see an overweight Olympic sprinter; she wouldn't have a chance. She'd have to go on a diet and shed the extra pounds—the baggage—to get back on her game. The same is true of someone who has, say, gone through a bitter breakup. Carrying the scars of a failed union into the next relationship can undermine it from the start. You must come to grips with the previous loss—shed the guilt, blame, and resentment—before you can find happiness or discover your new purpose. The chronically ill face a similar challenge. Therapists tell them they must accept their condition and lose the anger and frustration before they can move on and live their best life possible. They must adjust to their new reality and redefine their goals within the framework of what is possible.

Emotional baggage flows from many parts of life. Who hasn't had difficulties? We all carry around more psychological weight than is good for us—be it from an unrequited love, betrayal by a friend, an abusive relationship with a spouse or parent, or maybe a financial setback. Maybe you feel you've been held back at the office by a clueless or cruel boss, or by a colleague who has sabotaged your work. Such things are part of the ebb and flow of life. You don't have to like them, and you are right to do what you can to correct them. But we all must learn to accept setbacks and hurt, and deal with them rationally. Dwelling on failures and disappointments only sucks up time and energy that could be spent achieving a new goal. The longer you take to deal with your baggage, the heavier it gets and the harder it will be to achieve your new dreams.

Make peace with yourself and others. Part of reorienting your focus on new dreams is learning how to move beyond troubled or failed relationships. To do this it is helpful to forgive others for what they've done to you— and even yourself for what you may have done to others. Clear the decks. Get right with the world. Then you can move on unfettered and without hesitation.

Forgiving is a personal decision and one that does not depend on the approval or acceptance of any other party. You can forgive those who have wronged you without uttering a word to them; indeed, people who have done you wrong may choose not to acknowledge the wrong. They may not seek your forgiveness. It doesn't matter. You're the one who wants to get past the ill feelings. It's your decision. You don't necessarily need them to participate.

Likewise, you can forgive yourself for the wrongs you've inflicted on others even if they do not choose to forgive you. They may want to hold on to the grudge. They may want to carry that baggage forever. But you don't have to. If the person whom you have offended will not listen or cannot be reached, you can still forgive yourself and move on.

In the past few decades, researchers have documented the many benefits of forgiveness. Long acknowledged as the path to salvation in the Bible and other religious scriptures, forgiveness more recently has been put through the rigors of science, and has proved to be a potent elixir. Holding a grudge, it turns out, can literally kill you. Forgiving is the antidote.

In one study, college students were asked to focus on a grudge, and when they did, they registered higher blood pressure and a quicker heart rate. The students experienced increased muscle tension and heightened feelings of being out of control. They were asked to imagine forgiving their tormentor, and their vital signs returned to normal. In another study, people with elevated blood pressure due to anger saw their blood pressure return to normal after formal forgiveness training. And in yet another study, financial advisers who underwent forgiveness counseling boosted their monthly income by 24 percent Their minds were at ease, and they became more productive.

The toxic effects of anger are real. Forgiveness can lessen stress by 20 percent according to Dr. Frederic Luskin, a senior fellow at the Stanford University Center on Conflict and Negotiation and a leading forgiveness researcher. He found that the act of forgiving leads to far less depression, heart disease, panic, back pain, nervousness, restlessness, and sadness, and a stronger immune system. Forgiving leads to greater feelings of hope, peace, compassion and self-confidence. It may even open the heart to kindness, beauty, and love.

*   *   *

How do you go about forgiving? Here's a nine-step process based on the work of Dr. Luskin:

1. Examine how you feel about what happened, and understand exactly why it's not OK. Explain these feelings to someone close to you. A trusted sounding board will let you confirm your view or possibly reveal flaws in your thinking that deserve further reflection.

2. Make a commitment to forgive, and do so openly regardless of the response your act elicits. Forgiving is an act that will help you; it's not for anyone else's benefit.

3. Empathize with the person who has offended you. Forgiving does not necessarily mean reconciling. But envisioning why a person acted a certain way helps you get past it. You are after peace of mind; not atonement or assignment of blame.

4. Get the right perspective. Your ongoing pain is all about your hurt feelings—not about whatever first offended you weeks or months or years earlier. That's ancient history; let it go.

5. Hold on to forgiveness. When you feel like taking it back distract yourself quickly with exercise or thinking of things that make you happy.

6. Give up expecting things from other people that they don't want to give you. You can't control others. But you can work hard to provide hope, peace, love, and prosperity for yourself.

7. Stop mentally replaying the events that hurt you; use your energy to find new ways to achieve your goals.

8. Don't focus on your wounded feelings. That gives power to the person who caused you pain. Remember that a life well lived is always the best revenge.

9. Remind yourself that forgiveness is a heroic choice. Commit to it publicly and stick with it.

Be Open to Late Blooming

Middlescence may be the ideal time for fresh starts and late blooming with new dreams and goals, of intellectual growth, new relationships, vitality, and contribution. The rocking chair can wait. It has for John Glenn, who went back into space at the age of seventy-seven. After twenty years of directing, Clint Eastwood in his seventies began making the best films of his career, including award winners like *Letters from Iwo Jima*, *Flags of Our Fathers*, and *Million Dollar Baby*. Some of our brightest lights got off to a rocky start. "Can't sing. Can't act. Balding. Can dance a little," read a casting director's notes after an early audition by Fred Astaire. Walt Disney was fired from an early job for not having any good ideas. Mark Twain and Alfred Hitchcock produced their best work past the age of forty.

Late bloomers are everywhere, and among them are scores of ordinary people. We often presume energy and creativity to be the domain of youth. Yet that is not the case. In fact, creativity, a core trait found in many late bloomers, may be enhanced with age. That is the central finding in the groundbreaking work of economist David Galenson at the

University of Chicago. In his studies of creative genius he determined that creativity comes in two basic forms—conceptual and experimental. The conceptual genius is like Orson Welles or Bill Gates. They come on the scene at a young age with a bold new idea and change history. *Citizen Kane*, which Welles directed at the age of twenty-five, is widely held to be the most innovative movie of all time. Gates of course put the "personal" in personal computer. The experimental genius, on the other hand, matures over time and achieves greatness late in life—like Clint Eastwood or Louise Bourgeois or Mark Twain. They build on past successes and ultimately learn enough to produce genius-level masterpieces.

"In our society, if you talk about creativity you immediately think of the young geniuses," says Galenson. "These are the Picassos and Andy Warhols of the world; people who basically just have an idea—usually when they're very young. This is what we traditionally have called genius: the idea that God touches you on the shoulder and endows you with this quality that you don't understand but gives you remarkable insight, and which very often disappears as you get older." But there is such a thing as acquired genius too. It comes after years of learning through trial and error.

In Galenson's view, learning through experience leads to wisdom, which unlocks the creativity in experimental geniuses. The exact same mechanism is what produces all shapes and sizes of late bloomers—ordinary people who may not achieve fame and recognition but gain personal greatness through achievements that matter to them. He believes late blooming—like wisdom—is available to just about everyone. "Psychologists argue that wisdom and creativity are unrelated; that creativity is for the young and wisdom is for the old," Galenson says. "But this is obviously wrong. Wisdom is precisely the source of creativity."

An avid art collector, Galenson chanced on his field of study while walking through a gallery one day. He came upon a ten-year-old painting that he liked, and a friend cautioned him not to pay the asking price. The artist's newest paintings were selling for much less, he was told. To Galenson that seemed natural. A lot of artists' earliest work sells for more because they fall into the conceptual genius category—like Andy Warhol, Jackson Pollock, and Jasper Johns. Their earliest work broke with contemporary standards; it was revolutionary and regarded as highly innovative. Through the years these artists never found another mold to break; their newer work was interesting, but it didn't have the same impact. So collectors gravitated to their early work, which naturally commanded the highest prices.

Yet something troubled Galenson. Doctors and lawyers and bankers and many others tend to get better with age and command their highest fees late in life. Shouldn't it be the same with artists? Don't they get better with age? Looking at thirty years of auction data he found that there were indeed many artists whose latest work commanded the highest prices. These were experimental geniuses whose peak creativity surfaced only after years and even decades of building on past efforts to create exciting new works.

Galenson studied the price-age relationship in other creative fields too and found the same pattern. There were always young hotshots who produced their best work right out of the box. But there were vast numbers who just kept getting better and better—more creative—with age. The ability to create, to do new things, must be enhanced by age in many people, he concluded. "There's a form of creativity in which wisdom produces innovations," he says. "Every time a young person comes along and does something dramatic and gets rich and famous, people say, 'Well, that's a genius.' When someone shows creativity late in life they say, 'Well, that's really unusual, that's an anomaly. Louise Bourgeois. Anomaly. Clint Eastwood. Anomaly.' Well, no it's not."

We can't all be geniuses. But you can definitely learn and grow and innovate as you age. You can set new goals and have new dreams—and you can reach for them with an arsenal of lifetime skills that puts them well within reach.

Shedding your old skin, or turning into a butterfly, isn't effortless. You have to make it happen. A snake may take two weeks to rebirth and emerge as a bigger, brighter, shinier version of its former self. It's an incredibly exhausting ordeal. The caterpillar too must struggle to discard its old shell and bloom into something spectacular. It's no different for humans (except that it may take far longer!).

It's great that you have so much potential; as an adult you can still have new hopes and dreams and a vision for a new kind of success in the years still before you. But you're not going to just wake up one day like Sleeping Beauty and have the life you want. You can, however, wake up one day and begin to ask: Who do I want to be next? What dreams do I have for the rest of my life? What would fulfill me now and in the years ahead? How can I get there?

Empower yourself to think big. It's OK to consider things that are far different from anything you've ever attempted. It's OK to forget about chasing fame or money. You don't have to prove anything. And guess what? If you discover that gnawing feeling and decide that you'd like to do something new and purposeful; if you choose to go beyond your own self-indulgences, you just may open the doors to the most rewarding part of your life. "We must be willing to get rid of the life we've planned," said the mythology scholar Joseph Campbell, "so as to have the life that is waiting for us."

But as I said, it won't just happen by itself. Robert Chambers didn't wake up one day with a pool of capital and a list of honest-but-poor folks who needed a decent car at a decent price. He had to find bankers and credit counselors who were willing to work with him. He had to vet his prospective clients for honesty and commitment. He had to research and document how his organization would help his clients break the cycle of poverty and turn them into good credit risks. It took years to put together. Somehow, he figured it out. Katie Ginsberg didn't just wake up one day with a well-oiled organization preparing sustainable-living curriculums and seminars for students and teachers. The whole effort was a nearly anonymous labor of love for two years, during which she researched the subject and attended lectures and symposiums. She had to figure out what organizations were pursuing similar goals and might partner with her and how to set up an IRS 501(c)(3) charity. She learned how to approach the government and private donors for grants and why it's important to set up a board of directors with diverse talents in education, the law, writing, business, and publicity. She had to make all that happen from a limited knowledge base. Somehow, she figured it out.

I want to leave this chapter with another anecdote. I'll have more to say in the next chapter about my friend Augie Nieto. But this a good place to introduce him because his is a powerful tale of fruitful late blooming— not in the same sense as Clint Eastwood and Mark Twain, who enjoyed wonderfully creative success late in life, or even like Robert Chambers and Katie Ginsberg, ordinary folks who managed to break free from their auto-life rut by attacking social issues of personal importance. No, the story of Augie Nieto is vastly different; yet the lessons are universal.

Finding His Purpose Through Illness

Augie Nieto was a robust, driven, ambitious, and even Nieto would say, largely a self-centered man. He was a health nut who stayed in tip-top shape and was always supremely well groomed. He was rich, having founded Life Fitness of Chicago, a maker of exercise equipment that he co-owned and which was sold in 1997 for $310 million. A brilliant and driven entrepreneur, power and money were important to him. "Money was a way for me to keep score," Nieto says. "That's how I measured if I had won." By that standard, he clearly had. Nieto drove a Ferrari and lived in a cliff-side house in Corona del Mar, California. He and his beautiful family indulged their every passion, like exotic travel, scuba diving, and Arctic snowmobiling.

But Augie's fairy-tale life turned upside down in 2005, when at the age of forty-seven he found himself struggling to lift weights that were always an easy task for him. After a few weeks of uncertainty and terrible anxiety, he went for a checkup and was absolutely shocked to learn that he had amyotrophic lateral sclerosis, a degenerative and fatal illness better known as ALS, or Lou Gehrig's disease. Unaccustomed to setbacks that he could not pay his way out of or fight his way through, and envisioning the torturous decline that awaited him, Nieto became deeply depressed and suicidal. During that dark period he rethought all of his core values and concluded that his final hurrah, his legacy, needed to be about more than money. It needed to be about doing something important for the world.

Nieto might have languished in self-pity, or he might have decided that with so little time left he should live life large and indulge his "bucket list" fantasies. He could afford it, and he always enjoyed being flashy. But material things and self-gratification had somehow lost their appeal. With each day bringing more incapacity and misery and the end of his life in sight, a series of changes happened inside of him that led him to conclude that it was the things that he could not buy that were most important to him—his family and his relationships, and his potential contributions to others.

He dedicated himself to finding a cure for ALS, even though with his rapidly deteriorating condition he fully understood that such a thing was not likely in his lifetime. His new goal, he told me, was to create and endow a businesslike operation that would become self-funding and stay on ALS research long after he had passed—or until a cure was found. I'm happy to report that just such an operation is now in place, thanks to "Augie's Quest," which he describes in detail in his 2007 book by the same title.

As I was formulating my own thoughts for this book, I spoke at length with Augie in November 2007, when he had become wheelchair bound and ALS had rendered his speech almost unintelligible. He was a gentleman and took great pains to carefully enunciate so that I would understand his words. Virtually every sentence he uttered was a gem, and I could hardly believe the extent to which he had turned away from physicality and materialism and toward this larger more spiritual purpose. It occurred to me that this previously frisky caterpillar was transforming himself into a soaring butterfly right before my eyes.

"At first, I had no idea what ALS was," Nieto confessed. "It's known as Lou Gehrig's disease. But Lou Gehrig died a long time ago. A lot of people don't remember him." Believing that the disease needed a face in order to attract funding for research, this very proud man went public with an illness that was killing him an inch at a time and robbing him of his ability to perform the simplest tasks, like walking, bathing, or feeding himself. He pledged much of his personal wealth to the cause as well and took every opportunity to speak on the subject and draw attention to the illness.

Because of his entrepreneurial and team-building talents, Augie approached the usually disjointed and tedious process of global medical discovery with an intensity and ingenuity previously unseen. In a short time, Augie's Quest has been producing meaningful results, yielding clues from collaborative teams of researchers worldwide that should help to more quickly identify possible treatments. He has set in motion incentives, networks, and funding mechanisms that are literally speeding up the scientific process while ensuring that it will not slow down even after he's gone. This singular mission has brought great purpose to his life at a most difficult time. It's also taught him valuable lessons about not wasting time and living life with urgency, lessons that he freely passes on to those who will listen. "When you're healthy, life is like a marathon with no end in sight," he told me. "You can't see the finish line, so you slow down and pace yourself. But when the finish line is in view, you speed up because there is no point in saving your energy. This disease has taught me to run faster. I can see my finish line now, and so I run at a fuller tilt."

It's ironic that only when he had so little time left did Nieto realize what was truly most important in life. He sees what he has been able to accomplish on the ALS front, and it is so much more satisfying than the material successes he enjoyed before. If Nieto could speak clearly now I think he'd say to everyone in shouting distance that you should live your life with urgency, as though your time is running short. Find a dream and pursue it—with determination and passion.

Chapter 4

Your Marriage Is NOT the Most Important Relationship in Your Life

In the drought and heat of Berkeley, California, in the summer of 1991 fires ravaged the hillsides. Berkeley is a quirky and wonderful place where I lived from my mid-twenties to my late thirties. It's a college town filled with lots of interesting characters who are among the most highly educated and wealthiest people in the world. In their homes they have all the latest high-priced technology as well as exquisite handmade and restored antique furniture. These people are extraordinarily well traveled, and many of their homes are decorated with Persian rugs, rare paintings, and exotic tribal art. Yet as flames swept through the area, and thousands of residents were given about three hours to pack up and evacuate, almost all of these beautiful and precious possessions were left behind.

I love this story because three hours is plenty of time to grab a few paintings or roll up a rug. Yet three hours is not so much time that you can think for a while or make a second trip. Those who were fleeing had just one shot, and they had to make up their minds quickly; they had to decide what they would get from their home and stuff into their SUV on their way out of town. Their gadgets and their fancy and expensive stuff didn't make the cut.

What do you think they took? What would you take? In almost every case, the things piled into their vehicles were family pictures and souvenirs of interesting moments in their life. Photos and videos. These were their most cherished belongings. At the end of the day, isn't it the experiences we have, and our memories of them, that are our most valued possessions? I believe this episode offers a beautiful illustration of the importance of the close relationships and moving experiences that you have throughout your life. It is the people you have known and the special moments that you've shared with them that matter; not things. Does someone have to burn down the house for you to realize that?

Our lives can be busy. Making a living, raising kids, and keeping the household humming require tons of energy. Sadly, it's natural for relationships, even your closest ones, to slip to the back burner. How often do you call your parents or grown children? Have you lost track of a sister or a brother? What about nieces and nephews, cousins, a college roommate, or your Best Friend Forever from high school?

By the time you reach forty-six or fifty-two or sixty-six even most marriages could benefit from some refreshing. I have my own special way of doing that, which I'll share near the end of this chapter. For now, let me just say that if you put in the time it'll be worth it. Make the call. Send the e-mail. Extend the invite. You might be surprised at how rewarding it can be to reinvigorate not just your marriage but also other family ties and old friendships. Bonds forged many years ago are truly special. At one time, these were dear people in your life. Whatever happened since then doesn't matter. If your house was on fire it's their pictures and the mementos of them that you would grab.

But as important as those relationships are—especially the one you share with your spouse—it is the not-yet-made relationship that has the power to be most transforming. With family and old friends you enjoy familiarity, and that may foster comfort and trust. These are vital relationships. Take especially good care of them. But don't stop there. Don't be content with the relationships you already have because there is no promise greater than the one built into a new encounter.

New relationships come with uncertainty—but also excitement. They arouse your curiosity and sense of exploration. It is critical that you keep surrounding yourself with fun and interesting people who can help you discover and be what you want to be. I'm not saying your spouse and family can't help. Your husband or wife knows you best. Their understanding is definitely important. But nurturing and restocking your network of close friends is critical to the self-discovery and personal growth that will lead you down the road of higher purpose in the years ahead.

In the past few decades we have become increasingly isolated. Studies show that the number of confidants each of us can truthfully claim has dwindled from four to just one or two. That's not enough. Too few friends is limiting. You have the capacity to handle more without sacrificing anything in your marriage and family, and each one of your close relationships will fill you up in unforeseen ways. You owe it to yourself to keep opening doors. This isn't a popularity contest. You're not trying to register the most "friends" on Facebook. So don't overdo it. Experts say that four is a good start. Six or eight is better. Ten could stretch you too thin.

Great Partners, Great Results

How important are close relationships? History is full of examples of greatness that was only achieved through partnership—Laurel and

Hardy, Martin and Lewis, Abbott and Costello, Lucy and Ricky, Rogers and Hammerstein, Lennon and McCartney, Ginger and Fred, Gates and Allen, Ben and Jerry, Antony and Cleopatra, Lewis and Clark, Bonnie and Clyde, Pocahontas and John Smith, Roosevelt and Churchill.

These partnerships all surpassed what any of the individuals could have achieved on their own. "If we are together nothing is impossible. If we are divided all will fail," noted Winston Churchill. This human condition may be why so many important decisions in society are left to groups. For example, our laws are made by hundreds of politicians who were elected by millions of people. The Supreme Court rules by committee, as do juries. Central banks from the United States to Europe to Asia set interest rates via a majority vote. "Every prince needs allies," said Italian Prime Minister Silvio Berlusconi, "and the bigger the responsibility, the more allies he needs."

It may seem a stretch to devote a chapter to new relationships in a book about moving from material success to personal significance. But finding purpose in one's adult years is about many things—finding the job or pursuit of your dreams, replanting your time and money—and also developing the richest and most meaningful connections of your life, and through that support network reaching for your full potential.

Augie's Quest

Let me return now to the story of Augie Nieto. He found his purpose in life when there wasn't much time left for him to pursue it. But that's not all he found. With his days running short, he thought deeply about what matters most—and through his reflections gained a high degree of wisdom about many things. I was especially taken by his life-as-a-marathon metaphor. Nieto had been an avid runner before his illness; he competed in twenty-one marathons in all. He knew what he was talking about. His observation that in life, as in a long foot race, you speed up when you see the finish line is one of the most important things I've ever heard.

Am I making too much of his observation? I don't think so. As I've said, most people live their life like a climb up a mountain: The way up is exhilarating; the way down—the back side of life—is a long period of retreat and withdrawal. Nieto's vision is so much more hopeful. It holds the promise of ramping up your ambitions and contributions later in life, not withdrawing, and through a kind of existential time warp actually doing—and becoming—more as you get older, and in far less time. Knowing his days are numbered has given Nieto renewed momentum and changed his path. "I redefined normal," he told me. As he went from Ferrari to wheelchair, athleticism to near total paralysis, he clarified and accelerated his goals; he wiped away trivialities and focused on what was important to him and brought meaning to his life. "I didn't mourn what I couldn't do; I celebrated what I could do."

His quest for an ALS cure was just one of those things, and there he's already established a powerful global legacy. With his business savvy and turbo-charged fund-raising, Nieto has expedited potential breakthroughs for many years to come. His ultimate legacy in this area may well be having established a model for networked collaboration and funding of scientific research that will be duplicated in the quest for many other cures.

But along with his drive to make a difference in the world of science and medicine, he came to focus on something more personal—his connections to other people and especially with his wife Lynn. A strapping former football player and inventive and charismatic marketer, Nieto had always derived a large portion of his self-worth from being physically fit, charming, handsome, smart, savvy, and able to provide his family with a comfortable lifestyle. Without those attributes, he believed, he would be nothing; he would cease to be important even to the people around him every day. "I wondered 'Why me? What did I do to deserve this?'" Nieto recalled thinking after being diagnosed with ALS. His self-esteem devolved into self-pity, and he fell into despair and then one day purposely took an overdose of his medication.

But rather than die, as he had intended, Nieto was hospitalized and fell into a strange and revealing coma. For several days he could not move a muscle or communicate in any way. Yet his mind was alert, and he could hear everything being said around him. As his family and close friends kept a bedside vigil, they tearfully talked of their love for him and their hope that he would revive. Nieto was moved by their expressions of love for him, even as he lay in this comatose state with, in the best-case scenario, nothing but physical challenges ahead.

For the first time in his life he saw and felt that he was deeply loved by those closest to him regardless of his appearance, physical abilities, sexual prowess, business acumen, money, or influence. He reflected that his wonderful wife and kids and close friends seemed to love him unconditionally, which he had never suspected. This realization both liberated and empowered him—and helped him shake off the coma. And it ultimately totally reshaped his worldview. "I woke up and was able to accept my diagnosis," Nieto said, further reflecting that "your body is just an envelope. You and what you stand for are inside." Once he realized that, Nieto said, "I was no longer just reacting; I was able to act. With encouragement and support I was determined to make a difference—a big difference."

We too often seek in ourselves and in our friends superficial qualities. Yet appearances are not the root of meaningful relationships. Augie

Nieto had to fall desperately ill to realize that. Perhaps you've reached some nadir in life too. Hopefully not. But if you have hit a snag let the example set by Nieto—or quite possibly someone you know, a neighbor, friend, or family member—serve to reinvigorate you and enliven your personal quest for purpose in the relationships around you.

The wisdom that Nieto acquired through his illness proved of such ultimate value to him that he eventually grew to accept his multiplying physical limitations. Only through the lens of his illness was he able to see life clearly. "Here's a guy who defined himself by his physical body as well as his mind, and now his physical body is like the crate he was shipped in," his wife, Lynn, told me. "His focus is stronger now. He's not out doing the one-hour runs and the massive workouts. But he's spending that energy elsewhere, where it really counts."

Lynn Nieto says her husband's illness, and the revelations it stirred, actually drew the two much closer together. "I know things about my husband that most people will never know about their spouse," she says. "I know the way his beard grows. I know how to shave him. I know how to care for him in a physical way that I cherish. It takes forever for us to get ready in the morning. But I don't find that it's important that I'm ready to go at 7:30 AM I cherish the preciousness of each day." She says that "our marriage is stronger than it's ever been." Of course from time to time they disagree. "But there's a whole different thought process of how long you're going to stay mad," she says. "You ask yourself: How significant was that? Do I really want to pick that fight?"

This higher level of relating to those who matter the most is all part of speeding up as you reach the finish line. With time so dear, you come to realize that it just doesn't make any sense to lose a minute on trivial things or on trivial relationships. That's why I regard Nieto's marathon metaphor as so powerful. Look ahead to your finish line. You don't need to be ill to see it. You've probably got a bunch of good years left. But why not speed up anyway, and find and focus on the people and pursuits that really matter?

Speeding up transformed Augie Nieto. He realized that before his illness he had been spending too much time building a shallow circle of acquaintances to fill out his life with activities and fun. What was missing, he concluded during his illness, were close relationships that would help him discover what he was all about and pursue new paths. He chose another metaphor to explain this idea to me:

> Think of performing on a stage with all the people in your life seated in the theater. Some are in the front row. Some are in the middle section, and others are seated way back. Those in the back row can barely see what's going on, and they are only modestly involved in your life. They can't see you sweat or wink or slip—or nail your lines. They may be interested, but in a detached and easily distracted way. Those in the middle rows have a slightly better feel for your performance. But you're still not making eye contact; there's much that they too miss. The folks in the front rows, on the other hand, see your every expression and do not miss a line. They pay close attention and practically live your performance with you. They may even feel the spittle from your mouth as you approach the front of the stage and passionately belt out your words. It is they you are performing for. They are the ones who really count.

In life, Augie told me, focus on people in your front rows. "It's so easy to waste your time on the wrong people," he says. "Only when your time has grown short do you realize all of the lost opportunities. You could have spent your time with someone who really cares."

One Good Woman—or Man

If developing deep relationships and continually restocking the pool are so important, why is it so difficult? The Greek philosopher Diogenes spent his entire life searching for one good man, and by his account he never succeeded. Both Aristotle and Cicero considered a true friend among the most unusual of treasures. "The wish for friendship develops rapidly, but friendship does not," wrote Aristotle. "That such friendships are rare is natural . . . they need time and intimacy."

Oh, yes. We have many acquaintances; the average number of "friends" that people claim in their lifetime numbers in the hundreds. But you cannot possibly have that many "meaningful" relationships of the sort that Augie Nieto has come to value. We routinely substitute the sweet nectar of deep and genuine friendship for the artificial flavor of passing acquaintances. We have filled our lives with a revolving door of folks who serve a purpose for a while but vanish as quickly as they appeared.

Why is that? Harvard author and professor of public policy Robert Putnam documents this in his landmark book *Bowling Alone,* where he explains fifty years of growing isolation as the product of the mass penetration of TV sets into households followed by newer technologies like the personal computer and Internet. Putnam argues that we are so distracted by technology and life in general that we do not take the time to search for true friendship or nurture it where it has taken root. In our increasingly isolated world, the notion of friendship has become watered down.

You may have folks to shop with and to exercise with. You have fishing pals, and hang out with people at work. But few of these relationships rise to the level of genuine friendship—people to whom you can bare your soul and without whom your life would be significantly less full.

These kinds of relationships—whether there are two or ten—deserve your focus. "Companionship is only the matrix of friendship," wrote C. S. Lewis. "It is often called friendship, and many people when they speak of their friends mean only their companions. But this is not friendship in the sense I give to the word."

Nurturing new relationships is especially critical as adults. Eventually your parents, your partner and your siblings and other relatives may move on or pass away. Close friends can replace them in your life. In any event, good friends fill most of your emotional needs and can contribute to your sense of meaning. Hindu teachings say that friendship provides fulfillment in such psychologically critical areas as affection, romance, brotherhood, protection, guidance, and intimacy. Marlene Rosenkoetter, dean of the school of nursing at the Medical College of Georgia, identifies these virtues of friendship as well: playing a role in someone's life, feeling loved, feeling good about yourself, and having a support group.

We're moving into a world where friendship networks, which are not necessarily easy or natural for us to form, are of utmost importance. In earlier days you didn't really need to know how to make friends. You simply had them. They lived near you, sat next to you in church, or worked with you. You didn't often pick up stakes and move; so you naturally bonded with folks in the community over the common interests that put you near one another in the first place. The idea of someone, at age sixty-three, walking up to someone in an art class and saying, "Hi, my name is Claudia. What's yours?" and trying to jump-start a friendship that way is kind of new. But it's increasingly common and important.

What is going to most likely emerge in the years to come is people reaching out and seeking to form their primary connections with friends—not family. And women likely will take the lead in this mature friendship revolution as we begin to say good-bye to the Noah's ark style of living, where there is one man for every woman and they stay together for life. As we age, there simply won't be enough men to go around because they don't live as long. Millions of women are already discovering that it can be as nourishing to share life's ups and downs with a network of close friends as with one spouse. A trip to any geographic area with a high concentration of retirees will reveal the emergence of energetic and attractive groups of older women, who go to the movies together, enjoy investing together, and who care for one another when a health problem arises. Increasing numbers of women will choose to live together with their friends à la *The Golden Girls*, recapturing some of the communal spirit of their youth and blending it with the emotional and financial practicalities of their current lives.

Plan Your Relationships

If you're like most people, you've probably spent hours agonizing over and planning the financial part of your later years. Modern culture dictates it. You are raised and led to believe that your top priority in life is to achieve financial freedom; to quit work as soon as is practical; and to spend the rest of your days doing whatever you like. You literally grow up and grow old asking, "How much is enough?" Wall Street was built on this obsession, and plenty of others have tapped into it for profit as well. Author Lee Eisenberg enjoyed success with his thoughtful book on retirement preparation, titled *The Number*. But your happiness depends on so many other things. Boiling it all down to money can be a colossal mistake.

Living well is foremost about how you spend your hours, and who you spend them with. Sure, financial resources give you more options. But the real goal isn't money for money's sake—to keep score, as Augie

Nieto came to realize. It's finding quality time, and you can't have quality time without others to share it. "The experience of separateness arouses anxiety," noted the philosopher Erich Fromm. "It is, indeed, the source of all anxiety." So along with all of your financial planning you might try a little relationship planning too. After all, growing old and lonely is no more fun than outliving your savings.

Few have described the value of friends, relationships, and experiences better than Erma Bombeck, who penned these fabulous words:

If I Had My Life To Live Over

Someone asked me the other day if I had my life to live over, would I change anything.

My answer was no, but then I thought about it and changed my mind.

If I had my life to live over again, I would have talked less and listened more.

Instead of wishing away nine months of pregnancy and complaining about the shadow over my feet, I'd have cherished every minute of it and realized that the wonderment growing inside me was to be my only chance in life to assist God in a miracle.

I would never have insisted the car windows be rolled up on a summer day because my hair had just been teased and sprayed.

I would have invited friends over to dinner even if the carpet was stained and the sofa faded.

I would have eaten popcorn in the "good" living room and worried less about the dirt when you lit the fireplace.

I would have taken the time to listen to my grandfather ramble about his youth.

I would have burnt the pink candle that was sculptured like a rose before it melted in storage.

I would have sat cross-legged on the lawn with my children and never worried about grass stains.

I would have cried and laughed less while watching television … and more while watching life.

I would have shared more of the responsibility carried by my husband.

I would have eaten less cottage cheese and more ice cream.

I would have gone to bed when I was sick instead of pretending the earth would go into a holding pattern if I weren't there for the day.

I would never have bought ANYTHING just because it was practical/wouldn't show soil/guaranteed to last a lifetime.

When my child kissed me impetuously, I would never have said, "Later. Now go get washed up for dinner."

There would have been more I love yous…more I'm sorrys … more I'm listenings … but mostly, given another shot at life, I would seize every minute of it … look at it and really see it … try it on … live it … exhaust it … and never give that minute back until there was nothing left of it.….

We can all learn something from Bombeck's observations about the value of relationships and experiences, and take the time and devote the energy to create our own special moments.

Growing Close as a Vacateer

Elisa Sabatini decided to seize every minute after hitting her middle forties. She thought about the kinds of things that excite her, which include travel, cultural learning, and community service, and figured she was a good candidate to become what I call a *vacateer*—someone who goes on vacation to volunteer their time in the service of others. Through www.voluntours.org she signed up for her first trip, hoping to forge some friendships with people who share her passions. Sabatini, who is single and fifty-three years old, is now a veteran vacateer, and she remains close to many of those she met on three separate service trips over the past ten years. She cherishes the instant bond that people share when they take time out of their lives and pay their own expenses for the privilege of, say, working in fields or mixing cement as part of a project that will improve the lives of some of the poorest people on earth.

Sabatini's first experience as a vacateer was a six-week trip to Asia, where she toured India, Sri Lanka, and Bangladesh with fifteen other volunteers. They worked with a local women's group that taught nutrition and health, and found housing and improved security for the residents of poor neighborhoods. "The experience we had there of looking at that culture and then looking at our own culture was really a compelling thing," she says. "I remember one of the guys on the trip said to me that he was so impressed to see that many of the issues in these little villages weren't so different from the issues that everybody deals with—loving your kids, putting food on the table, being sure that you've got a safe house for your children and a decent school in the neighborhood."

Ten years later, Sabatini says, she remains in contact with every single volunteer from that trip. "I created relationships that are some of my longest term colleagues and friends," she says. One of those was the head of the local women's group in India, Bhavana Dee. She still lives in India, but Sabatini exchanges e-mail with her regularly. The two have coordinated service trips for other groups and visit each other. "We hang out, drink tea," says Sabatini. "She's one of those people I just have an easy connection with. Anytime she shows up she's welcome at my house for as long as she wants to stay."

Reach across Generations

In search of new and meaningful relationships, it can be enormously helpful to break out of the generational box where you more or less associate with and meet only people around your age. We have become an age-segregated society. The kids go to school all day and have carefully orchestrated extracurricular activities through the dinner hour, all with their peers. You spend ever longer hours at the office with no children or elders in sight. More older adults live in retirement villages or congregate in senior centers with people their age. And it's all exacerbated by our spread-out extended families, which only occasionally come together. When they do, family members sometimes find they have few touchstones.

The result is that the old have too few relationships with the young; and the young do not understand their elders or the aging process. This distinctly modern condition has consequences. In the absence of understanding, myths and stereotypes flourish. Young and middle-aged people see elders as feeble and intransigent. Elders see younger generations as disrespectful and possibly even evil or dangerous. We all lose in the process because our perspectives are needlessly warped.

Take a minute right now and think about the ten people you spend the most time with, other than your kids or parents. Is there anyone in the group who is more than ten years older or younger than you? How often do you even see a thirty-eight-year-old going out to dinner with their sixty-seven-year-old friend? Not often, right? This isn't the way things always were, nor is it the way things should be. Just a few generations ago, families lived together and worked on the farm, or at the family business. People were always dealing with and relating to children, young adults, heads of households, and grandparents. They saw births; they witnessed deaths. The old counseled the young and taught them valuable skills; the young challenged the old and offered new ideas. Everybody benefited.

But today the tapestry of the generations has been pulled into threads. Kids are preoccupied being kids, and with cell phones, the Internet, and Facebook—and parents often don't even know who the kids are talking to—or what they are talking about. Grandma and Grandpa may live four hundred miles away and be busy doing their own thing. You are left with your peers to ponder about how it all became so difficult to understand one another.

Intergenerational ties can keep your life interesting and keep you connected while providing enormous emotional nourishment. Young people feel like they are being mentored; old people feel honored and that they have some way to offer their unique counsel. A thirty-two-year-old woman who befriends a sixty-three-year-old woman can learn about childrearing and marriage without competitive spirits getting in the way, like whose twelve-year-old is the smartest or best athlete. The two can simply enjoy their shared love of, say, spy thrillers, gardening, or investing. It might even fill a void for the younger woman if she has lost her mother or grandmother.

Numerous studies, including one from Johns Hopkins University, have shown that adults who interact regularly with children report increased well-being and a healthier view of life. One study found that preschoolers in regular contact with adults develop better social skills. Kids who grow up exposed to the aging process tend to see it as natural. They are less fearful of aging and exhibit greater tolerance and respect for elders.

These kinds of findings have moved many communities to begin proactively joining the young and old by organizing activities at so-called shared sites. They include programs like the one at Heritage Day Health Centers, in Columbus, Ohio, which operates a program for older adults in the same building as a childcare center sponsored by the YWCA. Both sponsors pool their resources and promote activities including finger painting, cooking, and volleyball where both young and old participate. The nonprofit Generations United (www.gu.org) has as its goal matching different-aged people in an educational setting so that they can explore areas of common ground while celebrating the richness of each generation. The group's core belief is that young people can relieve isolation, loneliness, and boredom among older adults while the adults, in turn, can be a positive role model. There are many other options and organizations that will help you connect with younger—or older—people in an exciting learning environment, including programs at most universities or through mentoring groups like Community in Schools (www.CISNET.org) and Big Brothers Big Sisters of America (www.bbbsa.org).

Mentor Your Way to Meaning

No new connection, in my view, is more beneficial and personally fulfilling than the one that emerges when you invest a chunk of your time in someone else's future. What is a mentor? Generally, it is anyone who takes the time to share their life lessons with someone else who is typically younger and open to learning from the voice of experience. This is not just a guardian and her dependent or a teacher and her pupil, but any relationship where you are allowed to pass on a skill or your wisdom.

Mentoring occurs in many places and has been with us for centuries. It is one of the oldest forms of influence the world has ever known and has been traced to the ancient Greek storytellers. In his classic tales, *The Iliad* and *The Odyssey*, Homer tells of Odysseus, who asked his friend

Mentor to look after and educate his son Telemachus while he fought in the Trojan War.

Yet the term mentor didn't fully emerge in popular language until the eighteenth century French priest and educator Francois Fénelon put his own spin on the subject in *The Adventures of Telemachus*. This was a soaring work of fiction that told of Telemachus's many travels and the relationships he forged with various wizened elders, including his primary teacher, Mentor. Searching for his father, Telemachus embarks upon a series of adventures and encounters with extraordinary men who directly or obliquely provide him with important life lessons. He employs these lessons in his search and ultimately becomes reunited with his father.

Telemachus is little known today. But when it was printed in 1699 it became an immediate success and was the most frequently published modern work in the eighteenth and nineteenth centuries. The book was most important for the political views it espoused. But it helped shape intellectual development for a hundred years, and because the mentoring theme was so dominant throughout the story it solidified and gave a name to the act of being a role model and life counselor.

In more modern times, Mitch Albom's *Tuesdays with Morrie* has become a mentoring classic. In this heartwarming real-life tale, Albom tells of reconnecting with a favorite college professor he hadn't seen in sixteen years. After learning his old mentor was dying of Lou Gehrig's disease, Albom visits the man every Tuesday and soaks up his wisdom on love, work, marriage, envy, children, forgiveness, community, and aging.

Over the course of my career, I've seen a handful of seminal events that have lifted our youth-obsessed culture's aging awareness, such as John Glenn's trip back into space at seventy-seven, George Foreman retaking the heavyweight boxing crown at fifty, Jessica Tandy winning her first Academy Award for her role in *Driving Miss Daisy* at seventy-nine. But in some ways, *Tuesdays with Morrie* trumps them all. A runaway best seller, it presented a view of mentoring that caught the attention of millions of readers. It's not a Hollywood story about conquest or guy gets girl or coming of age. It's about the passing of wisdom; about the primal need for elder guidance and to pass along all that one has learned. There is something powerful about the passing of knowledge and wisdom and perspective from one generation to the next. Albom's book nailed it—and hit a global nerve.

I'll bet you've had a mentor, or life coach, at some point and possibly been one too, at least informally. My time helping students with public speaking is a form of life coaching, and in the coming years—when I'm more or less done mentoring my children (you're never really done, of course, but now that Maddy and I are empty nesters, they seem to need me less)—I envision devoting many more hours to that kind of thing. As I grow older and, hopefully, grow a bit wiser, passing on the fruit of my experiences to others is a role I'd really like to play.

Certainly, I've had mentors. In my case, they've been informal relationships at different points in my life. I long ago learned to value the insights and wisdom of people who are older than me. I've sought them out from time to time, and when I've connected it has always helped me work through specific problems or set a general vision for my work or my life.

One of my most profound mentoring experiences came several years after I had launched my consulting firm, Age Wave. I was struggling to find time to manage my staff and my investors and, frankly, not enjoying myself. On the one hand, I liked the idea of running a growing organization because it was a platform that would let me expand and have greater reach. But the headaches of hiring and firing, raising capital, and dealing with high-pressure investors didn't seem worth it. I expressed these feelings to an older woman in my field, Rose Kleiner, who urged me to speak with her husband, Eugene, about my business problems. At that time, I had never heard of Eugene Kleiner, but it turns out he knew a thing or two about business. He was the cofounder of Kleiner-Perkins, the highly acclaimed Silicon Valley venture capital firm that initially funded Amazon. com, America Online, Genentech, and other successful enterprises. In his seventies at the time, I primarily thought that he was a kindly elderly man and, perhaps, he'd have some sympathy for my plight. Little did I know that within a few hours he would emerge as my Obi-Wan Kenobe for that stage of my life.

So I met with Eugene—for just a day. It was both the start and the finish of a beautifully successful mentorship. I told him about my struggle with shareholders and my frustrations with capitalism; that I could easily walk away from the venture capital world and have a lot more fun. He listened patiently for hours as I whined away. Then I finally asked him what he thought.

"Well, Ken, if you walk away from your employees and your shareholders now, you'll be far more free and you may even have more fun. But for the rest of your life, you'll be known as a 'quitter.' On the other hand, if you stay and fight, even if you fail, you'll be known as a 'fighter' —and if you win you'll be known as a 'fighter and a winner,'" he casually reflected. Then he added, "One day you may want to hire people again or raise money for a new venture, and people will look back and judge you on how you handled this dilemma. They'll either see a quitter, or a fighter or a winner. Take your pick."

Bam! I knew I didn't want to be a quitter. That one day changed my life, and Eugene Kleiner probably never knew what a significant influence he had been. That's the way it works sometimes. What he said probably sounded trivial or obvious to him. It wasn't to me. If you make yourself available for this kind of role in others' lives you will have a bigger impact than you imagine.

Another extremely important coach in my life was Maggie Kuhn, founder of the 1970s activist group known as the Gray Panthers, which fought for nursing home reform and against all forms of age discrimination. She was one of my guiding lights for years when I first entered the aging field more than thirty-five years ago. Back then, there were few positive images of the elderly. The study of aging was primarily focused on loss, disease, and poverty. I wanted it also to be about wisdom, connections, longevity, and continuing contribution. I wasn't sure the world was ready for my positive spin and thought about switching to another field of study.

Then I met Maggie. We attended many of the same conferences, worked together, and often spoke from the same dais. She was a phenom known as "America's wrinkled radical." She was in her seventies, but she was beautiful, brilliant, and outrageous. She was in the media all the time at protests and sit-ins. She was on *Saturday Night Live*. She was a force, and she believed that what the aging field needed was a Paul Revere to ride in and sound the warning about how an aging population would change society. This rider would have to be young, she believed, so that young people might pay attention.

Maggie thought I just might be that person. She encouraged me to aspire to the role of social revolutionary. I'm not sure I'll ever live up to her hopes for me, but the thought of being influential, a change agent in my area of expertise, has been my personal North Star for decades. It's what got me thinking about the enormous social, political, and economic impact of aging-related issues and making the field my life's purpose. It's probably the reason I'm writing this—my sixteenth—book. It's partly because of Maggie. She made me think big. She told me I could. She believed in me.

The Coach Next Door

Mentors come in all shapes and sizes. Some like my parents are there for a lifetime; others—like Eugene Kleiner, for me—for just a day. Some are aligned with charitable groups like Big Brothers Big Sisters of America and the Boys and Girls Clubs of America (www.bgca.org); others are simply a friend, relative, neighbor, teacher, or employer with time, insights, wisdom, and guidance to share. Informal mentoring is by far the most common dynamic. But formal youth-oriented programs are rapidly expanding at schools and through national organizations like America's Promise—The Alliance for Youth (www.americaspromise.org), Save the Children (www.savethechildren.org), and Mentoring USA (www.mentoring.org). Meanwhile, executive-to-protégé coaching programs are proliferating in the world's largest corporations, bringing even more visibility and momentum to the concept.

Rey Carr is a Canadian who latched onto the mentoring movement early, and since 1975 has built his life around coaching others and helping others find coaches in every aspect of life. His firm Peer Resources (www.peer.ca) is the ultimate guide to understanding the movement and getting involved—whether you're seeking to be a mentor or looking to find one among your peers or superiors at work, school, or in the community. Carr's mission is to provide training, educational resources, and consultation to any person or organization that wants to establish or strengthen peer support, peer mediation, peer referral, peer education, peer coaching, and mentor programs in schools, universities, communities, and corporations.

A scholar with numerous degrees, including a doctorate in philosophy, Carr loves horses, chocolate, cycling, and Mexican food. He believes strongly in the value of humor and laughter—and the value of coaching at all levels. "When you look at the most successful companies, they are the most likely to have a mentor program, and when you look at the least successful companies, they are least likely to have one," says Carr. Likewise, he says that student mentors provide invaluable service to other students by helping with a variety of things that they've learned through their own experiences. One big one is transition.

Each school setting has its own vibe. A child could be highly successful and active in elementary school but lose that in a middle school that is four times larger. The issues only compound as kids work their way to college. "They may be going from a position of being well known and active and energetic and highly integrated socially to one where they know very few people," says Carr. "Now they're faced with a lot of older kids who might push them around or just make it more difficult for them to feel like they're part of things. By establishing a mentoring program to help with the transition you increase the likelihood that they're going to continue to be productive and get the grades that they need, and reduce the likelihood of social problems, particularly those associated with alcohol and drugs."

Whether at work, at school, or in your family or community, I'll bet you have skills and experience that others can learn and benefit from—and which will help you form mutually beneficial connections to folks outside your generation. The National Mentoring Database (look them up at www.mentoring.org) lists 4,100 organizations that specifically support youth mentoring programs. It is estimated that some three million adults in the United States have formal one-to-one relationships with kids who are not their own, and in polls virtually every last one of them say they would recommend to their friends that they become a mentor. These relationships last, on average, for nine months but many go on for years—and keep enriching all the parties involved. They need your help.

Making a Lifetime Friend

Michelle Mundy, thirty-eight, was in her first job in the advertising department at *Texas Monthly*, a magazine, back in 1992 when her employer decided to partner with Communities in Schools, a national mentoring organization. Mundy, who lives in Austin, Texas, thought it would be a good way to give something back. So she signed up to mentor a bright-eyed five-year-old with absentee parents, Angela Wilborn, who was being raised by her grandmother, and the arrangement flowered into a full-fledged friendship of seventeen years—and counting.

"I will never forget our first meeting," says Mundy, who was just twenty-two at the time. "This little kindergartner had the biggest smile. She was so excited to meet me, and that made me excited. There was definitely a connection for us right away." It doesn't always work like that, Mundy says. Years later, after her formal mentorship with Wilborn had ended, she tried again—twice—but never felt the same kind of connection. But with Wilborn it seemed natural, and the relationship ultimately brought meaning and perspective to both of their lives. With invaluable guidance from Mundy, Wilborn became the first in her family to graduate from college (with multiple job offers)—and Mundy was proud to be at the commencement with her own daughter at Johnson & Wales University in Providence, Rhode Island, to help celebrate.

It all started when Mundy began meeting Wilborn as a very young girl once a week to help with schoolwork, or eat lunch, or play jacks, or just listen. "She really looked forward to my visits," Mundy says of Wilborn. "If I had a conflict and couldn't make it, it was a really big deal to her and that made it a big deal to me. I had to show up." Says Wilborn: "Every Friday she'd show up no matter what. She'd congratulate me on my grades or talk to me if I was in trouble. Later, she motivated me to stay in school. There were times I thought I'd quit. But she wouldn't let me."

Over the years Wilborn's grandmother relocated a few times, usually within an hour of Austin. Mundy worried that the sudden departures would cut her off from Wilborn, so she and the child agreed to stay in touch via letters and the telephone. Mundy occasionally drove to wherever the family was staying in order to take Wilborn out to lunch or shopping. After Wilborn's grandmother moved back to Austin while the girl was in fifth grade Mundy decided that the official mentor designation was too restrictive. For example, she was limited to visiting only during school hours and on school grounds. So she chose to take a more active role in Wilborn's life.

Mundy began to take Wilborn shopping, to amusement parks and ball games, and out to eat. "I took her out to eat a lot because she never had that opportunity before," says Mundy. "Her family just didn't have the money. I'll never forget taking her to a restaurant. She had never had fajitas, which is unheard of for a fourteen-year-old Texan. When those fajitas came out sizzling in front of us, her eyes just got huge. It was such a simple pleasure for me to watch her experience something new that most of us take for granted."

Mundy opened up Wilborn's life in more meaningful ways too. She not only encouraged her to stay in school as a teen, but also helped her study and earn grades that would get her into college. She showed Wilborn, who had never been out of Texas, that she could go anywhere she liked—and even helped her fill out the college applications and loan and grant documents.

Now, when Wilborn visits Austin she stays at the Mundy home and babysits for Mundy's two children. She calls Mundy "Mama-Shell" (instead of her first name Michelle). "By the time I was in eighth grade she had taken the role of my mom," says Wilborn. "The mentor thing stopped. She became my mom. I needed school supplies, they were there; money for school clothes, it was there. If field trips came up I didn't have to worry about how I'd pay for them. She made sure I attended—if my grades were good. She made sure that I was in band and in basketball and active in school. It was awesome. When I introduce her to friends I say, 'This is my mom.'" Without Mundy, says Wilborn, "I'd probably be back in Austin doing nothing. I'd probably be a bum."

Yet this has been a two-way street. Mundy says that Wilborn's response to her efforts has given her confidence in her ability to be a good mother. She values the exposure her own children have had to a child born with less. It has kept them grounded and forced Mundy to answer some tough questions about life and fairness and materialism. "Our relationship shook me out of my little bubble world," says Mundy. "I can't imagine my life without her. She exposed me to things outside my world and opened my eyes; she put things in perspective for me. I have learned that no matter how bad a situation is you can always see the good in it. She does. Little things in my world that I used to see as a big problem I now see much differently."

Do You Have What It Takes?

Mentoring programs come in many forms, and there is a place for you. I guarantee it. "At any one point in time, I have three, or four, or five people that I am acting as a mentor for," says Deepak Chopra. "And I listen to them mostly. I listen to what's going on in their life, what's going on with their friendships, in their relationships. To be a mentor you need to understand what's going on in a person's life and you just want to have an internal dialogue that says, "How can I help? Because I really care."

When I asked Jill Godsey, marketing director of Big Brothers Big Sisters, how a person could tell if they were cut out to be a mentor, it was almost as though she didn't understand the question. "Do you like to watch movies?" she responded. "Do you like to play video games? Do you enjoy shooting hoops? Those are the kinds of things that our Big Brothers and Sisters do with their Little Brothers and Sisters. It is simple and fun, in addition to rewarding."

Sounds pretty darn easy, doesn't it? If you still have doubts, take this fifteen-question "mentor quiz" designed by Peer Resources. Award 5 points if your answer is yes; 2 points if your answer is sometimes; and 1 point if your answer is no:

___Do you know what it's like to have worries, frustrations, and concerns about your work?

___ Do people seek you out to talk about their worries, frustrations, and concerns?

___Is the amount of time you spend listening significantly greater than the amount you spend talking?

___ Has anyone ever helped you uncover a feeling or talent that, before then, you hadn't recognized in yourself?

___ Has anyone ever inspired you with a famous quote that influenced your thinking or behavior, and that you have since passed on to others?

___ Has anyone ever prodded you to an "aha!" moment that enabled you to grasp the core of meaning of some event, or a deeper understanding of yourself or someone else?

___ Has anyone ever helped you gain knowledge about how things work, about how to get things done?

___ Has anyone ever encouraged you to find a way to deal with challenges in your life or work?

___Has there ever been anyone in your life who had a profound positive effect on you, but you didn't realize it until much later in your life?

___ Has someone in your life provided just the right help to you at just the right time?

___ Has anyone in your life helped you to grow and deepen your character, moral or ethical integrity, or gain a stronger commitment to your values?

___ Has anyone inspired you to shift the direction of your life in a constructive way?

___ Have you ever reached out to a person in need, and made a difference?

___ Do other people reach out to you when they have important life or career decisions?

___ Have you ever felt a profound change in your values and goals after pondering something you observed, read, or experienced?

___Your Mentor Score

Now add them up. If you scored 60 to 75 points you not only have great potential to be a mentor but probably are also already acting in that capacity for one or more people. If you scored 45 to 59 points you are clearly a valued person in other people's lives and have what it takes to be a great mentor. If you scored 30 to 44 points you may have core mentoring strengths that likely will blossom through experience. If you scored below 29, you may still be right for this type of giving, but you may need some training.

Your Mentoring Choices

The vast majority of community-based mentor programs are geared toward at-risk youth, those teens and preteens who come from poor and often split families and are most vulnerable to dropping out of school and getting into trouble and living a life of low expectations. Yet there are ample opportunities to mentor all kinds of kids through athletics, tutoring, and programs like Junior Achievement (www.ja.org). You can mentor youngsters with disabilities, those wishing to learn a hobby or play an instrument, or how to write or take up a cause.

Mentoring opportunities extend beyond kids and the physical limitations imposed by geography—to virtual and professional communities of folks around the world with whom you share a value or experience. That might be your alumni association, a national civic group, your tribe, fellow ex-pats, activists, or coworkers.

A woman I know who recently retired from her entertainment law practice is putting together a group of retired Hollywood cameramen, newscasters, screenwriters, producers, actors, and actresses—to travel to third world nations and teach teenagers all how to envision and produce world-class media. Imagine their impact? A troupe of highly skilled communications professionals heads off to, oh, Kenya to share their skills with people who are just developing their ability to publish local newspapers and film documentaries—and who can really benefit from this type of knowledge. Being a mentor in this more flexible, modular world outside your own immediate community can be both satisfying and liberating.

Whatever you try, give it time. The fit may not always be perfect at first and it will take time to work out the kinks. But don't be afraid to move on if something doesn't feel right after a few weeks or months. Mentoring should be an experience you enjoy. Give yourself permission to explore various options until the right connection falls into place.

There are formal mentor programs geared toward seniors too, who may be struggling with finding new friends, a purpose, or a pastime and who may be encountering aging issues like immobility, medical care, loss of a spouse, financial difficulty, or loneliness. Such people can benefit from a surrogate child or grandchild. But often the best mentor for a senior is another senior who's already faced one or more of the same issues. One organization making such matches is the Senior Companion Program (www.seniorcorps.org). Senior companions serve adults who need assistance to live independently. They offer companionship, assist with simple chores, and provide transportation. Generally, senior companions are sixty or over and must commit to at least fifteen hours each week. Some training and expense reimbursement is available. But the real benefit to the volunteer is the joy of helping others.

Here's John Glenn on the subject of retirees giving back: "When I was in space the second time, I was seventy-seven. When I came back I heard from every old folks' organization in the United States. Most of them were just congratulatory things but some of them wanted advice, and my best advice is, I think you do better when you wake up every morning with something you're looking forward to, something productive. Older adults sometimes just sit and do nothing, and I think that's the worst thing they can do. They've had a lifetime of experience. They've had education. They've had on-the-job training. They've been business executives. They've been farmers. They spend a lifetime learning how to do these things. I don't think it has to end. At the least we can have people who take these experiences and use them to mentor young people, advising and counseling them so that maybe they don't have to make some of the same mistakes we made in getting through our own lives.

"A mentor gets a lot of satisfaction. They're doing something constructive, so they feel good about that, and when they see the results with the young people they're working with it's very, very rewarding. Also, they have a feeling that their own experiences aren't just ending because they're old. They're able to sort of provide a new base through their own experience; they provide a new base for a young person to start from and that gives you a great deal of satisfaction."

Faith-based programs. Religious organizations account for 43 percent of all volunteers who mentor youngsters and thus are a major force in this movement. Much of their effort centers on spreading their philosophy and reinforcing their values. These can be gratifying outlets for folks who share the same religious zeal as the organization.

Some years ago one of my former executives at Age Wave, Mark Goldstein, rediscovered his faith. Mark is a terrific public speaker with a deep understanding of how to craft marketing plans to appeal to maturing boomers. But his life changed after his mother's death. He began attending temple more regularly and started requesting private visits with his rabbi. While attending these sessions, he couldn't help but notice that the services and programs seemed to be out of touch with the middle-aged men and women in the community. One day he was asked to speak at a gathering of Jewish leaders, and he talked about the fact that many boomers were turned off by organized religion and how congregations might approach this generation to reengage their faith. The audience loved him, and now he spends most of his time counseling Jewish leaders on how to better appeal to a new generation of congregants. He has become a marketing guru for a nonprofit sector, all based on the knowledge and skills he learned during the course of his primary career.

These kinds of transitions from the for-profit world to the nonprofit world are becoming common and have immense value. In Mark's case, the skills and knowledge he brought to his faith-based consulting wouldn't necessarily strike anyone on Madison Avenue as earth-shattering. But within this particular nonprofit sector they just didn't have his level of sophistication. What he brings to them is enormously valuable, and Mark's profound sense of contribution provides incalculable satisfaction.

Civic Programs. Nondenominational mentor programs also abound. Again, they tend to have a strong focus on youth and fall under a national organization like the Foster Grandparent Program (www.seniorcorps. org), Boy Scouts of America (www.scouting.org), Girls Scouts of the USA (www.girlscouts.org), Girls Inc. (www.girlsinc.org), National Black Child Development Institute (www.nbcdi.org), Kids and the Power of Work (www.kapow.com) and YMCA of the USA (www.ymca.net). The central aim of these types of programs is to impart skills that will help kids throughout their life.

There are also many locally operated nonprofit mentor programs run by a highly energized founder, which makes them fun to work for if you are a volunteer. The key is matching your passion with the right organization.

Helping Inner-City Youth

A longtime supporter and mentor through Big Brothers Big Sisters, Gerald Chertavian wanted to step up his service commitment after striking it rich during the dot-com mania in the late 1990s. He never forgot the essays he wrote to get into Harvard Business School, where he later graduated with honors. He had espoused on the need to teach low-income young adults basic business skills. "So I decided it was time to make good on those essays," he says.

Chertavian, forty-two, grew up in working-class Lowell, Massachusetts but enjoyed a successful career on Wall Street before starting a software development company that, when sold in 1999, put $27 million in his pocket. Long active in Big Brothers Big Sisters, he turned his thoughts to the four million young adults aged eighteen to twenty-four who, he says, are disconnected from society because they've never been given a chance. "That's totally unacceptable," says Chertavian. "This is a solvable problem."

In 2000, he launched Year Up, a nonprofit that gives disadvantaged young adults one year of training in what Chertavian calls ABC: attitude, behavior, and communications. This interpersonal training is complemented with technical training, usually in computers. Students are paid a stipend of $180 a week and get docked if they're late for class. Some 85 percent find meaningful work directly out of his program; 60 percent of those who enroll have been referred by former students.

Wilfredo Pena came to the States from El Salvador as a teen refugee, went through the Year Up drill, and found work in the back office at Fidelity Investments. "He's now finishing college and has bought a house," says Chertavian. "He's living the American dream."

Year Up now has seventy employees and an annual budget of $13 million. It operates in four cities and graduates five hundred a year. Cherta-vian, who just began taking a salary at the insistence of his board, is now raising $18 million to expand into four more cities. "This is incredibly satisfying to me," he says. "I have a real desire to mentor and see other people reach their potential. I'm so blessed. I get to find meaning in what I do every single day."

People like Michelle Mundy, Mark Goldstein, and Gerald Chertavian have enormous impact, and so could you by finding a group like theirs, or starting one, and coaching someone who might benefit from your in-terests, experiences, or particular set of skills. And as each of them points out—you'll benefit too from fresh perspectives that can only come from people who are not part of your age or economic or ethnic demographics.

The Win-Win

I've described mentoring as a two-way street, and it really is. You get as much as you give. I recall a project decades ago when I was asked to teach a group of elders how to take better care of their health. I would engage them in yoga and meditation for a while, and afterward we'd just sit and talk. These elders loved the time they spent regaling each other—and me—with tales from their younger days. It was a joy for them to voice their memories.

The strange thing was that the more I indulged them the more I found myself enraptured by what they had to say. I often felt that what they had to say to me was far more interesting than what I had been teaching them. They had so much stored knowledge. When I got be-neath the surface—to their stories and insights, and the moments that had changed their lives—there was so much for me to learn from them. Experiences like that are what propelled me into the aging field.

Today we have a society groping for wisdom and guidance, as illustrated by the explosion of self-help books and self-appointed media gurus. Yet it may be the person living in the apartment next door who has the answers you really need. By not seeking that person out; by not setting up mechanisms for that kind of exchange, collectively we're letting some of the greatest wealth of our time go to waste. Meanwhile, as individuals we're failing to explore a gold mine of potentially transforming yet-to-be relationships.

A Confession

OK, so even though the title of this chapter suggests that our marriages might not be the most important relationship in our lives, the truth of it is—in mine it is. That might be the case for you too, if you are married or have a longtime partner. The title is not to be taken literally. I'm just saying you need to shake things up and keep pursuing other relationships even as you take care of this paramount one. Over the long haul, there's no question that my connection with my wife, Maddy, ultimately towers over all other relationships in my life. But this special quarter-century love affair doesn't always just "fall into place," and there are times when we're ready to strangle each other or when it feels as though the other activities of our lives have formed jungle vines that threaten to cover—or even bury—our connection.

In fact, Maddy and I have found that to make our marriage work, we have to continually bring "purpose" to this relationship, just as we've been discussing with regards to work, or charitable involvements. I've come to notice that for so many people, their marriage can simply get lost within the pushes, pulls, and pressures of their everyday lives. It appears that many marriages wrongly assume that automatic pilot will keep things in place. I truly don't think it happens that way for most of us. In fact, I'm convinced that just as a garden regularly needs replanting or a business may need continual infusions of investment capital, our marriages also need to be refreshed—even rebooted—on a regular basis. There are lots of relatively easy activities that can help to refresh our romance: simple acts of kindness during a stressful period, an unexpected gift, a playful dinner for two—and so on.

However, one of the key ways that we repeatedly remind ourselves of the sacredness of our bond is by getting remarried every year—again and again. Yes, that's right. Maddy and I have gotten remarried every year on or near our anniversary for twenty-five years—and counting. When we originally married, on Thanksgiving in 1983, we had such a great time at the ceremony and on our honeymoon that I asked Maddy if she'd consider remarrying me every year. And, to add a bit of spice to this ritual, we set the rules that we would do so in a different religion and in a different location each year.

We haven't missed a year yet, and so far, we've been remarried in a castle in Bath, England, by an Anglican priest; in a Hopi ceremony in Sedona, Arizona; and at Marie Antoinette's Chapel of Love in Versailles, France. We've been married by the skiing judge of Vail on the high slopes of Vail mountain; in a tai chi ceremony (followed by a nude soak in the mineral hot springs) at Esalen Institute in Big Sur, California; by a tribal chief and his toddler grandchildren in a Navajo ceremony in Tucson, Arizona; and by the ship's captain while cruising through the Sea of Cambodia off the coast of Thailand. We've recited our vows in Grace Church in Greenwich Village; in a Buddhist ceremony in Berkeley, California; in a Mayan wedding at the top of the Chichen Itza pyramid in the Yucatan; and, of course, at the Chapel of Love in Las Vegas (and I'm a bit embarrassed to admit that I was dressed in a white Elvis jumpsuit with red trim—gold medallion and all). We've even been "married" twice by our children—once in Zihuatanejo, Mexico, and a few years later on a secluded beach on the remote island of Anegada in the British Virgin Islands.

We also had our kids perform a formal remarriage ceremony for my parents in celebration of their sixtieth anniversary at our home in California. When my dad strolled down the aisle in his white dinner jacket arm in arm with my beaming mom and then our kids launched into the service that they had written together, it was an incredibly powerful moment in all of our lives—for every reason you can think of.

For Maddy and me, getting remarried each year is definitely a lot of fun. But we also have found that these occasions are like valuable sanctuaries when we can look critically at the year that just passed and openly discuss what went wrong and what went right. These moments have become punctuation points in our relationship when we can stop the train, take a deep breath, and rechart our course. When I was younger, I believed that the nouns and verbs of our lives were what mattered most. Maddy and I have both come to appreciate the special importance of the punctuation points!

Some years, we've concluded that everything is going just fine, while others require serious discussion—maybe even an argument or two— before we can align our needs and commitments again. We also have practical discussions of what our relationship needs more of or less of. As our lives have unfolded, these "pauses" have focused on everything from our anxieties over the impending birth of each of our two children, a few work failures and humorous successes, the death of Maddy's dad, and most recently, how we intend to cope with becoming empty nesters and the painful financial reckoning that has seized the world. This annual ritual has proven a great way for us to stay connected, and when the moment comes when we face each other and say "I do," it never fails to help us remember the things that made us fall in love in the first place while allowing us to take notice of all the reasons we love each other still.

We try not to make a big chore of these occasions and have found that the simpler we keep them, the more we can focus on each other and on the continually evolving purpose of our bond. From time to time, when people learn about our remarriage history, they ask us why we would do something as odd as that. We simply respond, "You should try it! We bet you'll be moved by the experience."

Chapter 5

Giving—It's Also about What You Get

Life is without meaning. You bring the meaning to it.

—Joseph Campbell

In June 2006, Warren Buffett, the second richest person alive, pledged 85 percent of his personal fortune—$31 billion—to the Bill and Melinda Gates Foundation. The world of philanthropy had never seen anything like it, and Buffett was roundly applauded not just for his outsized generosity but his humility as well. He could have built himself a shrine in Dubai, or he could have established the world's largest foundation in his own name to live on forever as a monument to his riches. He could have pulled a Leona Helmsley and left $5 billion "for the care and welfare of dogs," or whatever his handpicked goals might be. But Buffett chose otherwise; he handed his money to a friend whom he trusted to more effectively distribute his life's accumulation. In the eyes of the world it was a singular act of selflessness, and a clarion call for others to follow his lead.

So only a refreshingly honest and irascible Scotsman like Sir Thomas Hunter, a self-made billionaire philanthropist himself, could see Buffett's largesse as anything less than magnanimous. Buffett, argues Hunter, may have taken the easy way out. "If you've been clever enough to make $31 billion, you're wired differently from 99 percent of the population," Hunter explained to me. "And I would love to have your thinking in trying to solve the world's seemingly intractable problems."

In other words, if you'll indulge an American football metaphor, Buffett is the quarterback who drove his team to the goal line and then left the game, handing off responsibility for gaining the final yard—the toughest yard—to another teammate. Gates is no ordinary teammate, for sure. But Sir Tom's point is worth considering: Someone with unusual ability owes it to others to stay with the job until it is finished. In Hunter's view, making a fortune is the easy part; distributing it for maximum good (getting over the goal line, to complete the football metaphor) is the real challenge. "I really believe there's nothing that you can't solve with the right brain power," says Hunter. "I would love to get Warren Buffet's brain engaged in some of these challenges. And, by the way, he would also get so much out of it."

Taking on Goliath comes naturally to the direct and enthusiastic Hunter, forty-seven, who enjoys playing drums with a local rock band and usually sports a "make poverty history" wrist band. His earliest role model was Wal-mart founder Sam Walton, and he later fashioned himself after a fellow countryman, Andrew Carnegie—whose name Hunter endearingly pronounces as only a Scot would, with the accent on the second syllable (Car-NAY-gee).

Hunter is the son of a working-class grocer from the Ayrshire mining village of New Cumnock, about an hour south of Glasgow. After a bitter miners' strike in 1984 his father's business failed, which proved to be a valuable early lesson for Hunter in the importance of becoming self-reliant. He was an average student. But he developed a knack for buying and selling things and after college he went to work for a newspaper that he audaciously offered to buy after being there just a few weeks. He was fired by the enraged owner.

But Hunter found his mark soon enough, striking riches in the global athletic apparel business. His company grew into the U.K.'s top sports retailer before he sold it for $600 million. He was just thirty-seven at the time, and soon after selling the apparel company he opened a private investment firm called West Coast Capital, which provides seed money to entrepreneurs. By age forty-five, Sir Tom had become Scotland's first—and wealthiest—homegrown billionaire.

It was around then that his personal journey from success to significance took wing, springing somewhat ironically from a strategy to shelter his wealth from taxes. Shortly after selling his company, he established the Hunter Foundation with no clear vision of what it might do other than keep the tax man out of his pockets. From this bit of self-interest, though, emerged a new worldview. Hunter began to transform from driven businessman fixated on lavish living into devoted, roll-up-your sleeves philanthropist.

"When I became rich, I found I didn't have anything to do anymore, which was kind of scary," Hunter recalls, after selling his company. "And, of course, as my profile grew so did my mailbag. People would write me and ask if I could do this or that for their football team, or their church, or their hospital. Some of the letters really pulled at my heartstrings. So I'd send them a check. But then that was it. I didn't know if the money had made a difference. I didn't know if it was even real, and it wasn't fulfilling. Who would have imagined that giving out money would be so boring?"

He began to research ways he might give that would have more meaning and satisfaction for him and came upon Andrew Carnegie's famous *Gospel of Wealth*, which states that "a man who dies rich, dies disgraced." Those pithy words hit Hunter like a bolt of lightning. After many long and intimate discussions with his wife Marion about what they might possibly do with the rest of their lives, they both began to feel energized by the idea of working as hard and as smart at giving their money away as they had worked to make it in the first place—for the betterment of others and their own fulfillment.

To better understand the challenge in front of him, Sir Tom met in New York with the head of the Carnegie Foundation, Vartan Gregorian, who urged Hunter and his wife, Marion, to think about what they wanted to accomplish. Gregorian also gave Hunter a whole new way to think about his wealth. "He challenged me," Hunter says. "He said it wasn't really my money; I just held it in trust for the common good. That was a big shock for a Scotsman—being told my money wasn't actually mine."

Hunter took those words to heart, though, and in 2007 announced that before he died he would give all of his money away. One of his principal benefactors so far has been the Scottish educational system, which in his view needs a dramatic overhaul to prepare students for draconian changes in the Scottish economy. Sir Tom became determined to introduce enterprise and entrepreneurship into school curriculums to prepare the nation's youth for the information-based world they would graduate to. He invested in pilot school programs that proved so successful that the government agreed to adopt and fund them.

Hunter has other acclaimed philanthropic interests as well. For example, he is investing $100+ million in Africa through partnerships with the Clinton Foundation, UNICEF, and others. He mobilized popular support for aid to Africa and is committed to sparking substantial and sustainable economic growth there, beginning in Rwanda and Malawi, where governments have pledged their full support for his programs. Hunter's mission, in concert with the Clinton Foundation, is to develop programs that produce profits from agriculture and provide greater access for the poor to better nutrition and health care and clean water. In one year his efforts helped Rwandan farmers increase their crop yield by 240 percent.

What's most fascinating and exemplary about Hunter is that while he has worked so hard to make his fortune, he doesn't simply want to give it away. Instead, he approaches all of his giving as an investment—not charity. He sets goals and demands measurable results, much like running a for-profit company. He says he would have cut off funding for his Scottish education initiatives had they not shown demonstrable progress. In this way, he embodies the new breed of twenty-first-century philanthropreneur, who seeks social change through targeted investments in people. You can be a philanthropreneur too—for as little as $25—through innovative organizations like kiva.org and microplace.com, which fund third world business start-ups. I'll talk more about those in chapter 7.

An interesting thing about Hunter is that when he got jazzed about philanthropy it reignited sparks in other parts of his life too. He redoubled efforts in his profit-minded investment firm, seeing the profits he would be earning there as a means to further his philanthropic ventures. "What I'm doing now is a bigger buzz than any business deal," Hunter says. "When we help farmers in Rwanda get a better price for their coffee, it's their success—not ours. We are just a catalyst. But you can see the results. When a farmer one year can barely feed himself and the next year he can feed himself and his family and take care of his kids because of something you did—that's a hell of a thing."

Yes it is—a better-than-business buzz that Sir Tom playfully but ear-nestly chides Warren Buffett for missing out on. Are you missing out too? "Listen," Hunter says, "I'm not someone who wants to preach to anybody else and say you should do what I do. I just feel a bit sorry for those who don't give something back because they're missing out on the best fun of their life."

Giving Isn't a Chore

Forget for a moment that Sir Tom is a billionaire. The epiphany he expe-rienced was real, and you can experience it too. You don't need boatloads of dollars. You just need time, desire, and compassion, and you may never have those things in greater abundance than you do right now. Perhaps your kids have moved out, or soon will. You are staring down the road at your empty-nest years, relieved of many family responsibilities. Retire-ment—or partial retirement—might beckon you. You are no doubt eager to explore the vast leisure opportunities before you. But you have the time and personal abilities to devote to a higher purpose too, and however you choose to give back you can be sure that in one way or another you'll get as much as you give.

Don't undervalue the skills and connections that have come to you through your life experiences. Not everybody knows how to weld a pipe, run a procurement division, write a press release, raise money, give an injection, pilot a plane, interpret law, teach a class, organize a brainstorm-ing meeting or fix a computer. Someone out there can benefit from what you know, and it can be a blast passing it on. Your personal skills and assets can help you launch out in new and exciting directions. Now is the time to step up and rethink how you want your life to function, and how you might fit service to others into it. You can choose how and when. You may choose to become a vacateer, mixing fun and adventure with personal fulfillment. Why not skip Club Med this year and sign up the whole family for a virtuous vacation with Habitat for Humanity? It's tough to connect with your kids these days, and you may just find that this kind of time is the most rewarding experience of your life.

Giving isn't like a spoonful of castor oil, that notoriously ghastly cure-all that was so hard to swallow that TV's Little Rascals—Spanky, Buckwheat, Darla, Froggy, and the gang—were always comically scheming to avoid their dose. The horrible taste certainly loaned credibility to castor oil's perceived medicinal value. Anything that bad must be good for you, right? Well, too many people view giving the same way: the right thing to do, but painful. It doesn't have to be that way.

You don't have to soullessly give on command at the office, or only support your place of worship. The nonprofit world teems with organizations that can use your donations of time or money for specific purposes that you care about. We're way past the days of large charitable organizations with mostly soup-kitchen roles to offer. Such volunteers are still needed, of course, and quite valuable. But you might get a lot more out of dreaming up a charity's new slogan or rescuing injured wildlife in the mountains—or using your business skills to make an organization run more efficiently.

In the Dychtwald house we give in various ways, and much of it is so enjoyable that we don't think about what we're doing as a service to others. My wife, Maddy, contributes untold hours at school. She coordinates team dinners, supervises training sessions, and has driven a lot of other parents' kids along with our son to distant water polo matches. Maddy and I also mentor students learning to speak in public, and we judge school speaking tournaments. Some folks might call such gratis efforts a chore. The hours certainly can stack up. But we love watching all the kids interact and grow, and making new friends. We do it mainly for the joy it brings to us.

The afterglow from helping a person or an organization that benefits from our contribution is a wonderful payoff. Although psychology and gerontology have been my fields of study, public speaking about these topics has been a big part of my livelihood. It's terrific and satisfying work. But it's not easy. There's a lot of preparation that goes into my presentations that no one but me sees. Still there are some groups that I just want to help at no charge because I'm interested in contributing to their mission or their future. For example, some years ago, I volunteered to help the Alzheimer's Association devise a new marketing strategy. That was work. But it gave me a great chance to make use of something I know a bit about for a cause that had captured my attention. I always keep some of my personal bandwidth in reserve for that kind of thing. Volunteering shakes me out of my rut and lets me express myself in ways that don't happen at the office. Everyone has skills and causes that speak to them. What are yours?

For me giving is both routine, and it is not. That is, I'm always searching for the next way to contribute a little something—yet I have a few special causes or steady habits that I stay with year after year. This keeps the mix varied, my options their widest, and allows me to keep learning about new things and meeting new people. At this point in my life (I'm approaching sixty), I don't yet have as much time as I'd like for giving back. Not yet retired (of course I may never retire), my central focus is still my career and my family. But now that Maddy and I have just become empty nesters, we can envision expanding our volunteer efforts in our personal quests to find purpose by doing things for others. And in a few years, I think I'd like to cut back my workload to about 50 percent —providing even more time to do all sorts of new things with my time and with my life. Lots of us are in this phase of life, and it sure doesn't hurt to start thinking now about the possibilities for when that day arrives and you have a little—or, conceivably, quite a lot of—extra time.

A Dear Old Friend—and Role Model

I briefly mentioned my affection for Habitat for Humanity. Let me explain where it comes from. A few years ago I went to Houston to take part in Jimmy Carter's signature annual home-building project. The experience was unusual in ways that I would never have imagined. I'd gotten the idea to join the Habitat build through my meetings with President Carter in Atlanta, where he had invited me to help him brainstorm the topics for his *The Virtues of Aging* book.

It was a steaming Sunday in early June when Maddy and I arrived alongside some five thousand other volunteers. I was naturally anxious; other than a bookshelf or two I had never built a thing with wood. During the orientation that day we learned that the plan was to build a hundred houses in just five days. There would be about forty people on each house. The rest—some one thousand volunteers—would cook meals, run errands, and haul trash.

President Carter respectfully reminded everyone that he was there to work, not to socialize, and it soon became apparent that he meant it when he told the gathering, "I have a job to do." Like all of the volunteers, I had brought my own tools and paid a $250 fee to be part of this unusual experience. Each house had four adept crew leaders, ten to fifteen construction pros, around ten somewhat handy volunteers, and another ten or so folks who were like me—pretty much unsure which side of the hammer to hold.

Anyway, we showed up at 6:30 AM on Monday and Maddy and I were thrilled to learn that we'd be working on house number 1 with Jimmy and Rosalyn Carter. Our team gathered in a circle. President Carter offered a short prayer and we got to work. Early in the morning it was already so hot and humid, within an hour I felt like I was going to have a stroke. But I put my discomfort aside and joined the torrent of hammering, lifting, and nailing that had commenced. Remarkably, near sunset the entire frame was in place. I, however, was ready to go AWOL. It was now over a hundred degrees, and my arm ached from swinging a hammer all day. I glanced at the seventy-something former president. He was banging away like a pro, and I wondered how long he could keep it up.

After another work break, I was spent. But the president was still pounding away. First thing the next morning, we had a lot of wood that needed cutting. But with only two power saws on the site, some would have to be cut with a handsaw. You guessed it—President Carter stepped up and had hand-cut twenty two-by-fours in the time it took me to cut ten. By 4:30 PM of the second day, the crew was spent. Nearly all my fingers were damaged and bleeding. Carter kept right on toiling, well past the dinner hour.

House number 1 was proceeding so fast that by the third day all eyes were on us. I was fascinated that our pace was being driven by an "old" man who said so very little. It became clear to me that Carter's leadership style did not involve barking at people or being critical, but making everybody on the site want to work to keep pace with him.

Wade and Shalina Gibson, the young couple who with their three children were going to live in the house, worked with us. You could see it dawning on this low-income African-American couple that they were soon going to have their own house, and that it was being built by a former president! While on the site I liked to ask my fellow volunteers why they were taking part in the build. Almost everybody had the same answer: They didn't feel whole inside unless they took some time to help others. And for this group it wasn't about writing a check; it was about giving a chunk of their life.

By twilight on the fourth day, we were laying sod and planting trees, then finally installing carpets and appliances, and at 3:30 PM on Friday—right on schedule—we were finished. President and Mrs. Carter brought us inside the house for a ceremony, and as our group of forty coworkers and new friends stood together in a circle holding hands it hit everyone pretty much at once that we had just done a wonderful thing. Exhausted and filthy but with full hearts, we huddled as President Carter said a prayer and turned to Wade and Shalina and gave them a white linen-covered Bible—the first book for their first house. The gesture was so powerful; the emotional intensity in the room went up a notch, if that was possible.

"Do you know what Jesus did as a young man?" President Carter asked. "He was a carpenter; he worked with his hands. By allowing us to build your house, in a small way you've allowed us to do the work of the Lord." Although three hundred pounds of muscle, Wade started to cry like a baby, as did Shalina. Pretty soon we were all crying. It didn't even matter what particular religion any of us subscribed to—the feelings we all shared were deeply spiritual

Before our group broke up President Carter urged all of us who are fortunate in life to never forget those who are not. He spoke of the blessing of giving, how the harder he and Mrs. Carter work the more blessed they feel by the results.

I just find Carter's thinking on the subject so compelling that it bears frequent mention. Giving of himself, the president has told me, makes him stronger. "Every time we thought we were making a sacrifice for others, it has turned out to be one of our greatest blessings," he said.

"In other words; we have gotten more out of it than we have put into it. You just try it, even if it's nothing more than going to a public hospital and rocking a baby for two hours a week. It's an expansion of life, an encounter with new people who are potentially friends. And so, it's a learning process, an exciting process that gives new and expanding life experiences."

What We Get When We Give

Exactly why and how people choose to give is a complex equation. But it's clear that giving can be very, very good for you—so good for you, in fact, that through time philosophers and others have wondered if giving might not just be among the most selfish of all acts! De Tocqueville, for one, described philanthropy as "self-interest, rightly understood." The Chinese Zen master Chuang-Tzu as far back as the fourth century BC, argued that most philanthropy is meant to further one's personal, business, or social agenda. Philosopher Friedrich Nietzsche (who viewed charity as demeaning to the recipient) worried that people of wealth exerted too much control over society through charity that mostly furthered their own interests. Scandals erupted in England in the 1950s over the tax-exempt status of mammoth charitable foundations run by families like the Wellcomes and Nuffields.

Philosophical questions linger today. Would the public missions that philanthropists take on be better left to government? When Bill Gates directs his foundation to buy millions of computers for public libraries in poor neighborhoods is he being generous, or furthering his own business interests? Theologian Reinhold Niebuhr cynically summed up such concerns like this: "The effort to make voluntary charity solve the problems of a major social crisis results only in monumental hypocrisies, and tempts selfish people to regard themselves as unselfish."

I readily concede that there is a selfish element to giving. Yet, to me, it seems silly to attack generous acts on that level, especially in the realm of Everymanthropy, where what you give most of is your time and energy. So what if you get something back for your efforts? Doesn't that just lead you down the path of more giving? Embrace the rewards. It's OK. Generally, these rewards can be lumped into eight basic categories. You may experience all of them, or just one or two. At some level, though, when you give it's because you seek to gain one or more of the following eight benefits:

Do the Right Thing. The highest level of giving is altruism, generally defined as an unselfish act for the welfare of others without regard for oneself. Altruism is a core teaching in most of the religions of the world. In the Jewish Torah and Christian Gospels, for example, there are many references to loving your neighbor as you love yourself. Yet, unfortunately, true altruism is extremely rare. Even people of faith will admit that in treating their neighbors as they would treat themselves they hope to gain everlasting benefits—like, say, entry into heaven, which is no trifle.

Dwight Burlingame, professor of philanthropy at Indiana University, has said, "It is nearly impossible for someone to act with pure altruism." He argues that "every act of goodness toward another person is a combination of altruism and self interest." Still, there are those rare people who willingly give without regard for themselves. Consider Wesley Autrey, the construction worker who was christened the "Subway Superman" after his split-second decision to dive onto the train tracks in Harlem and rescue nineteen-year-old Cameron Hollopeter, who had stumbled in front of a train. As Autrey lay on top of Hollopeter, holding him in place, a train roared overhead so close that it left grease on his cap. Autrey said later: "I don't feel like I did something spectacular; I just saw someone who needed help. I did what I felt was right." That was Autrey's reward—he felt good about doing what was right.

I can't resist pointing out that Autrey's act of unusual selflessness paid off in very material, yet unexpected, ways. He received: $5,000 in cash for him and $5,000 in scholarships for his daughters from the New York Film Academy, where Hollopeter was a student; $10,000 from Donald Trump; a $5,000 Gap gift card; tickets and backstage passes to a Beyoncé concert; season tickets to the New Jersey Nets and a signed jersey from Nets star Jason Kidd; a new Jeep Patriot and two years of car insurance from Progressive; a one-year free parking pass for use anywhere in New York City; new computers for his daughters every three years until they graduate high school; a year of free subway rides; and a weeklong trip to Disney World and tickets to see *The Lion King* on Broadway. Finally, Mayor Michael Bloomberg presented Autrey with the Bronze Medallion, New York City's highest award for exceptional citizenship. Said the mayor: "Wesley's astonishing bravery—saving a life in the face of an oncoming subway car—is an inspiration not just to New Yorkers, but the entire world."

Do the rewards of altruism often bear such tangible fruit? Of course not. Do good Samaritans anticipate payback before helping others? Probably not. But that's not what giving is all about. If you do it for the right reasons, it usually comes back to you somehow. It just does.

Make a Difference. When you really dig into why people give it's pretty simple most of the time. They want to bring some sense of meaning into their lives by making a difference to someone someplace in the world in some small or large way. In an AARP survey of people forty-five and older, half of all respondents called making a difference "a very important reason" to volunteer or donate money. Making a difference, especially one you can see, feels good. That's why Sir Tom quit sending out checks for causes he was unfamiliar with. It was unfulfilling.

Most people looking to make a difference try to tie their efforts into a cause near their heart. Think about Augie and Lynn Nieto again. Their drive to search for a cure for Lou Gehrig's disease started when Augie was crushed with the illness. It's not uncommon for the families of cancer victims to adopt cancer research as their pet cause. Maybe you know a battered or abused victim and want to fight for tougher laws, or have seen school kids sharing books in poor school districts and want to lead a book drive. If you are searching for a place to make a difference, the first things any good charity or wealth adviser will ask you are, "What have you seen that bothers you? What would you like to fix? What do you care about?" When you can answer those questions, I assure you that you'll be able to find related organizations in need of your time and talent, or money.

Give Thanks. You have much to be thankful for, and expressing that thanks through a donation of time or money can give you a sense of settling a debt and make you feel a little more in balance. Some people give to their alma mater or place of worship or sorority. Others may have come through rehab and choose to volunteer as a substance abuse counselor or Big Brother or Big Sister. Look at your life. Your giving doesn't have to be traditional. Was there some group or some organization that provided for you in a way that was positive and important and maybe you can give something back now? For example, if you have enjoyed PBS shows during your life, maybe you can send them some financial help during one of its pledge drives. Giving thanks can both help others and be a powerful character builder.

With Very Little, Still Giving Thanks

Money gets tight near the end of each month for Debb Snyder, a disabled fifty-five-year-old who lives on Social Security in Vancouver, Canada. So when she saw a flyer in her mailbox one day advertising heavily discounted canned vegetables at the corner grocer, she asked her in-home caregiver to run out and buy as many as she could carry—to eat over the next few months. The caregiver did just that, and while at the store she picked up an entry form for a sweepstakes in which you could win a year's worth of food, valued at $2,600.

Snyder filled out the form, and a few weeks later learned that she had won the grand prize. It was enough money to relieve the strain on her budget for a year or longer. Except that's not how she saw it. She wanted to give thanks to her creator for providing for her.

Her good friend George Kaufer, whom she knew from church, runs Vancouver FISH, the second largest food bank in the county, and with tough economic times his free food and clothing service was being tapped by more and more area residents. His pantry was close to bare. Snyder, barely able to make ends meet herself, called Kaufer and said she'd like to share her small bounty with the shelter. She wrote him a check for $300, enough for FISH to buy crates of ramen noodles, an easy-cook starch that is a staple in the food bank's gift baskets.

Doesn't sound like much, does it? But FISH wasn't the only beneficiary of Snyder's modest sweepstakes winnings. In all, she gave away $1,600—more than 60 percent of her little windfall—to a handful of local charities and friends in need. One of those recipients was the Reverend Duane Sich, a nearby pastor who had just penned—but not yet published—an essay titled "Give 'til It Feels Good." In his view, people should see giving "not as a sacrifice but as a celebration."

That's the way Snyder sees it too. "I have the things I need, and God always provides," Snyder told her local paper, the *Columbian*. Added the Reverend Sich: "You just sow seed, and some hits the good soil. You don't know where the good soil is. If everybody would do the same thing that Debb does, the message would get out there, hit the right places."

Stay Engaged. Giving something back, especially in retirement, may be the best single way to stay involved in the world. Volunteer work can take you far from the normal day-to-day things to places and endeavors that you might otherwise never experience. You'll get to express yourself in ways that do not present themselves in other areas of your life, and you'll meet new people in exciting new environments. Connecting with others as part of an activity that means something to you is like pouring nutrients into your veins. You have the chance to keep using your skills, but perhaps, in a different way and for a different purpose. If you've been a project manager you can volunteer to organize a charity struggling for direction. If you know how to write a business plan you can mentor a team of young entrepreneurs. You are an influential force; so use what you have learned. It's a great feeling to wield your influence for the benefit of others, and it can be a real kick to stretch, or replant yourself beyond your normal boundaries.

Build a New Social Network. It may not be foremost in your mind when you first volunteer. But a productive new endeavor is a natural place to find new and possibly even better friends. I certainly enjoy the contacts I've made through my volunteer efforts. Thanks to my work with Habitat I have a friendship with Jimmy Carter. I've recently met new friends Deepak Chopra and Robert Reich at the Esalen Institute, where I often volunteer. Most volunteer organizations are a melting pot of different people; you come as you are and then become part of something much bigger.

Cooperation and teamwork can work wonders. There are things you just can't do alone. Yet with minimal effort on the part of many individuals, great deeds get done and important needs are resolved. Like an old-fashioned barn raising, there is enormous satisfaction in communal efforts that draw all participants closer. At Esalen, we all toss in a single ingredient—a skill, a strategy, maybe some money—that we are best able to provide. Over the years we have developed an ever widening network of friends whose relationships enrich us all.

The same thing happens every day at churches and on community works projects. A small collection of people who may be very different in their lives and in their families and in their circumstances come together out of a common interest or respect, and without trying often end up as lifelong friends.

Get Some Recognition. There are many ways to think about recognition— a plaque on the wall, your name on a building or a foundation, public thanks at a dinner or ceremony. This kind of acknowledgment, however, is not what most people are after when they donate their time or money. Even Steven Spielberg, who can afford to give enough to have his name put up in lights, once said, "Eighty percent of what I give is anonymous and the other twenty percent is only where my name can help attract other moneys." I believe in anonymous charity too, unless the publicity itself generates more aid. Giving isn't necessarily about getting noticed; it's about the impact it can have and how it makes you feel inside. It's its own reward.

Yet there are subtle forms of recognition that flow from good deeds and help drive the philanthropic spirit. With my volunteer work at Habitat and Esalen has come a certain gravitas that I command in those organizations, along with a comforting sense of community that I share with the countless others who have been through the programs. I value the influence and connections that come with my involvement. That's not why I give. But it's part of what I get back. It's nice to be thanked, have your name on a charity's letterhead, or be greeted warmly by those who appreciate your efforts. You might go to a dinner and sit with others who have given. It's almost as if your contribution has gained you entry to a club. If that matters to you, it's OK. Your efforts are still making a difference.

Feel Good about Yourself. I guess that at the end of the day, there's nothing wrong with feeling good. You know that natural high you wake up with or go to bed with every once in a while. You're never quite sure what caused it. Maybe you had a great day at the office—or expect one. Maybe you simply had a great night's sleep or finally made a big decision, or maybe your child overcame some social or academic hurdle. Life is full of little satisfactions like that, and they contribute mightily to your overall happiness. Here's something else that helps: doing good things for others.

Some of my best moments, outside of the time I share with my family, are the times I'm immersed in my volunteer efforts. Stepping outside your normal world moves you further toward the Erikson ideal of wisdom and giving. You allow your non self-absorbed dimensions to flourish. You meet people who might be struggling, and from that you gain a better sense of all you have and can offer. There is a fortitude that grows in a person when they have helped others or seen a wrong and righted it. You grow and become stronger as an individual.

Volunteering even has physical benefits. In the late 1980s, Allan Luks, executive director of Big Brothers Big Sisters and author of *The Healing Power of Doing Good,* surveyed three thousand adult volunteers—and 95 percent of them reported a "helper's high," or feelings of energy and euphoria. Many also noticed they were suffering fewer aches and pains and even fewer common colds.

In 1999, a University of Michigan study actually found that elders who volunteer live longer than those who don't. In a comprehensive review of existing data, the Corporation for National and Community Service in 2007 concluded that volunteers have greater longevity, higher functional ability, lower rates of depression, and less incidence of heart disease. Students who participate in community service programs have stronger ties to their school, peers, and the community. They show greater aptitude for interacting with authority and more readily develop the skills, values, and sense of empowerment necessary to become leaders, problem solvers, coaches, and public speakers. Volunteerism promotes good citizenship as students early on experience the rewards of giving back to the community. Through firsthand experiences they learn empathy and gain exposure to different cultures, and develop an appreciation and awareness of the struggles that some individuals face. Community service builds their self-esteem, self-confidence, and sense of social responsibility.

"There is now a convergence of research leading to the conclusion that helping others makes people happier and healthier," says Dr. Stephen Post, a professor at Case Western Reserve University School of Medicine and coauthor of *Why Good Things Happen to Good People: The Exciting New Research That Proves the Link between Doing Good and Living a Longer, Healthier, Happier Life.* "So the word is out: it's good to be good. Science increasingly says so." Civic engagement, adds Thomas Sanders, executive director of the Saguaro Seminar at Harvard University, "is the new hybrid health club for the twenty-first century."

Save on Taxes. A lot of people assume this is one of the biggest reasons people give money. But it's a surprisingly small motivator. In virtually every survey on the subject, those who give say that the tax benefits are among their least important considerations. In an AARP survey, just 13 percent noted tax deductions as a reason for giving. The only factor cited less often was being asked to give at the office—a curious finding that deserves further comment. Traditional office giving still raises billions of dollars annually, but it's clear that most of us don't like the arm twisting. Raising money at work will become increasingly difficult in the years ahead. The charities that rely on such giving must find other ways to appeal to a new class of giver, one that views its donations in a more personal light and as a potentially exciting way to be involved—not as a duty to be quickly discharged.

That said, there's nothing wrong with a little tax planning. In fact, it is a critical and prudent component of wealth management, and especially important for people with a lot of money or a big income. Deductible contributions cut your tax bill. But even more important, at least from a giving-back point of view, is that deductible contributions afford you much greater control over the causes that your money supports.

Look at it this way: If you earn $100 and are in the 35 percent tax bracket, the government will take $35 and leave you with $65 to parcel out as you like. But you can control the entire $100 if you choose to give it to a charity—and avoid the $35 tax. Think of your after-tax income as "personal" income, which is yours to control, and your tax payments as "social" income, which goes to the greater good—to support social programs and public works through government spending. Charitable giving simply lets you control more of your social income.

This is by design, and governments actually welcome your taking control. Deductions for charitable giving have been on the books for decades. "Federal and state governments understand that the tax revenues they lose through charitable deductions will be used more efficiently and effectively by local charities to support social infrastructures than if those same dollars were passed through the government's hands," the Federal Reserve Bank of St. Louis has concluded. Indeed, "charitable activities can be accomplished in the private sector at about one-third less than what the government would have to spend to accomplish the same goals."

I've always paid my taxes willingly and I may even be a bit loony, but I feel a sense of patriotism when I do. I use the highways. I benefit from the security that our defense spending creates. I visit museums and believe in public education. But when I first chanced on this notion of personal and social income, and how I might gain a bit more control over my social income to benefit the causes that are dearest to me, it changed my thinking. I encourage an honest approach to tax planning—but also one where you can make the biggest splash possible in the waters where you choose to swim.

Multiple Rewards

As I said, in your giving you probably enjoy one or two of these rewards. But Wilson Goode hits on six of them—altruism, making a difference, doing the right thing, recognition, feeling good about himself, and giving thanks. It could be argued that his giving returns so much that it is entirely selfish. Yet if you ever meet the man you'll know that is not the case.

Finding Purpose among Inmates' Children

Wilson Goode was the mayor of Philadelphia from 1984 to 1992, and upon retiring from politics he earned a doctorate of ministry before becoming the director of Amachi, a nonprofit that mentors the children of parents who are in jail, on parole, or under state or federal supervision. It is a role that Goode was well suited to. When he was just fourteen his sharecropper father was sent away for assaulting Goode's mother, and Goode experienced firsthand the psychological trauma of growing up with an incarcerated father.

He once thought that his own experience was not a factor in his attraction to the Amachi program. He thought he had moved on. But long after he took over the program it dawned on him, he says, "that I was being used by God to help children who had suffered an experience similar to mine; that I could speak with authority on this issue."

Amachi is a Nigerian word that means "what God has brought us through this child." When it was launched in 2000 Goode had just received his doctorate of ministry, and his dissertation was on how to get congregations more involved in their community. "The research showed that a congregation would become involved in the problems of a community if asked to by their faith leader," he says. Amachi seemed the perfect way to test his theory. He joined the organization as its director and instantly reached out to the religious community, recruiting leaders regardless of their denomination, to rally their congregations to serve as mentors for the children of inmates, a group that—without intervention—is highly likely to end up in prison themselves at some point in life. Amachi met with quick success and has inspired hundreds of other programs that today serve 30,000 children between the ages of four and nineteen.

"When I was young, I thought I could do everything," says Goode. "Now that I'm in my seasoned years I'm content to pour my energy into establishing a sustainable program that will help rescue these children from a sure life in prison. Age gives me the sense that I don't have fifty years for a project, but that while I have the time I should do all I can to create something that wasn't there, to leave a legacy."

Find Your Mark

Look, I'm not a Rockefeller. When it comes to giving something back I put myself somewhere near the middle of the pack. Could I do more? Probably, and that's the direction I'm heading. When I teach a student the speaking skills that I've developed and watch her develop the confidence to command a room—well, it's pretty great. Whether she does anything with her new skills, I do not know. But that's not the point; I'm trying. You may get the same kick out of teaching dance, music, drama, art, or clay spinning or coaching Little League or mentoring a small business or rescuing wildlife or . . . whatever makes you feel more significant.

I look at my life just a few years ago and I can see how, without any conscious decision, I've stepped up my giving game for the enjoyment of it, and I can see how I'll step it up even more in the years to come. The day is coming when my mom and dad won't be alive and my kids will be grown, and the chunk of time I now give to them will be up for grabs. What will I do with it? I'm beginning to see endless exciting possibilities in the service universe. Retirement is not for disappearing; giving is not just for the rich. Your time is coming. What will you do with it? As Winston Churchill said, "We make a living by what we get; we make a life by what we give."

Chapter 6

WHO DO YOU
THINK YOU ARE?

Trust yourself. You know more than you think you do.

—BENJAMIN SPOCK

Fred Sievert wasn't the man he always thought he was. He had unrecognized passions that he slowly came to understand, and nearing the age of sixty he also found that he had skills that he had acquired during his life, almost without knowing it. When we spoke, his hidden personal assets were just coming into focus; his journey from success to significance was still a work in progress. But this much was certain: after leaving a high-powered insurance career and beginning to explore his spiritual and creative sides, Sievert was perhaps as happy as he'd ever been. He wasn't sure where he would end up. But he was enjoying the trip, confident that what he was learning about himself would open exciting new doors and keep him productive and engaged for many years to come.

Sievert has had a lot of big moments over the years. He's a smart, affable, stylish, and highly polished executive who joined the New York Life Insurance Company as its chief financial officer in 1992 and worked his way to president of the company. From that perch he took New York Life to the top of its industry, achieving the number one ranking in market share and soaring profits. But one moment in particular changed Sievert forever. He talks about it often. In fact, it became a prominent anecdote in his two dozen farewell speeches after announcing his retirement.

New York Life had entered into a joint venture with a hospital company in India, and while visiting there some years ago Sievert was invited to observe an open-heart procedure at a new facility in New Delhi. "I didn't really want to go because of the travel, but said, 'all right, let's go take a look,'" Sievert recalls. "I'm thinking I'm going to be up in some amphitheater thirty feet above the operating table. But they take me into the scrub room. I strip down and they put on the gowns and the mask and the hat and booties and all that stuff, and they walk me into the operating room."

Positioned near the patient's head, Sievert got a surgeon's view of quadruple heart bypass surgery. He found it both unnerving and riveting as he watched the patient's heart in an open chest cavity doing its thing—beating so near to him that he could have grabbed it. The throbbing heart was practically speaking to him. "That was a profound spiritual experience for me," Sievert says. "I'm thinking: you don't really think about how or why your heart beats. Yet it never stops as long as you are alive. How could this happen? Is it evolution? Is it chance?" Sievert thought long about that experience. It unsettled him in ways he could not imagine. He concluded that "there has to be a higher power" and that it just might be time for him to explore that world and what it means to him.

That singular moment stoked a spiritual fire from within and led him to start his search for a new definition of success—one that had nothing to do with money and things and everything to do with personal growth and uncovering the person he had become. He decided he would retire and enroll in the Yale Divinity School, where among other things he would reflect and study the Bible. Yet Sievert's story is not simple; this is not the tired tale of a man who found God and decided to spread His good word. Sievert has never had designs on joining the clergy or preaching from a pulpit. He has lofty goals and complex new passions. As he discovers the new him he wants to make good use of all of his skills, all of the things that made him a superstar in the business world as well as those life skills that only now are becoming evident.

For almost his entire time at New York Life, Sievert was a contemplative and religious man. He tried to live by his core values. He tried to pay employees well and give customers good value for their money. But the thing that really set him apart in the secular world of business was his open expressions of faith. He never proselytized. But he did frequently and publicly credit his faith in God for his material successes. "We had 50,000 employees and agents around the world representing every imaginable ethnicity and religion, so I had to be careful," Sievert says. "But I did mention my strong faith in large group meetings."

Indeed, Sievert believes that his most important legacy at New York Life was not profits or market share gains or business lines that he opened or closed—but his commitment to family and the public embrace of his faith. "I see these as coping techniques that helped me be the best I can be," he says. "In my position I was able to reach and influence a lot of people. They all knew about the praying and the Bible study. I wasn't trying to convert people; it wasn't like an Evangelical pursuit. I just wanted them to know about what I felt mattered in life." Ultimately, Sievert says, he wanted to know himself better too. He was burdened with an inner voice telling him that something was missing from his daily experience. He couldn't quite define it. But in time he came to recognize in himself what I too had recognized in my moment of truth after Hurricane Katrina: it was that gnawing feeling. Some unexplainable force inside was restless; he craved more than a beautiful house, a bigger bank account, and further professional accolades. He felt his spiritual development needed more attention, and that's when he retired in order to attend divinity school and in doing so, made his own very personal choice to transition from success to significance.

Who is Fred Sievert? On paper, he's is a numbers guy. As the top financial executive at a *Fortune* 100 company his principal craft was in balancing assets with liabilities, keeping costs down, and profit margins up. He had to analyze risk and manage staff. His talents included understanding financial and consumer markets, and knowing the nuances of tax law, budgets, regulatory filings, and economic forecasting. These are valuable stores of knowledge that can be applied at just about any organization—perhaps as a board member or manager or strategist. Certainly, if he chooses one day to build his own congregation or a nonprofit his hands-on experience running a company will prove invaluable.

But Sievert now knows that he is so much more than the sum of his primary work skills. In fact, he believes it's his hidden skills that will be most important as he goes forward. Let's face it; you don't need a lot of financial acumen to interpret the Bible. He's more likely to lean on the things he's become good at through the trial and error of everyday life and that he practiced at work even though they were not his primary responsibilities.

First among those, says Sievert, is writing. "Even though I was president of a company, I had to do a lot of writing," he says. "I had to take some very complex matters and simplify them." Sievert wrote innumerable speeches, memos, letters, and reports during his career. Looking back now he realizes that writing is something he has always enjoyed even though it was a peripheral part of his job. "There are things you do that you enjoy so much that you lose track of time," he says. "For me, it's writing. I sit at my computer. I just love doing it—even lengthy reports. I'd give them a lot of thought and write out ten or twenty pages of text that I wanted people to really stay interested in. I could spend hours doing that."

Another skill he acquired almost without knowing it was the ability to communicate effectively to groups. Any leader must become adept at offering direction and being clear about goals to small groups of top managers. But Sievert went way beyond that and found himself in front of large crowds of employees and insurance agents several times a week, explaining complex insurance issues or offering sales direction. "It was a different presentation to a different audience almost daily," he says. "So my presentation skills became highly refined." Needing to communicate also taught Sievert how to distill information, get at what's important quickly, and sharpen his analytical skills.

Sievert also found himself heading up big projects, where he had to track and chart progress and get the cooperation of a variety of people from around the world, many of whom did not report to him. This required detailed organizational skills and the ability to negotiate and see all sides of an issue. As a leader, Sievert was also a teacher and mentor to those who worked for him. "I love mentoring young kids too," he says. "I taught when I first got out of college. Now maybe I'll find out if I want to pursue that again."

But what Sievert seems to have learned most about himself is that he wants to touch people and have a big impact, no matter what he does with the rest of his life. That's why simply heading a congregation or teaching probably isn't in the cards for him. He wants to share his deep faith with a mass audience and hopefully help millions of others find the peace that comes from religious conviction.

So he's a work in progress and he's currently weighing two options. The first is writing a book that would reconcile the vindictive God of the Old Testament with the merciful God of the New Testament. "I've been keeping a list of forty or fifty passages from the Old Testament," he says. "I call it my list of Bible stories that you'll never hear from the pulpit because the stories are so inconsistent with most peoples' view of God. I'm already starting to think about what the outline of the book would be and what might be of most interest to readers."

His second option is joining with the Yale Divinity School's Center for Faith and Culture, whose mission is to explore ways to help people practice their faith responsibly in all spheres of life, including the workplace. Any role there likely would be management and strategy, and include expanding the organization's footprint globally; it would call upon many of Sievert's primary skills as well as his secondary organizational, speaking, teaching, and communicating skills.

Whatever he decides, says Sievert, "I know there's something more down the road for me. It's like being back in college as a twenty-year-old trying to map out my career. Well, here I am in the same mode. I've got a lot of good years left. What am I going to do with those years? It's exciting to be in that mode again."

Who Are You, Really?

As Fred Sievert is learning, it may take years to understand the real you—or perhaps, the new you. Some things are clear enough, like the work skills that have served you so well. But you have also learned things outside of school and the workplace; you have acquired core competencies through your day-to-day battles and passions. Upon self-examination, Sievert found he was more than an insurance executive. He was a budding philosopher with a deep fascination with life's biggest questions. You have talents hidden just beneath the surface too. Discovering them is key to transitioning to a life of significance.

You are trained to think of your skills and talents as what you do at work. But if you think of them as core strengths instead you can begin to see how they are more widely applicable. You're not just an administrative assistant; you're someone who gets things done. You're not just a retail manager; you're someone who can spot the strengths in others and suit them to the task. You're not just a nurse; you're someone who is gentle and caring and understanding and compassionate. You're not just an athlete; you're someone who works well with a team.

At this stage of life, odds are you are pretty good at whatever interests you have simply because you enjoy them and have done them as often as possible. So in thinking about the new you look first at your core interests. If you want to approach this exercise in a systematic and scientific manner, you may want to consult a career counselor or life coach. They have sophisticated "interest" models to help you discover what you most enjoy and where your hidden skills may lie. You may also go online for a nominal fee and in about forty-five minutes complete a detailed evaluation known as the Strong Interest Inventory or the Myers-Briggs Type Indicator (both at hollandcodes.com/strong-interest-inventory.html). But you can approximate these types of evaluations through simple reflection.

Think about how you spend your time. Most of us tend to be drawn— either directly or indirectly—to the settings, activities, and people that allow us to express our interests. Search the courses you liked in college and the things you most liked about your primary career. Think also about your hobbies, and what exactly makes them exciting. Is it research?

Add to webinar

Is it management? Is it competition? Is it the physical or mental exercise? The challenge? Do you like writing? Do you like being around children? Animals? The outdoors? Fig~~ure out~~ what inspires you. What makes you get out of bed in the morning with a smile and eager to start the day? What do you enjoy doing? What do you care about? What really stimulates you?

These are the kinds of questions that will help you focus and understand how to find your purpose. "Chance favors the prepared mind," said Louis Pasteur. Yet most people never take the time they should to get to know themselves. Giving of your time can eat into your personal and family life and take you away from many other things that you enjoy. Service to others can be demanding and difficult. You won't stick with it if you don't love it. But if your cause sings to your heart you almost cannot go wrong. "When you're using your business acumen to help

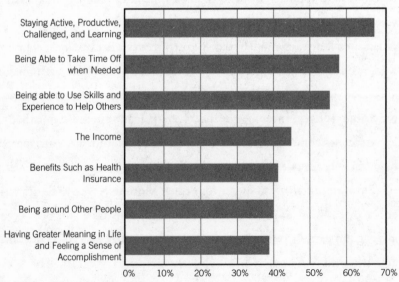

Most Important Factors in Post-Retirement Work

Source: Civic Ventures 2008 Encore Career Survey

people struggling with mental illness, get homeless youth off the street, or work with abused kids . . . you may sometimes go home frustrated over work or finance problems," says Jim McClurg at the Social Enterprise Alliance. "But you never go home wondering why you went to work in the first place."

The New You

Fred Sievert embodies a generation of individuals who long to make an impact by applying their life-learned skills to previously undefined passions in creative new ways. In fact, half of fifty- to–seventy- year-olds say they want a job now or later that helps their community. They want to put their primary and secondary skills to use as a volunteer, or in a purposeful new career—getting paid in both money and satisfaction.

What motivates do-gooders? Most want to help the poor and elderly, address health or environmental issues, teach or otherwise work with youngsters. Strikingly, in surveys many people who have taken a job at a nonprofit say they don't need the income; they took the job mainly to exercise their skills, pursue new passions, and make a difference. They see meaningful "good work"—running a food bank or providing elder care or simply performing administrative duties for a charity that advances a cause dear to them—as their best way to find purpose in their lives.

Today's Everymanthropists (and Everywomanthropists) generally have less interest in stuffing envelopes and ladling soup, and more interest in leading an effort or at least applying their professional or life skills to the task, and really leaving their mark. Seeing the good you do and reaping the personal rewards is so critical that nearly half worry that they will never find a service job that suits them.

Indeed surveys show that just one in eight nonprofits does a decent job of aligning the tasks they assign with the specific skills of their volunteers. This is a tragic disconnect. It leads to frustration and resentment, and often to short-lived volunteer experiences. And it only begins to illustrate the gulf between many of our venerable charitable organizations and today's new generation of philanthropreneurs. Most nonprofit leaders regard raising money as their biggest challenge and consider a financial contribution the best form of support anyone can offer them—attitudes that fly in the face of your desire to get involved and reveal the extent to which they may undervalue your ability to make a difference through your time and talent.

Some large organizations are starting to get it. I've spoken with local chapters of the United Way of America that have made great strides in giving volunteers more authority to choose their tasks and even help set priorities for their chapter. Some large British organizations like Oxfam seem to get it too. But change is coming slowly, which is why so many of today's experienced men and women are taking matters into their hands and forming groups to tackle the problems in front of them—head-on. Why give to a jumbo charity that only wants your money and then does as it pleases when you can give instead to a group right in front of you, choosing your mission and seeing the good you've done? "In a world of rapid change, if you're not a change agent, you're not a citizen," says Bill Drayton, founder of the pioneering social innovator group Ashoka, which is a global nonprofit that funds innovative and practical ideas for solving the world's most urgent social problems. Drayton redefines success at this stage of life as causing change that helps others, saying, "You should be a white blood cell just looking for something to attack."

We can't all be as committed (or as brilliant) as Drayton in the realm of social change. But collectively we are beginning to move mountains. Two out of every three "downshift" jobs that adults aspire to qualify as good work—work with a higher purpose—says Civic Ventures. Notably, this rush to significance is being led by women, where 70 percent say it is "very important" that their work "gives you a sense of purpose" (just 48 percent of men say so). Those who say they are planning to work for pay in their retirement years cite five primary reasons: to stay involved with other people; to hold on to a sense of purpose; to keep some income; to put their job skills and life experience to productive use; and to help improve the quality of life in their community. Notice that only one of those is about money. They are mostly about service and living up to your potential, which is remarkable in a survey of folks who expect to be working for pay in later life.

It is becoming commonplace in the nonprofit/volunteer world to be paid for your good works, either in funds for training, a stipend to offset expenses or, increasingly, a flat-out salary or hourly wage. Indeed, many of the people I cite throughout this book get paid in one way or another for the good work they do—albeit at a far lower rate than they could command elsewhere. This is a distinctly modern trend: paid volunteerism.

As the later-life worlds of work and volunteerism have begun to merge, experts have studied what aspects of service are most rewarding and most likely to keep you interested in serving, whether you're paid or not. The chief finding: if you believe your effort will have a moderate or big impact on other people, you are far more likely to jump at an opportunity to serve than the person who feels their impact would be minimal. Nonprofits must meet this desire head-on; they must give you a chance to exercise your abilities. A mind-boggling 31 percent of folks who volunteer one year do not return, according to the Corporation for National and Community Service. Rather than being energized and motivated by their volunteer activities, they too often are turned off and become disinterested.

The higher your emotional attachment, the longer you'll stick around and the happier you'll be. This seems obvious. Yet many nonprofit managers view your commitment as a time for dutiful service—not as a time for personal growth and excitement. That's their mistake. Don't settle for a role that is significantly less than what you had hoped for. Of course, you'll need to bring some common sense to the equation. You have to be qualified—or trained—before you can take on important roles that are outside your skill set. You may have to be patient too, while you demonstrate your know-how. But don't waste your time with an organization that can't ultimately fulfill your needs.

Boomers have a higher volunteer rate than past generations did in this life stage, and the number of fifty- and sixty-something folks who want to give back will swell around the globe over the next twenty years. So the revolution is just heating up. It's in everyone's interest that society find ways to harness service-minded individuals' talents and passions and turn their unique blend of energy and ability into something worthwhile. But to keep this group in the game, charities and others will have to do better at catering to each of our desires to make our mark in our own way.

Finding Your Niche

If you want purpose to be a big part of your life, you should take the time to figure out what you have to offer and who can make the best use of your time, wisdom, or resources. It may take a little patience and experimentation to get it right. You may have to try on a few dresses. But eventually you will find one that fits. Here are some guideposts to get started:

Walk before you run. Try a few things out before leaping headlong into a commitment. Volunteer for a modest role at several nonprofits or work part-time at a good-work job just to explore your options. Even within the same field, cultures and practices vary greatly among nonprofit agencies. You should be willing to start at the bottom. The volunteer world is like any other in that it has its own pecking order and infrastructure. You may have to accept some things you don't like—for a while, before changing them or hitting the road. If you want a paid position, consider volunteering as a stepping-stone. Be sure to let your supervisor know your ultimate goals, and keep reassessing your progress toward them.

Know when to make a change. You may find it's more rewarding to try something completely different from your former day job, or you may be better off sticking with what you know. Finding the right volunteer work can be tougher than finding the right job. Often, expectations are impossibly high: you're eager to make a difference and convinced that your talents are needed and welcomed. But you still run into roadblocks. Remember to never let go of your desire to have an impact that is on your own terms. There are countless groups out there that would be thrilled to have your time and input. Give it an honest try but be ready to move on.

Think about compensation in a new way. Nonprofits do not pay well—at least not in monetary terms. But low-paying and volunteer positions offer an experience you can't find anywhere else. So let go of any vision of self-worth that is based on income. Be ready to trade your business standing and high income for the freedom to work on interesting problems and the rewards of spending time doing something important. Base your new life on significance and service—not money—and surround yourself with people who think that way as well.

Value your life experiences. Make sure any organization that wants you understands what you have to offer, and don't sweat it if the experience you are looking for doesn't fit perfectly with your demonstrable skills. Life experience and wisdom are now part of your core strengths. You've had success, failure, and challenge. You've managed your family, dealt with financial issues, handled medical problems and life transitions, and coped with rapid technological change. These experiences have helped make you reliable and worldly; they've given you good judgment, problem-solving skills, the ability to navigate a crisis and negotiate a compromise. You've learned to listen and to assess cost-benefit trade-offs. You probably have greater comfort working with all types of personalities, a sense of responsibility and purpose. Trumpet these skills. You can add a positive, new dimension to any diverse organization.

Hire yourself. If you just can't see yourself meshing with another organization be willing to hire yourself. Strike out on your own. People in their forties and fifties and sixties are doing it all the time, leaving the corporate ladder not only for a more meaningful day-to-day routine but also for the opportunity to mold an experience that is just right for them. This is what the social entrepreneurship trend is all about. Everyday people still in the prime of life are identifying causes that are not being addressed as they would like, and they are quitting the for-profit world to launch their own, typically nonprofit, operation and taking a salary to make ends meet.

Finding Her Niche with Immigrants

Jane Leu has always enjoyed working with immigrants; it evoked a sense of purpose inside her and brought out her extraordinary abilities to empathize and advocate for those who are unable. Leu, thirty-nine, had staked out a path in the nonprofit sector early on. Among her first jobs was one with the Lutheran Immigration & Refugee Service, a national nonprofit that in the mid–1990s was dedicated to helping Bosnian refugees settle in America. Her job was to help immigrants find immediate work, so that they could become self-sufficient. But the nonprofit that employed her "was narrowly focused" on immigrants' first few months—not the long term, Leu says, adding "we were taking bankers, lawyers, architects, computer experts, and skilled researchers and putting them to work as cabdrivers, nannies, and security guards."

Her most vivid misplacement was a Bosnian surgeon who was assigned to work on a chicken cutting line. "There was a real need to match these people with their skills," she says. She first went to her employer to see if the outfit would broaden its scope but got nowhere. So she began to research an idea for a new nonprofit, one that would pick up where Lutheran Immigration stopped—namely, helping skilled, legal refugees transition from self-sufficiency to a level of professional success that was commensurate with their abilities. She first identified this need in 1996 and spent the next several years plumbing her professional networks to learn if anything like the idea she was germinating already existed. It didn't. In 2000, at the age of thirty, she quit her job and "with a healthy dose of optimism and naiveté" founded Upwardly Global, a San Francisco-based nonprofit that helps white-collar immigrants network, prepare resumes, and search for suitable work.

She started by working from a desk in her basement, inviting individual refugees in for counseling. To make ends meet, she also worked thirty hours a week as a bookkeeper. Slowly, she began to make a difference, placing skilled immigrants in high-paying jobs. With her successes she began to seek and eventually land small grants from local foundations. Today, Upwardly Global has fifteen paid employees, dozens of volunteers, hundreds of clients, and a second office in New York. Leu is planning to open a third office, this one in the Midwest, and go national from there.

Sure she's ambitious, and as her nonprofit grows so will her professional credentials and the salary she takes as head of the organization. Is that bad? Upwardly Global maintains a data base of immigrant resumes that employers can view online. It teaches its clients valuable job-hunting lessons, including the value of a firm handshake and looking an interviewer in the eyes. Clients include immigrants from Bosnia, Belarus, Kenya, Syria, Russia, Bolivia, and Sierra Leone. "UpGlo," as Leu calls it, also works with employers to educate them about the immigrant labor market and the skills that are available there. Everyone wins.

Pursuing a career as a nonprofit founder is hard work. "You have to be passionate about your cause, willing to work for free for a while and able to take rejection," Leu says. Even now, she adds, she gets only about one grant for every twenty applications. "But it's a life rich in purpose," she

Most Appealing Jobs in Post-Retirement

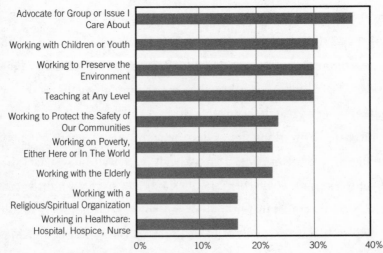

Source: Civic Ventures 2008 Encore Career Survey

says. "For anyone who may be looking for a second act, it's about the best choice they can make."

Your Primary Skills

Your primary skills are usually obvious. You may know the law. You may know medicine. You may know accounting. Maybe you can write or speak or manage a project or drive an 18-wheeler or teach kindergartners. If you are good at organization, you can help organize a board of directors. If you are a gifted salesperson, you can help raise some money. If you are an advertising veteran, you can help put together a publicity campaign. You may find a whole new level of satisfaction doing what you are good at for a group that needs you and that you truly want to help.

When you take your core skills and redirect them for a greater purpose it doesn't feel like the same old thing you've been doing your entire career. And you can mix things up if you choose—if you've been a manager in your career, you may not want that pressure in a volunteer capacity. Let someone else worry about the big stuff while you just do your thing when asked. Conversely, if you've been taking directions all your life this may be your chance to take charge and fulfill your management ambitions—after your career is over! At work you might have been just one of many with a specific skill or expertise. In your volunteer life you can be special—a superstar.

There are many volunteer or good-work organizations that want to capture your primary skills, especially if they are in business, medicine, or the law, through mentoring organizations like the Executive Service Corps Affiliate Network (www.escus.org) and Senior Core of Retired Executives, which I've already mentioned, as well as pro bono groups like Doctors Without Borders (www.doctorswithoutborders.org) and the

American Bar Association's Second Season of Service (www.abanet.org/secondseason).

But virtually all professions and avocations (including homemaking) incorporate and build skills that transfer to the volunteer world—things like problem solving, consensus building, negotiation, understanding, handling budgets, developing relationships, and managing projects. Lawyers, speakers, financial experts, operations managers, administrators, writers, and marketing professionals are always in demand for director slots and other volunteer roles. A former director of operations for a manufacturing company would be a hero at a food bank that needs to coordinate moving perishable items to widespread pantries in a timely way, or for the Red Cross, which needs to get disaster-relief equipment to people in unexpected locations quickly. A cabdriver might drive disabled or elderly citizens to meetings or doctor's appointments. A computer specialist might teach the elderly or at-risk youth how to use a computer. Your job has equipped you with the talent that some organization needs. You just have to find the right fit. Following are the types of people most in demand at charities:

Managers The nonprofit sector is growing rapidly and desperately needs people who are able to translate their for-profit functional skills and management experiences across sectors. A middle or senior manager in almost any industry, or an office or retail supervisor, should have the basic tools—organization, interpersonal skills, ability to set goals and manage people and projects. Some things are different at a nonprofit. They have far fewer resources than you may be used to and can't always hire a consultant to solve a problem or buy a new piece of equipment to become more efficient. But they can summon their recruiting skills to attract volunteers with experience in needed areas and you can use your procurement experience to find a substitute or discounted piece of machinery.

Nonprofits have a different set of stakeholders than you may be used to as well—from volunteer staff and board members to leaders of the communities they serve. You can't simply give orders and make demands. But you can call on your motivational skills and ability to build consensus to get everyone working together. Volunteers aren't in it for the money. So you must call upon your assessment skills to figure out the individual talents of a diverse volunteer workforce that wants above all to be suited to the task.

Entrepreneurs. Because of their more limited resources, nonprofits need can-do executives and volunteers who are willing to get their hands dirty. You may need to do the little things, as well as set strategy and manage people. The ability to find creative solutions and perform many different tasks is critical. These are skills that almost anyone who has started or run a small business may have. Secretaries and administrative assistants are also trained to get a wide variety of things done. If you've worked as an engineer or in design you probably have natural or acquired skills at finding innovative solutions that would serve you well in a nonprofit.

Team players. Because there are so many stakeholders in the nonprofit sector and decision making power is widely dispersed, it is important that you work as a team member and can manage your task through influence and consensus building and compassion and empathy. Nonprofits need leaders who can inspire by example and roll up their sleeves to get things done. Again, many middle or retail managers have such skills, but so do many nurses and home health aides and schoolteachers. Athletes and coaches and those with a military background may also be well suited to nonprofit work.

Chameleons. Keeping an open mind and being able to change as needed is critical. Projects vary greatly, and there is typically a revolving door of volunteers. So you may have the expertise and manpower you need one day but not the next. Nonprofits need people who manage through changing circumstances. But you may not need management experience to possess these skills. Pilots have to adapt their flight plans to suddenly changing weather. Sales people and financial advisers must adapt to changing markets and the changing needs and resources of their clients. A background in human resources, where you have worked with a diverse labor force, might also translate.

Communicators. With their many stakeholders, nonprofits have a large need for people who can communicate well and can get across their message without ruffling too many feathers. You must deal with staff, board members, communities, and often peer organizations. They all need to know what's happening and may want a voice in how your group proceeds. In the nonprofit world, there is more emphasis on process. You have to get your ideas across differently. A background in management consulting and business development probably gives you such skills, though you need to be careful not to come on too strong with business rhetoric. Writers and speakers are natural communicators. But so might be a real estate agent or other sales professional, customer service representative, or public relations expert.

Your Secondary Skills

It might be that you're a terrific salesperson or accountant or administrator. To have achieved in such careers, though, you may have had to become proficient at speaking, PowerPoint, writing, editing, negotiating, or communicating. Maybe you have a skill that you acquired much earlier in your life, possibly during college, and you want to flex those muscles again. Or maybe your most basic life skills—patience, empathy, understanding, and wisdom—were acquired through dealings with a spouse, your children, or their schoolteachers, and these are the most important qualities you'll need for your transition. Don't underestimate the value of your secondary skills. Now may be the time to exercise them.

Finding Her Purpose in Conflict Resolution

That was the case for Nina Meierding. She was a schoolteacher and, later, a lawyer. But the domestic skills and knowledge she acquired over thirty years of marriage and family are what best prepared her for her transition to significance. Meierding, fifty-four, is the daughter of an engineer. She earned a master's degree in education from the University of California and then taught special-needs students for seven years. She went back to school to get her law degree and ultimately opened a family practice in Los Angeles. Later, she and her husband (a retired educator) moved to Bainbridge Island, Washington.

Making a lot of money was never her thing. Meierding became a schoolteacher out of a sense of purpose. Her law practice also sprang from a desire to help people figure out their problems, and she abandoned it just as it was beginning to take off. Why? She had seen too many disputes lead to empty resolutions where one or both parties felt cheated. The so-called resolution only further poisoned the relationship. "You might win a case and get custody of a child or ownership of a car," she says. "But then the other party says, 'OK. I guess I'm going to just take my kid and move out of town, or destroy the car before handing it over.'"

Those aren't good outcomes for anybody and only add to the likelihood that you'll end up back in court. "In the legal system you get a judgment," she says. "You don't necessarily get a resolution. The dispute lives on." Meierding wondered if there might be a consistently better way to resolve conflict, one that really ended the matter. She firmly believed that the only good resolution is one that is negotiated, and where both sides feel satisfied. That's what led her—after just a few years of practicing law—to become a mediator, helping families talk out their problems and arrive at lasting solutions.

Having a law degree certainly didn't hurt. But as she reflected on how to help resolve family disputes her thoughts instantly went, not to any legal precedents, but to the many conflicts she'd had to referee over her years as a wife, mother, stepmother, and grandmother. She thought about all of the emotions she has experienced in those roles, and the beliefs and feelings of others that she has had to skillfully navigate. "Dealing with death and grief, the dynamics of being married, working with special-needs children—it teaches you things like patience and perspective," she says. "The more experiences that happen to you, the more you learn from them and can use them to help others through their disputes."

For Meierding, becoming a mediator was the answer to her yen to serve. She's so passionate about mediation that she now trains others and says almost anyone past forty or fifty can hone the skills needed to be a good mediator. The most important traits are curiosity, a sense of calm, and the ability to listen—skills that practically define being a good mother. "We see people in our programs all the time who say, 'I've seen enough in my life. I know what life is about. I have patience that I didn't have when I was younger.' There's a maturity of life that I have found very valuable in this role, especially since reaching forty."

How else might your secondary skills come into play? Here's a sampling of service-oriented work suited to mature adults primarily because of the skills they've acquired through their nonwork routines:

Fund-raiser. Most people in a position to donate money are older and more likely to trust someone closer to their age. If you don't have the guts to ask for money, don't worry about it. There's less of that kind of confrontation than you may think. Fund-raisers spend most of their time developing relationships. By the time the relationship is strong, you may not even need to ask for donations. Most important: you get to work for a cause you believe in. If you want to look into this option, start with the Association of Fundraising Professionals (www.afpnet.org) and the Chronicle of Philanthropy (www.philanthropy.com).

Geriatric care manager. Older folks often get overwhelmed by the mountain of paper in their lives: medical bills, tax forms, investment documents, and government forms. Family members often live far away or are too busy to help much. A geriatric care manager is much more than a bill payer. You help elders find the right doctor, ensure they get needed social services, and simply check in to be sure everything's OK. A good starting point: the National Association of Professional Geriatric Care Managers (www.caremanager.org).

Politician. No, you don't have to run for Congress—or anything else if you don't like that aspect of public service. Local governments typically have a dozen or more boards or commissions, and they are eager for volunteers to step up. Just contact your local governing body. Volunteer service of this type is a great springboard to elected positions where you can have even more impact, like mayor, town board or city council, and the school board. You'll need a winning personality and may need some ability to speak in public. But what will serve you best is the basic wisdom, empathy, and common sense that most folks over fifty can easily summon.

Personal coach. People in need of a little advice are increasingly forgoing a visit to the shrink and instead seeking the services of a personal coach, who may be seen as more approachable and less judgmental—and definitely less expensive. If you know anything about things like retirement planning, healthy living, career switching, volunteer opportunities and the adult dating scene—and you are willing to hang out a shingle and market yourself—you'll likely find lots of clients. Again, your key skills here are lots of practical knowledge, common sense, and strong listening ability. Start at the Web sites of the International Coach Federation (www.coachfederation.org), Coach U (www.coachu.com), Choice magazine (www.choice-online.com), and with *Coaching Manual: The Definitive Guide to the Process, Principles and Skills of Personal Coaching* by Julie Starr.

Add to 19 website?

Celebrant. Ministers for all faiths are in demand. You may want to spend the second part of life developing your spirituality, like Fred Sievert, and possibly becoming a faith leader. But there is a baby step you can take in that direction right now: without having to be an ordained cleric or justice of the peace you can arrange and preside over weddings and funerals. Look into this option at www.celebrantusa.com.

* * *

Nonprofit board member. Like local governments, small philanthropic organizations are always looking for volunteers, and they crave a wide range of skill sets. With years of experience and a Rolodex of contacts under your belt you may be well equipped to fill a critical a role. Small nonprofits, for example, usually run on spartan budgets and need lawyers, accountants, speakers, writers, fund-raisers, and managers on their team both as advisers and doers. Experience in public relations, human resources, marketing, and special events are in demand. So is expertise in government relations, proposal writing, and strategic planning.

Most nonprofits have Web sites and list openings online. Some places to get acquainted with the nonprofit world include these Web sites: www. independentsector.org, www.bridgestar.org, and www.guidestar.org. To see where your small business experience might fit in check out the Social Enterprise Alliance Web site (www.se-alliance.org). Consider posting your profile at boardnetusa.org to let local boards know you're available.

Get the Training You Need

Let's say you ask yourself all the questions and do a thorough self-examination, and you conclude that you don't have the skills you need to volunteer in the way you'd like, or to find paying work that serves a purpose. OK. This could easily be the case if you are looking for a totally new experience. Here's the great news: you can acquire the skills you may need. In most cases training is just a phone call or a mouse click away.

Consider Nina Meierding, again. Even as a lawyer she had to tiptoe into her new role as a mediator. She took three years to transition her practice into full-time mediation. During that time she became active in various trade groups, attending symposiums and workshops and getting better all the time. Ultimately, she served on the ruling body of the Academy of Family Mediators and the Board of the Association for Conflict Resolution, and became a teacher and trainer herself.

For most volunteer roles you won't need to be retrained. Remember that everyone is good at something, and every talent has a purposeful application. But you might want to try something out of your comfort zone, and for that a little help can go a long way. Here are some places to get the training you want:

Nonprofits. Hundreds and possibly thousands of nonprofits will train you in return for a specific commitment to serve ten or twelve or sixteen hours each week. Experience Corps. (www.experiencecorps.org), for example, is a national program that engages adults over fifty-five to help at-risk grade school children learn how to read. Volunteers are offered extensive training in how to relate to young people of different cultures and needs. Those who put in at least twelve hours a week are also eligible to receive a small stipend. Consider the program in Minneapolis/St. Paul, Minnesota. In this program, adults tutor struggling students in nine public schools from kindergarten through third grade. The volunteers work with students one-on-one or in small groups under supervision of the classroom teacher. You must have a high school diploma and demonstrate an ability to relate to children, and be flexible and patient. You are required to give no fewer than four hours a week.

"The Experience Corps training program, its structured environment and its responsiveness to very real needs in our public schools and urban communities makes this an ideal model for the growing number of older adults who want to be productive in retirement," says David Jones, president of the Community Service Society of New York (www.cssny.org), which hosts such programs. "For communities in need, this is tantamount to finding a goldmine in the backyard."

*   *   *

For profit. You can find plenty of training in the for-profit world too, especially if you are contemplating early retirement from a large company. With so many folks redefining what retirement means, many companies have been sprucing up the services they offer to departing workers. Increasingly, they aim to help them find a second act—to become, say, a consultant or mentor or independent contractor, or a small business owner or a volunteer. They do this through workshops and seminars; they may also offer financial support and a sophisticated Web site that posts job and volunteer openings for folks past the age of fifty. "We haven't seen it yet in large waves," says David Certner, legislative policy director at AARP. "But there's increasing demand for these programs." And, he adds, more companies are stepping up all the time.

IBM, a frequent benefits trailblazer, launched its Transition to Teaching program in 2005. The company pays tuition and other costs for those who want to leave to teach math and science in school. Hewlett-Packard recently formalized an alumni outreach program that, among other things, helps to match retirees with meaningful bridge jobs and volunteer work. HP takes the view that their former employees are a vast pool of potential partners, consultants, and community leaders. They are proud to send them out into the world as ambassadors for the company and its products. The company recruits former employees to mentor young workers, and to staff "demo days" events where they may spend a few hours explaining HP products at retail sites. "We're just at the cusp of employers understanding that the transition into retirement isn't the final chapter," says Marcie Pitt-Catsouphes, director of the Center on Aging & Work at Boston College. "Retirement may not be the end of their relationship with people who work for them."

Nearly one in five large companies has begun to provide training for older workers interested in moving to the nonprofit sector; a third have expanded their retiree programs to include workshops on bridge careers and volunteerism. If you're exploring leaving your full-time career for a bridge job or volunteer role, or already did, get familiar with your company's resources. They're changing all the time and may now include things like a retraining allowance, paid leave, and job or volunteer matching services. Among those offering some kind of transition service include Shell, Disney, Boeing, Pfizer, Procter & Gamble, Verizon, Home Depot, and Goldman Sachs. There are many others, and your employer (or former employer) may be one.

College classes. Virtually all colleges and universities have something to offer adults who want to go back to school and retrain or get another degree in order to pursue what Civic Ventures's visionary leader Marc Freeman has coined as their "encore career"—a productive new pursuit in adulthood that capitalizes on your wisdom, and life and work experience. Indeed, to lure adult students back to campus universities around the world are even developing special housing designed specifically for the fifty-plus market. Adults who move back to campus can often audit classes for little or no fee—or choose to pay full boat and take a full course load, and earn a master's or maybe a law degree. This is one of the more exciting trends in higher education, and thousands of adults are taking advantage of it. Universities welcome older students not just for the revenue they provide but also because these adults round out the university population with an interesting and informative mix of ages. Adults also make fantastic mentors for kids who may be away from home for the first time.

But community colleges are the real sweet spot for adults looking to retrain and to repurpose their life—as opposed to those who just want to relive their campus days. Community colleges have deftly combined academic programs and vocational training since the 1960s, when they blossomed specifically to meet the needs of boomers hitting college age. Now they are changing again—to cater to boomers again, as they engage in middlescent career-switches. The affordable fees, flexible programs and schedules, and online coursework at community colleges are a good fit for anyone who wants to get in, get what they need, and get on with their life quickly. Today, more than a million adults are enrolled at a community college for the express purpose of retooling for a new pursuit. Millions more are expected to follow as the global age wave crests over the next twenty years.

Virginia's statewide community college system, for example, is filling some of the state's 1,300 teaching vacancies through a "career-switcher" certification program for professionals who already have a bachelor's degree and work experience. The goal is to put them in the classroom as teachers in fewer than six months. At Collin Community College near Plano, Texas, you can get certified to teach math through fast-track training. Collin also arranges for mentoring support from retired teachers to help your transition. Broward Community College in south Florida has a similar program. Don't overlook this valuable resource in your own backyard.

Get the training you need to get on with the next stage of your life. You aren't the same person you've always been. You've grown and evolved. You might need a push to recognize that—or even some further training to round out your emerging interests and talents. But discovering—and developing—the new you is critical to your new life of purpose.

Chapter 7

WITHOUT TIME AND TALENT—
MONEY IS JUST PAPER

What we have before us are breathtaking
opportunities disguised as insoluble problems.

—JOHN GARDNER, SOCIAL INNOVATOR

I haven't talked much about money in this book, for good reason. First of all, while most of us have the means to lend some financial support, you likely do not have a big enough bank account to really make a splash—to build a new shelter for the homeless, put a classroom of underprivileged children through college, clean up polluted waterways or buy mosquito nets for millions of poor villagers in Africa. Certainly, we can help. Even modest contributions are important.

You may, however, wonder if you are doing enough. So I'd like to address the issue—ever so briefly. We live in a largely capitalist world where money matters a great deal. Indeed, not much is possible without it. It's wonderful to donate your time and talent to a charitable effort.

It's fantastic to dream up and set up innovative new solutions to age-old problems. But without money very little gets done.

Giving cash or other financial assets as you are able is every bit as much a part of Everymanthropy as giving your time. The two actually go hand in hand. Surveys show that people who give time are more likely to give money as well—and vice versa. That's why, if you have ever volunteered your time to a local charity, you've likely been solicited for money from that same charity as well. Nonprofit leaders understand this giving dynamic quite well.

So, how much is enough? Obviously that is a personal question, and it is one that has stirred considerable debate since the dawn of civilized man. In today's world, as a benchmark, 10 percent of your income is a decent starting point. But ultimately what you can afford to give depends on your personal circumstances and your sense of commitment and urgency. As long as you try to do something you shouldn't judge yourself too harshly or worry about how others may judge you based on the level of your charitable giving. Still, a few guidelines might be useful.

Some years ago the philosopher Peter Singer laid out an aggressive giving grid, which helped me put my personal level of giving in context. More importantly, though, it opened my eyes to just how solvable so many global problems really are—if only the funds were offered to address the solutions. In Singer's view, it is the responsibility of the super-rich, rich, wealthy, and affluent people of the world to give enough to completely wipe out poverty, and what he showed was that it can be done—right now—if everyone in the world would adhere to his formula.

Using targets for minimum living standards set by the United Nations, he calculated that the super-rich (top .01 percent of earners, who average $13 million of income annually) should give a third of their income, or the staggering average sum of $4.3 million annually. The rich (the rest of the top .1 percent, averaging $2 million annually) should give a quarter of their income, or $500,000. The wealthy (the rest of the top .5 percent, averaging $623,000 annually) should give a fifth of their income, or $125,000. The affluent (the rest of the top 1 percent, averaging $327,000 annually) should give 15 percent of their income, or $49,000. And the rest of the top 10 percent, earning an average of $132,000, should give 10 percent, or $13,200. Everyone else with income above the poverty threshold should give at least 1 percent. That would do it. That would generate enough money to raise the living standard of every person on Earth above the U.N.-defined poverty threshold.

I leave it to you to decide how much you can or should give. Certainly, 10 percent or more of your income may seem like a tall order. But consider that one billion people currently live on less than $1 a day, and ten million children die every year from avoidable, poverty-related causes. The need is great and you can see how your donations could help. By yourself you could double the annual income of nearly a thousand people if you are affluent and hew to Singer's formula.

Outrageous giving is not out of the question. Indeed a quiet movement spearheaded by Christopher and Anne Ellinger and their Web site www.boldergiving.org hopes to change the perception about what is normal or reasonable when it comes to giving away money. The Web site profiles more than fifty members of the "50% League," which is made up of people who have given away either half of their assets or half of their income in each of the last three years.

Motivations for these folks vary, but often swing on the desire for a simpler life and less materialism, or for achieving maximum impact on a cause near their heart. They are a diverse and surprising lot. The league includes many common people, including a math professor and a retired insurance claim examiner who never made more than $45,000. Yet most typical of its members are older folks who are giving back after years of financial success in their profession or business, and the heirs of modest fortunes—like Grigor McClelland, a Brit whose family made its money in the grocery business nearly a century ago.

McClelland, an only child, was born in 1922. As a young man he joined England's storied peace activist group, the Quakers, and became a conscientious objector during World War II. He later joined the grocery business that his father had started in 1907 and helped build it. In 1988, he retired and sold the business for about $12 million. With those proceeds he endowed a family foundation, which now has assets of about $8.5 million and gives away some $250,000 a year, mostly in northeastern England, where the family money was made. McClelland favors volunteer-dependent agencies that provide vital services to needy families, children, the elderly, and the homeless.

"Each year I reduce my taxable income to the lowest tax rate band by making charitable gifts," McClelland says. "My descendants have reasonable financial security, and I enjoy living comfortably but not extravagantly."

Yet, in my view, simply writing a check—while certainly generous and even noble—isn't enough. It is incumbent upon all of us to consider the causes that matter most to us and focus our attention and resources accordingly. When you care enough to research and learn about a cause, and ruminate over it and think about solutions and understand what can and should be done—that's when your giving can do the most good. By adding your passion to your money you help make all of philanthropy more efficient. This new "philanthropy is more agile," Bill Gates has said. Yet it isn't just for Gates or Bono or Oprah. It's for you too. You can be a philanthropreneur with the best of them.

Finding Purpose in Early Retirement

Ram Gidoomal, a Londoner, concluded that he should be doing more when he reached age 40 and retired to focus on charitable activities. Charitable giving had always been a part of his life. He was raised in both the Sikh and Hindu faiths and attended a Muslim school as a child in Kenya, and he later became a Christian. So he was certainly well rounded and grounded in the concept of faith and service to others.

But it wasn't until after he had climbed the corporate ladder to become U.K. Group CEO of Inlaks Group, an international conglomerate, and was on a business trip to India that it all sank in. There, he visited a slum in Mumbai, and the shocking experience prompted him to think about what he might do—not just with his money; but with his energy—to make the world a better place. He realized how fortunate he was and how little it would take to have a positive impact on those who were severely disadvantaged. "Seeing this deprivation firsthand put my own financial position into context," he says in a profile on Philanthropyuk.org. "I realized that I was financially secure—and privileged. I asked myself: 'Why am I working for this money? What good is it?'"

He was inspired, along with three friends, to set up the Christmas Cracker Charitable Trust, which had a novel approach to raising money for charitable purposes. The group sought to create temporary food businesses that would be run by teenage volunteers for one month each year before Christmas, with all profits donated to relief projects in the developing world. "I wanted to use my business and entrepreneurial experience, but also to motivate youth; to make them aware of what is going on in the world, and to get involved," Gidoomal says.

Christmas Cracker was a fabulous success. It partnered with youth groups around Britain to run local "Crackerterias," which were eateries that served mostly donated food and employed slogans like "bite for right" and "justice, not just us." The eateries raised $850,000 the first year to benefit impoverished parts of India. Over the next six years Gidoomal launched similar projects, including newspapers, radio stations, and retail stores. All volunteers attended a training weekend, where they learned basic business skills and were allowed input on how the money they made would be distributed.

In all, Christmas Cracker projects have raised more than $8 million for charity, mobilizing over fifty thousand youths. Gidoomal initially intended to run the charity for only one year. But the success and the enthusiasm of the volunteers led him to stay with it year after year. "It was a very rewarding experience," he says. "We were changing lives while motivating young people to get involved." He never loses sight of what drives him. Recalling the Mumbai slums, he says, "Don't let what you cannot do stop you from doing what you can do."

From Mutual Aid to Philanthropreneur in Four Steps

Philanthropy is like any classic institution; it changes over time to meet the needs of society. We are now witnessing an important rebirth of the ages-old and honorable tradition of giving, and it can be instructive to examine how we got to a point where virtually all of us have the means to make a difference. So let's give it a quick whirl.

Phase 1: pass the animal skin. Man has always shared. Cavemen didn't have to ponder the greater good of sharing bodily warmth under an animal skin. They just did it. Clans and barbarians may have lived in brutal cultures where the strongest fared best, but they instinctively shared food, resources, and shelter and joined in the defense of their stores and their community. This most primitive form of philanthropy is likely what enabled our species to survive and evolve.

There can be no denying the harsh landscape of prehistory, which constituted a daily battleground with the elements, predators, and rivals. Within each clan was a clear pecking order, arranged principally on a hierarchy of brute strength, and there wasn't a lot of concern for the truly weak. Yet even Charles Darwin, who championed survival of the fittest, conceded that within primitive societies there must have been some sense of community. Otherwise women and children wouldn't have stood a chance, and man would have become extinct. In *Descent of Man* Darwin argued that early human communities "which included the greatest number of the most sympathetic members would flourish best."

Phase 2: do unto others. As civilizations began to form four thousand years ago, man's survival became less of an issue, so philanthropy took a different turn. Philosophers and organized religions began to preach good deeds to please the gods, which would earn you earthly rewards (healthy children, rain for your crops) and eternal life in the afterworld. In the earliest Greek civilizations giving was regarded as a religious duty. In Hindu scriptures giving was a duty that earned the donor a higher place when reincarnated. Buddha taught that giving was a personal virtue and his followers in 450 BC established the first hospitals for the needy.

Concern for the unfortunate was written into the Hammurabic Code, and the Egyptian Code of the Dead held that a good man is "one who had given bread to the hungry, water to the thirsty, and raiment to the naked." The impulse to relieve suffering through personal service was most noteworthy among the ancient Hebrews. In Judaism, the idea of righteousness figured prominently into ultimate salvation, and in the twelfth century Jewish philosopher Moses Maimonides offered seven ascending levels of charitable giving, which strike me as relevant today:

Giving cheerfully but too little.

Giving cheerfully and in plenty, but only after being asked.

Giving without being asked (though this ceases to be a good deed if advertised).

Giving publicly without knowing the receiver.

Giving anonymously to one you know.

Giving anonymously to one you do not know.

Giving in a way that helps a person help himself.

In the final step—the highest level—we see a foreshadowing of the modern social entrepreneur who seeks to give time and money toward finding sustainable solutions to the problems of the less fortunate. "He who aids the poor to support himself by advancing funds or by helping him to some lucrative occupation" fulfills a higher degree of charity "than which there is no higher," Maimonides wrote.

Early Christians also linked good deeds to everlasting life. To be pleasing to God, gifts needed to be motivated by genuine love, not by self-interest, taught Saint Francis of Assisi. Saint Paul taught that the rich man was not the owner but merely the steward of his riches, and he must therefore use it for the good of many. In fifteenth-century Christendom, it seemed to matter less how one collected wealth than how you shared it. This is when the first stories of Robin Hood surfaced in England, cementing the notion that giving to the poor—even if you had robbed the rich—was a worthy endeavor.

Phase 3: choose a cause (particularly if you're rich). With the rise of personal fortunes during the Industrial Revolution, philanthropy was ready to take a pragmatic turn. Self-made millionaires felt empowered to use their wealth to battle nagging social issues like poor health and illiteracy.

They had vast amounts of money to disburse as they saw fit and were invigorated by the challenge that social engineering presented. They built hospitals and libraries so that the less privileged might stay healthy and learn, and thereby lift themselves up with their own effort.

Much of the new thinking about charity emanated from the United States, where a unique spirit of shared values and cooperation had taken root among settlers in the 1600s. The first known fund-raiser in America occurred before it was even a country, in 1643, to benefit Harvard University. This ethos of communal help thrived on the frontier where, philanthropist Daniel Gross notes, "if the pioneers were to have a church, they would have to build it; a school, they would have to build it; hospitals or roads or courthouses, they would have to build them." This proclivity to give for social causes remains unusually strong in America, where charitable contributions each year total nearly 10 percent of the national budget and where some 70 percent of households make yearly charitable cash contributions. Over half of all adults in the United States volunteer an estimated twenty billion hours each year—a rate that is five or six times greater than most countries in Europe.

Phase 4: Everymanthropy emerges. The act of giving is undergoing yet another radical reincarnation. You don't need a bursting wallet to lend your time and energy to a cause that stirs you. Giving is for everyone and is beginning to be seen widely as a richly satisfying path to personal fulfillment and significance, particularly for those who are in the second half of life. In fact, the new philanthropy is becoming the new activism. Millions of ordinary citizens around the globe are reaching out to make a difference and are watching the ripples they create wash across space and time, building enough momentum to create meaningful change.

This revolution is being led at the big-money level, as technology entrepreneurs and self-made billionaires use their wealth to stir change. When the obituary of Bill Gates is written many years from now there may be less said about Microsoft than about his accomplishments as the self-appointed physician to the world who is trying to eradicate disease. Pierre Omidyar, who cofounded eBay, has started a pair of "social innovator networks" with the stated mission to "enable individual self-empowerment on a global scale" and employ "business as a tool for social good." Omidyar believes fixing world problems is a good business model and cites "trust between strangers" as the very foundation of eBay's success. Google cofounders Larry Page and Sergey Brin have said that they hope that their philanthropy may one day "eclipse Google itself."

There can be no question that some of the super-rich are setting new ground rules and establishing a new moral tone around the world. Warren Buffett has said he expects his entire pledge to the Gates Foundation to be spent within fifteen years of his death. Gates has suggested his foundation wind down within fifty years of his death. The idea is to focus as many resources as possible on the issues of our time; to make life better today for as many people as possible—and leave future issues for future billionaires.

The real emerging stars, though, are people like you and me—ordinary folks who weave acts of giving back into the fabric of our lives and have a big enough cumulative impact to change the world.

Helping the Homeless on Just Pennies

Walking along the Upper West Side of Manhattan in 1991, Teddy Gross and his four-year-old daughter, Nora, had to side-step a homeless man, which prompted the child to say to her father: "That man is cold. Why can't we take him home?" Gross suggested that they start saving their pennies and asking others for their pennies too in order to help the homeless, and from that sprang the nonprofit Common Cents (www.commoncents.org) and its hallmark program the Penny Harvest, the largest child philanthropy program in the United States. Nationally, over half a million children participate in the Penny Harvest and have raised over $5 million. Students typically organize a Penny Harvest at school and use the money they raise to support neighborhood service projects. These often center on sexual abuse, issues surrounding homelessness, animal cruelty, and immigration rights.

The Common Cents mission is to tap the innate kindness and generosity of children, which ultimately leads to helping communities and schools nurture a new generation of capable and caring young people. Teachers report that kids involved in a Penny Harvest are given real responsibility, and they rise to the challenge. In a study of the impact of the Penny Harvest program, Columbia University found that the students— aged four to fourteen—gained the self-confidence and the self-awareness that they can make a difference. The program sharpens their teamwork, communication and leadership skills, and increases their effort academically, all while serving the community.

Not Your Father's Style of Giving

People like Teddy Gross are the tip of the iceberg in solutions-oriented, roll-up-your-sleeves giving. You are part of a hands-on generation. You are willing to put in the time and do things the way you want them done. This embedded can-do spirit, which for so long had been funneled into personal gain and consumption, is today spilling over and forming the base of Everymanthropy. "Earlier generations of benefactors thought that social service should be like sainthood or socialism," wrote *New York*

Times columnist David Brooks. "But this one thinks it should be like venture capital . . . the new do-gooders have absorbed the disappointments of past decades. They have a much more decentralized worldview. They don't believe government on its own can be innovative."

Making "Womenade"

At a potluck dinner with friends one evening, Amy Kossoff and Lisa Herrick got to talking about the plight of the homeless in their hometown of Washington, D.C. A physician who works with the poor, Kossoff spoke of her patients' simple needs—$3 to fill a prescription, $10 for a few groceries, or maybe $20 to help with the rent. Kossoff couldn't resist reaching into her own pocket, time and again, and confided to Herrick that over the past few years she had probably given away $10,000 that way. Nearing the age of fifty and with a family and a hundred-year-old home to renovate, she told her friend she just couldn't go on like that.

One patient had lost electricity because after paying the rent she could not afford to have her utilities turned on. Kossoff wrote the check. Another patient desperately needed dentures, having had all his teeth pulled at a free dental clinic. The clinic could do the dental work, but could not provide the dentures. Kossoff wrote the check. The stories went on and on, and Kossoff was overwhelmed.

Herrick, a psychologist, thought about the group's annual potluck dinner, typically held in the dark of winter to bring a little light into the routines of a half dozen or so friends. She suggested that the next time they gather they each kick in $35 and give the money to Kossoff to help her struggling patients. Herrick even had a name for the effort—in a dream, an airplane with an advertising banner said: "If you have lemons, make lemonade. If you have women, make Womenade."

This idea was so big, Herrick and Kossoff figured, that they decided to reach out to a much bigger circle. Each friend invited as many friends as they could think of, and in March 2001 the first Washington Womenade potluck dinner drew nearly one hundred women who had a meal together and raised $3,500, which was ultimately spent on items such as dentures, groceries, and heating bills for the local needy. The group raised another $5,000 with a second party and $7,000 with a third. Now, whenever their account is empty, they just throw another potluck party.

"Helping people on a small scale makes a huge difference," Herrick told the alumni newsletter at her alma mater, Swarthmore College. "It doesn't cost much to keep someone from being evicted or to fill a prescription." Once, a man with both legs amputated held out fifteen medications and asked Kossoff which of them he really needed. He only had $20 to last to the end of the month. "I would try to give him money, but he would never take it," Kossoff told the *Washington Post*. "Now I say to people, it's not my money. It's a bunch of rich women in Chevy Chase, Bethesda, and Washington who'll feel really good if they help you out."

Kossoff has always fought for the poor and downtrodden, going back to the fourth grade in Los Angeles where a teacher called her parents to a conference for getting into fights on the playground as she stuck up for unpopular kids. Many years later, having graduated from George Washington University Medical School, Kossoff became a staff physician for an agency that serves the homeless. She credits her parents with instilling in her their sense of compassion and duty. "They always wanted to help people in need, animals in need," Kossoff told *Jewish Woman*. "I was always bringing home stray dogs, and they always found a place for them."

Women in twenty-three other cities have since formed their own Womenade chapters, repeating the successes of Herrick and Kossoff. In

Salt Lake City, Utah, for example, Womenade's $35-a-head parties have helped a Somalian refugee, victims of domestic violence, and a nursing student down on her luck. In Waukesha, Wisconsin, Womenade has bought pediatric ambulance supplies.

The Womenade concept is simple, without bureaucracy, and is founded on the friendship and generosity of women. Not one penny of the money that the women raise goes toward overhead; everything goes directly to people who need help. The women have funded medical supplies to homeless shelters, security deposits for apartments, utility costs for the indigent, furniture, groceries, bus passes and subway cards, and Internet access at halfway houses.

You can start your own Womenade chapter. No approvals are needed. Start by checking out www.washingtonwomenade.org. But basically, it's as simple as organizing a group of friends, finding a worthy cause in your community, deciding what kind of party you want to throw—potluck, picnic, barbecue—settling on where to keep your funds (a separate checking account is best) and how to parcel them out, sending out invitations, and throwing a party.

I take one look at my own family and I can easily see how, as a society, we have shifted away from trust in government and authority to take care of us, and toward self-reliance and activism. My mother and father, for example, wouldn't dream of questioning the president on something like sending troops overseas, or even question a doctor on his diagnosis. I'm more skeptical than that but still have a healthy respect for authority. My children, on the other hand, feel that no one is above question. With the Internet at their disposal, they are growing up empowered to get the information they want and advocate for themselves and make big decisions on their own, even though those decisions may sometimes run counter to what the experts tell them.

For example, my daughter Casey is now in her early twenties and is a member of a generation with a very different attitude toward power and authority than my parents'. For example, when she was just fourteen she needed and got braces on her teeth, like many kids that age. No big deal. Displaying a tinsel smile in high school is practically a badge of honor. But Casey didn't love it, and on her own began searching on the Internet for alternative solutions. Then one day, she sat her mom and me down and presented us with various printouts about a pioneering surgical procedure that would realign her bite and allow her to get the braces off almost immediately. As she argued the advantages of this new approach, Maddy and I were impressed, and mildly amused—until Casey informed us that she was fully serious and had even already spoken with our insurer to make certain the costs of the procedure were covered. Fighting for a little time to prepare our response—we asked, "Where is the oral surgeon who is the expert on this thing?"

"Boston," she told us.

"Well, that's about three thousand miles away," we returned. "Doesn't this seem a bit extreme?"

"I thought you might say that," she responded. "So I found a surgeon here in California who was trained by the Harvard doctor and does the same procedure just as well."

Then Casey told us, "and I have an appointment scheduled for Thursday. Which of you would like to take me to it?"

Well, after we caught our breath, we did go with her to the appointment, and after we all learned about everything involved in the surgery, we decided against it. However, the experience taught us that our daughter and tens of millions of kids just like her are quite comfortable taking matters into their own hands and don't always feel they need to wait for "authorities" to explore their options.

The sixty-five-plus years between my parents and my kids has brought incredible change to the world, but none more incredible than in the way younger folks feel empowered to learn, think, and act when things really matter to them. Perhaps it's the Internet effect, or the eBay effect, or the iPhone effect, or the Match.com effect, or the Facebook effect, or the customize-your-own-Website effect. Whatever. But there is no doubt in my mind that yesterday's obedient regard for social institutions and bureaucratic leadership is giving way to tomorrow's hands-on self-empowerment.

This same attitude shift can be seen in the emerging actions of so many people who are currently looking for the right level of involvement and the right social causes—and the right experience to make it all worthwhile. It's all part of the same trend. We want to arrange and customize the activities of our lives the way that best suits us—from choosing medical options to how we ultimately choose to give something back.

"In the nonprofit world we keep trying to shunt people into roles that were comfortable for people forty years ago but that hold little chance of capturing the imagination of the current generation," notes Marc Freedman at Civic Ventures. "I think of a physician I interviewed who had been the chair of a medical school department and one of the leading researchers in her field. She was retired for six months, got bored, and approached the local hospital, and said she was willing to provide her expertise free of charge. Well, they were delighted—and called back the next day offering her a job refilling water pitchers."

Big, staid institutions are misreading your aspirations in the worst way. It's making a lot of people angry and leading to a new class of givers who are remaking the system. The way you give and who you give to has long been dictated by the rich. But this system is now being democratized. Sure, most big financial gifts still come through megafoundations that bear high-society names like Ford, Carnegie, Mellon, Rockefeller, and Kellogg. The wealthiest 5 percent of donors account for 40 percent of all donations. Yet in the generally well-off developed world many people today have the means to give something. They are taking the time to find out where their financial contributions and their talents will have the greatest impact.

Changing the World $25 at a Time

Jessica and Matt Flannery, both thirty, perfectly embody the movement I've been describing. Just out of college they embarked on research and leisure travel to some of the poorest regions of the world, and while there they were struck by the simple unmet needs of countless tradesmen and small business operators, from fishmongers to goat herders to beekeepers to taxi drivers to fruit-stand operators. In many cases, very small amounts of money that could surely be repaid would make an immense difference in their businesses. The Flannerys wondered how they might help.

Jessica had always been interested in international development. That's why they were visiting the third world in the first place. But Matt was an entrepreneur at heart. He had tried his hand at several dot-com start-ups in the late 1990s and wasn't ready to give up. Before they married, "we actually went to a preengagement class and she said, 'I want to live in Africa and work with the poor.' And I said, 'I want to live in San Francisco and start a dot-com,'" Matt recalls. "We really had this dilemma. But we loved each other so much we just decided to get married and work it out."

Their solution didn't just save their love; it also brought relief to tens of thousands of struggling entrepreneurs in poor villages in places like Nicaragua, Cambodia, and Bangladesh. With a little investigating, the couple learned that a loan of as little as $500 would be enough for a small retailer to set up shop. Yet there are almost no banks to make such loans—or no bankers willing to take the risk. So the Flannerys sought to fill that void and created the remarkable nonprofit Kiva (www.kiva.org), which makes small loans to tiny businesses and in so doing helps lift people out of poverty.

In one case, the Flannerys took note of a fishmonger named Elizabeth. She was buying just a few fish each day from a dealer, and reselling them for a very small profit. "She had kids she couldn't put through school," says Matt. With a loan of $500 (through Kiva, which is Swahili for "agreement"), Elizabeth was able to afford a daily bus ticket. She used it to travel a couple hours to a wholesale fish market. By avoiding a middleman, she was able to buy three times more fish and sell them for twice the profit. Now she's putting her kids through school and has repaid the $500 loan.

In another case, the Flannerys found a small village in Tanzania that was in sore need of a general store. The villagers had to walk thirty minutes each way to buy basic goods. Despite this hardship, no one had opened a store nearby. "There was no question that a new store would succeed," Matt says. "People were buying the goods. They were just walking an hour to do it. So I asked myself, What would it take to start a store here? The answer was about $500 for the first purchase of inventory. There was no question that you'd get paid back. This, for me, was when I really started getting jazzed about starting Kiva."

On the Kiva Web site there are literally thousands of small business operators in need of loans from $500 to $1,000. You choose a client and, with a credit card or through PayPal, lend as little as $25. Within months you start getting small payments back, and usually within a year the loan is fully repaid. You do not collect any interest—only the principal amount. (That's part of what makes Kiva a nonprofit.) After you are repaid you can withdraw your money, though only about 10 percent of lenders do. Most leave the money in the Kiva system and lend it to another client.

Join the Movement

You don't have to start your own nonprofit to be a philanthropreneur. Here are some other ways to do your part:

Join a giving circle. Informal groups of friends who pool a modest sum of money and decide which local cause to support is the latest rage in philanthropreneurship. These friendship networks tend to remain relatively small—twenty or fewer—and they meet either monthly or quarterly and raise money from their own pockets. They discuss how to put their kitty to work in the community. Giving circles—like the Womenade circle put together by Lisa Herrick and Amy Kossoff—work a lot like the investment clubs that become so popular during bull markets, only instead of picking stocks to invest in, the groups pick charities to fund or support through volunteering, or both.

Some 12,000 people in the United States, mostly women, have joined a giving circle, the number of which has doubled to 800 in the last few years. The groups have collectively granted $100 million to local causes. They may hold potluck dinners at someone's home and donate what it would have cost to eat out, or hold a wine tasting where everyone chips in what it would have cost to buy the bottles at a restaurant, or simply assess membership fees that range from $10 or $20 per meeting to a $10,000 annual commitment, or higher. This is truly grassroots, hands-on Everymanthropy with groups tackling the full spectrum of community needs. Learn how to start your own giving circle by exploring the Giving Circles

Network (www.givingcircles.org). But fasten you seatbelt; this maneuver might alter your future!

Make a person-to-person (P2P) loan. Another area of explosive growth is what's known as microlending, which is best illustrated by the Flannerys and the nonprofit they started, Kiva. There is a vast new frontier out there, enabled by the Internet, where ordinary individuals in need of capital are forgoing the bank, and ordinary individuals with a little extra to invest are shunning stocks and bonds. Instead, they are finding one another online and cutting out the bank. Most of these "P2P" Web sites, like www.Zopa.com and www.Prosper.com, are commercial, profit-focused operations that aren't necessarily looking to do something good for mankind, other than make it easier to get a small loan. But Kiva and one other, MicroPlace (www.microplace.com), are set up expressly to facilitate small and desperately needed loans to the world's working poor in an effort to alleviate poverty.

An estimated 500 million people run microbusinesses around the world, yet fewer than 10 million, or just 2.5 percent, are able to obtain loans from traditional lenders. Those who are able to borrow in the micromarket have an incredibly solid repayment rate of 97 percent. Many wealth advisers have become familiar with this market and can help their generally well-off clientele find targeted microlending opportunities. But you can do it on your own too through Kiva and MicroPlace (a subsidiary of eBay). MicroPlace sets a minimum loan at $100; Kiva's is $25. You earn market-rate interest at MicroPlace; Kiva pays no interest.

Buy with impact. Big companies have been linking their products to one or more charitable efforts since the early 1980s. That's when American Express invented "cause-related" marketing, promising to contribute a small portion of card-members charges to help restore the Statue of Liberty. The campaign ultimately raised a then-impressive $1.7 million (and enough goodwill to turn American Express into an icon of corporate philanthropy). Today cause-related sales campaigns are everywhere. Some are permanent, national efforts like McDonald's support of Ronald McDonald House for families of seriously ill children. Many are temporary branding efforts, often around the holidays, like a Banana Republic offer of 30 percent off on a new sweater when you trade in an old one that will be given to the needy.

Such opportunities also abound in the U.K., where there is a strong desire to align business with the community through philanthropic activity. Food retailer Sainsbury's, for example, runs the Active Kids program, which raises money for sports and exercise equipment in local schools. Shoppers get Active Kids vouchers when they shop there and pass those vouchers on to the school of their choosing. The program has been a stunning success—some 85 percent of U.K. schools are registered, and on average they each receive about $1,300 worth of sports equipment from Sainsbury's each year, roughly three and a half times more than their average total physical education equipment budget.

The biggest new cause-related effort on the planet is Bono's Product Red, begun in 2006 to raise money for the Global Fund to fight AIDS, tuberculosis, and malaria in Africa. Companies pay a licensing fee to market some of their products as Red, and send a portion of those sales to the Global Fund. Partners include Dell, Microsoft, Converse, Apple, Gap, Motorola, Armani, and Hallmark. Combining consumerism with altruism, Red has so far raised $22 million, which has been used to build thirty-three testing and treatment centers and to supply medicine for more than six thousand women to keep them from transmitting HIV to their babies.

In all, marketers spend nearly $1.5 billion each year on cause-related campaigns and by raising awareness raise five times that amount for the causes they champion. Consumers are warming to the greater-good sales pitch. According to a Cone Millennial Cause Study in 2006, 89 percent of Americans (aged thirteen to twenty-five) would switch from one brand to another if it was associated with a good cause—up from 66 percent in a 1993 survey. Numerous other studies have shown that these campaigns increase company profits, which means of course they are here to stay.

Invest with a conscience. You expect former U.S. vice president Al Gore, who in 2007 won an Oscar for *An Inconvenient Truth*, his eye-opening documentary on global warming, to invest his newfound riches with a green conscience—and he does. He has an estimated $35 million with the Capricorn Investment Group (www.Capricornllc.com), which is a socially responsible investment fund for the wealthy. The fund, launched by eBay founder and environmentalist Jeffrey Skoll, invests in hedge funds that invest only in "makers of environmentally friendly products."

Don't have $35 million? Well, socially responsible investing is available to everyone and has evolved over the years to let you choose the goals and missions you most want to support (or avoid) with your investment dollars. The best news is that you do not necessarily give up investment returns when you follow your conscience. Assets held in socially responsible mutual funds are growing six times faster than assets held in all other funds.

The Domini 400 Social Index (a benchmark of socially conscious investments) has risen an average annual 10.9 percent since inception in 1990, versus 10.4 percent for the Standard & Poor's 500 over the same period. The companies in the Domini Index avoid significant involvement in alcohol, firearms, tobacco, gambling, military weapons, and nuclear power. They tend to score well on environmental issues like climate change and alternative energy, on social issues like human rights and workplace diversity, and on governance issues like executive pay and honest accounting. The most trusted mutual fund families in this area include Calvert (www.calvert.com), PAX World (www.paxworld.com), Domini (www.domini.com), Sierra (www.Sierraclubfunds.com), and Parnassus (www.Parnassus.com). But there are many others. To get started go to www.socialinvest.org, www.socialfunds.com, or www.morningstar.com.

Don't fear profits. The newest horizon in philanthropy is probably the advent of widespread for-profit ventures seeking to serve the public good. This is happening at the colossal end of the spectrum with the likes of Google and eBay getting into the for-profit, make-the-world-a-better-place swing of things. At the World Economic Forum in Davos, Switzerland, in 2007 Bill Gates called upon big business to engage in "creative capitalism" and use market forces to address poor-country needs. "We have to find a way to make the aspects of capitalism that serve wealthier people serve poorer people as well," he said at the conference. He challenged business leaders to create products and services for the poor. "Such a system would have a twin mission," he said, "making profits and also improving lives for those who don't fully benefit from market forces."

Lance Armstrong is mining the for-profit world to further his quest to cure cancer. His Lance Armstrong Foundation, which spends $40 million a year on health services and cancer research, recently entered a for-profit venture with Web site designer Demand Media to launch a health and wellness Web site funded by advertising (www.livestrong.com). Armstrong believes that the for-profit site will increase awareness of his foundation and promote its core mission of helping people with cancer. To cite one more example: the Susan G. Komen for the Cure charity, which raises money to fight breast cancer, has more than 170 corporate partners.

Take full advantage of tax breaks. If you are going to give money or other things of tangible value you might as well do it in a tax-efficient manner, which allows you to maximize your contributions. There are entire books on the subject and a sprawling industry of estate planners, advisers, and lawyers to help you get it right. I simply want to make the point that you can be creative with your giving even if you do not have a lot to give. There are strategies and products that let you give right now without giving up the income or control that comes from ownership.

The best known of these tools is the venerable charitable remainder trust, which allows you to donate property or money now and get it out of your estate. You get an income tax deduction and can continue to use the property or collect income from the cash for as long as you live. Any financial planner can set this up. But if you'd like to better understand how this all works, start by visiting www.charitableremaindertrust.com or www.npt.org.

One of the newer wrinkles in giving are donor-advised funds. These act as a family foundation for people without the millions of dollars you need to justify setting up your own foundation. They came into being in the early 1990s and are now the fastest growing corner of philanthropy, with more than 100,000 donor-advised accounts holding $18 billion in assets. The largest of these is the Fidelity Charitable Gift Fund. But virtually all mutual fund companies offer them. In simple terms, you can put money in a donor-advised fund today and take an immediate tax deduction. You keep control over the assets, investing them as you please (within the options offered by the fund company), and can parcel the money out whenever you like. If you donate appreciated assets to the fund there is no capital gains tax. There are some restrictions and minimums. But this is a wonderful tool if you want to establish a family legacy of giving while you are alive.

One other strategy worth mentioning here is giving away real estate—land, an apartment, a time-share—in return for a tax break. The charitable remainder trust mentioned above is one option. But you can also deed the property to a charity at current market value, avoiding tax on the appreciation, and take the full deduction. You can sell the property to a charity at less than full value and take a deduction for the difference. Or, say you own a thousand-acre farm in Montana. You can keep the land, but if you place certain conservation easements on it—dictating, for example, that the ground may never be developed—you can take an immediate deduction for the decreased market value of the land that results from the easements.

Tax laws vary. But these are a few of the ways that you may be able to introduce the giving of money or assets to your life sooner than you may have planned, and in the process reap some tax benefits while establishing a living legacy of generosity that your offspring may one day emulate.

Get Involved

Thanks to hundreds of innovators in giving, you can be a philanthropreneur on almost any level that you choose, pursuing whatever you most want to pursue. Wilma Melville is an animal lover who decided to rescue dogs from the pound and train them to search for survivors of hurricanes, earthquakes, and other disasters. She wound up founding the National Disaster Search Dog Foundation, which now has a $1 million budget and has sent dogs to New York City after September 11, 2001, and New Orleans after Hurricane Katrina. "I'm a different person now," says Melville. "This made me into a driven, knowledgeable, capable, very self-confident person." Sharon Rohrbach is a neonatal nurse who watched too many healthy infants suffer from neglect. She started raising funds to pay for nurses to spend time in the homes of newborns to help new mothers understand how to care for their baby and ultimately founded Nurses For Newborns, which today has an annual budget of $3.6 million and estimates that it saves more than a dozen lives a year. Says Rohrbach: "I feel like God's calling me to do this; to be my authentic self—all day, everyday—and there's a great satisfaction in doing that."

Partying with Purpose

One peculiar example of how inventive folks can be with their giving styles actually has to do with drinking and partying. Scott Delea has found the perfect blend of fun and purpose for his life. If there's anything he enjoys, it's a good time, mixing it up with friends and networking with friends of friends over drinks at happy hour or at a backyard barbecue or beach volleyball game. In that sense Delea, thirty-eight, a sales executive in Hoboken, New Jersey, is like any other charming and outgoing young professional. But back in 2000 he had begun to tire of the party circuit. It's not that he wanted to stop having fun; he just wanted the good times to count for something more than a few laughs and light conversation. "My theory was that my friends and I were pretty darn good at having a good time," Delea recalls. "Maybe we could find a way to use that to give something back to our community."

Delea, who has a political science degree from Syracuse University, began volunteering in various capacities at local charities. He tutored third graders for a while. "That was satisfying, but I wanted to do something bigger," he says. "There was always an excuse. You know: I'm too busy building my career, but someday I'll have enough time and money to make a difference. Just not right now. It got to the point where I was, like, I have to do something."

So Delea began surprising his friends by occasionally inviting interesting and lively members of local charities to join them at the bar and talk a little about their mission. That immediately began to make the conversation more meaningful, and soon he was turning these informal gatherings into bigger, formal affairs. He'd arrange with the bar owner to set aside space and give him a discount on food and drinks, charge a $35 fee to attend, and donate the profit to a specific charity. Not only was he raising money with his closest friends for a worthwhile local cause, but Delea, a bachelor, was also having more fun than ever and meeting new and fascinating people as his circle expanded. "It made for a very satisfying social event because the conversation was more substantive," Delea says. "You could meet people and have conversations that you wouldn't have while grabbing a few beers at the bar."

After the first event, which benefited a local Alzheimer's Association, Delea says he was flabbergasted at the follow-up e-mail from folks he had met at the happy hour. "Topics like Alzheimer's don't come up except when someone is in crisis mode," he says. "But I started getting emails from people with their own personal stories, and I never anticipated that. With my friends I thought it was just something that I cared about. But it made it that much more important to me; it helped to build a better connection between me and others in our group in a way that never would have come up before."

After the 2001 terrorist strikes, Delea decided to take things up a notch. "I didn't have a lot of time and I didn't have a lot of money," he says. "What I did have a lot of were friends. They didn't have a lot of time or money either. But I figured there was a way I could pull that together and make it count by adding it all up." In 2002, he formally launched Party With Purpose (www.partywithpurpose.org), a nonprofit that organizes fund-raising parties for community projects and charities.

Delea has held some thirty events raising $125,000 to benefit a diverse array of local organizations and causes. His efforts have helped set up a computer center at the Boys and Girls Club, pay for tutoring at the Jubilee Center, and clean up the Jersey shore, where he likes to spend his summers. The events that he coordinates now still include happy hours where a local representative will speak briefly about his or her organization's mission and go home with the proceeds (and possibly a few volunteer commitments). But he's also broadened out to things like beach volleyball and 5K races. "Each time they are for different charities, so we get a lot of exposure to different groups in our community and there are great connections that are built as a result of that," says Delea, whose e-mail list (which has grown from 100 to 1,500) is the main tool for getting the word out on events and bringing people together. "I've been to the weddings of people I met through Party With Purpose. We've all made a lot of great and special friends."

Starting and running a local nonprofit has changed almost everything about Delea. He's now on the boards of other local charities. He is often on local radio and in the local media, and he is considered one of Hoboken's go-to guys on the fund-raising circuit. He's met local decision makers in business, government, and the nonprofit world and believes he has a much deeper understanding of his community's issues and needs. "It's just snowballed," he says. "Most of the significant relationships and connections I have today I can somehow weave back to the founding of Party With Purpose, and that first event that we did with Alzheimer's."

Everyone sees something about their world that needs fixing. Not everyone knows quite what to do about it. But people like Scott Delea offer a good example of how easy it can be to become a philanthropreneur; to raise and direct money—and make a difference—by doing something that you care about and enjoy. Becoming a philanthropreneur is all about getting involved and getting things done in ways that produce real results. When you tackle a local issue with your time and energy and money you become more than a passive member of the audience; you become an actor on the big stage. This is no time to be bashful. You're ready, and the best part of becoming a philanthropreneur is that it can be fun and empowering and personally and professionally expansive all at the same time.

The old style of philanthropy has grown rusty; today there are innumerable interesting, hands-on ways to make a difference and just as many reasons for doing so. Your options will continue to multiply as a new crop of retirees looks for ways to stay relevant and make good on promises they made to themselves long ago. There's a spot for everyone in this revolution.

This, then, is the new face of philanthropy—it's philanthropreneurs like Wilma Melville and Sharon Rohrbach and Teddy Gross; like Scott Delea, Lisa Herrick and Amy Kossoff, and the Flannerys. These people don't have a lot of money. But they've got great ideas and a lot of heart. And they are directing millions of dollars to causes that matter.

It used to be that when people reached fifty or sixty, they had their greatest accumulation of skills, knowledge, and abilities but were also running out of steam. But today people reaching that age have not only an enormous concentration of ability but also vitality and lucidity to spare. They are realizing they may not grow old until they are eighty-five or ninety-five and are rising up to ask what might be their next act. What am I going to do? Is this all there is? Or can I find a way to make my heart sing? Can I find a way to give something back—and make the transition from success to significance?

Chapter 8

YOU THOUGHT YOU MADE A DIFFERENCE—BUT NOW YOU REALLY DO

Never confuse motion with action.

—BENJAMIN FRANKLIN

Back in the 1960s, while in high school and college, Marian Kramer was a civil rights activist with the best of them. An African-American woman from the South, she joined picket lines in front of diners that wouldn't serve folks of color. She marched on city hall over segregated schools, dared to sit in the front of the bus, and once spent eight days in a Baton Rouge jail for demonstrating in front of a local shop owned by a white man. Yet today, at age sixty-four, she freely admits that much of her energy back then was ineffectual. Take those eight days in jail. The shop owner (who had been accused of shooting a young man of color) may have lost some revenue. But after a brief hiccup he reopened, and it was business as usual. He never did face charges.

That doesn't mean her time was wasted. The civil rights movement accelerated all kinds of historic social change. School segregation ended. African-Americans registered to vote. Job discrimination and equal housing laws came into being. Still, Kramer says today, "Our problems didn't go away. We still have a hard time being integrated into society as equals when it comes to housing, education, and jobs." Legal rights are one thing, she says. But to a significant extent society has become economically segregated and African-Americans are still at a disadvantage. What good did she really do?

Kramer is rightfully proud of her young activist days, proud that she was part of a movement that means so much to history. But she is even more proud of her modern-day activism; proud that her many years of experience has given her the wealth of skills and perspective to target specific fixable problems and get things done, and enjoy the benefits of seeing the many positive results of her efforts.

Kramer is now the codirector of the National Welfare Rights Union in Detroit, where she fights for the rights of that city's poor. By working her connections and throwing the spotlight on some bad practices, a few years ago she was able to force Detroit Edison to stop shutting off the heat of residents who had fallen behind on their bills during the winter months. She scored an even bigger coup after that—gaining the rights to running water for some 40,000 low-income residents who couldn't afford to pay. The water issue was personal. Kramer had been hearing sporadic reports that residents were living without running water, and when a neighbor asked Kramer if she could run a garden hose from Kramer's house to hers, confiding that her water had been shut off months earlier for failure to pay, Kramer took up the cause. She ended up crafting a Water Affordability Plan that was blessed by the Detroit City Council—and which guaranteed no shutoffs.

"When I was younger I would have just demonstrated," she says. "Change would have been slow to come, if it came at all. Now I know how to appeal to authorities and who to go to, and they know me. They know who I am and what I stand for. I can get a lot done." Kramer says she's also benefited by becoming more open-minded with age. She says she understands competing interests, particularly the profit motive of commercial organizations, and that you can accomplish more when you listen to both sides. "I've grown patient over the years," she says. "Back then I didn't understand that you have to sit down and plan things out. Today we have a well conceived three-pronged approach to all of our efforts—we work through the legislature, the courts, and the streets— with rallies."

Kramer also says she has learned the value of great relationships. In her water battle, for instance, she was able to bring environmentalists into the fray on her side by showing that commercial interests were doing more than shutting off those who could not pay—they were bottling water for resale outside the region and putting a strain on the area's water resources. Most important, she says, "You have to pick a team. I work for the poor. I focus my energy on their behalf. I do not lose sight of that. I believe that by lifting them up the whole of society benefits."

Marian Kramer is doing more measurable good on behalf of others than at any previous time in her life, and she attributes it all to her continuing passion to fight for people who can't fight for themselves—and the maturity and experience that she now brings to her causes.

It's Your Right—No, Duty—to Do Something

Not so long ago I had the great pleasure of attending an event put on by the American Legion called the National High School Constitutional

Oratorical contest. My then sixteen-year-old son Zak took first place in the state of California and moved on to the nationals, where Zak faced off with fifty-two of the most amazing kids I'd ever seen. As they each expounded on the meaning and context of specific parts of the U.S. Constitution these young women and men were poised, clear, and insightful. I beamed with pride as Zak took his place among such exceptional young men and women.

Yet what really caught my attention was the substance of what the kids were saying, not just how well they were saying it. In Zak's case, I had spent many hours listening to him develop his ideas. But I didn't know exactly what angles he would take. In the end, he not only surprised me but prompted me to think hard about what makes a democracy tick. In America, we tend to take this grand document for granted. Before the competition I had never paid much attention to the Constitution and would even confuse it with the Declaration of Independence. But as I sat there listening to these young orators, I began to appreciate the brilliance of the Founding Fathers who wrote it.

I learned that the Constitution is at once fixed and fluid; firm yet malleable. It was devised as a clear set of guiding principles for our legal system, for our government, and, of course, for our exciting new experiment in democracy. But it's not so rigid that it can't be tinkered with and updated and reinterpreted. In fact, Zak's thesis was that the Constitution could be compared to the genetic code for a human organism that has the ability to grow, improve, and develop throughout its life. And he argued that the Founding Fathers purposely designed a partially ambiguous document to allow—even encourage—future citizens to adapt the legal environment to the changing mores of society.

The young men and women I observed in this contest all reflected that this remarkable document illustrates almost unimaginable foresight:

it provided every generation with the ability and the opportunity—even, as many of the kids argued, the duty—to adapt it to the times while still hewing to a set of basic principles. For such a system of laws to work best, though, every voice with a stake must join the debate. In other words, our democracy works best when there are vigorous and ongoing discussions and debates that include all corners of society.

Viewed in this light, it's fine for you to get up on your soapbox and advocate for something you believe; in fact, it's admirable and mutually beneficial, so long as you respect the rights of others to oppose you with equal intensity. Through dissent and discussion open societies thrive. This is clearly true in the realm of politics, where all free nations engage in public discourse over things like defense spending, human rights, school budgets, or zoning restrictions. But it is no less important to debate and advocate for changes in policies that affect the environment, the economy, health care, education, and social inequities—any venue, really, where you feel you have something to contribute. Your voice is important, whether you are leading a march through the capital or tapping out an e-mail to your congressman.

Let me give you a simple example. Not far from my home near San Francisco there is a privately owned hillside visible from the highway for miles. When President Bush sent the troops to invade Iraq in 2001, the owners of this property decided they would plant a white cross in the ground on that hillside every time an American died in battle. The owners didn't put up a billboard or publish an essay or take out an ad to explain what they were doing. They didn't seek out reporters or go on TV. They just did it; they spoke out—their way.

So what's my point? Well, this quiet antiwar protest turned up the volume all over town—in fact, all over California, as this protest landed on news broadcasts around the state. My own father, a proud veteran of

World War II, thought the mock graveyard bordered on treason. Others thought it merely disrespectful or in poor taste, while others were respectful of the point being made. Lots of people had something to say about it. Yet the residents were clearly within their rights; they were simply expressing themselves in a manner that appealed to them. Yes, they made a few folks uncomfortable. But that's the point. This act ultimately stoked conversation among families not just in our neighborhood and throughout the state, but also on a higher level—about the U.S. role in international affairs and how best to fight terrorism. This act raised important questions and in one very small corner of the universe elevated the discussion.

At a very basic level, that's what activism is supposed to do—raise awareness. If you do nothing more, at least you've made a few people squirm and opened some others' eyes.

Of course, the history of democracy is the history of activism. Many of today's current boomer pre-retirees came of age during a particularly outspoken time in modern history—the 1960s and 1970s. I'm sure that some of these individuals had an influence on your own development. I guess I had my own collection of activist heroes from that chaotic era, including Bob Dylan, whose protest poetry dazzled and confused me—and made me think outside the confines of my urban upbringing; Ralph Nader, whose *Unsafe at Any Speed* boldly challenged America's biggest corporation and led to safety advances throughout the global car market; Rachel Carson, whose *Silent Spring* led to a reconsideration of our sensitive relationship with our environment; Bucky Fuller, whose novel ideas about design and geometry transformed our thinking about energy and architecture; Betty Friedan, who with the publication of *The Feminine Mystique* made us all—men as well as women—wake up to the sexism and its many indignities that had prevailed for centuries; Mario Savio, who on the protest-ridden Berkeley campus pushed the limits of what "free speech" really meant (and he was a stutterer!); Alan Watts, who thoughtfully reflected on the distinctions between religion and spirituality from an Eastern as well as Western perspective; Arthur Clarke whose mind-stretching writing established new borders and more elastic boundaries between science and fiction; and, of course, Martin Luther King Jr., whose impassioned sermons called for an end to the horrific and shameful racism that had strangled America since its inception. These kinds of activism, to me, are powerful personal examples of how individuals can make a dent in the world's problems. And while these particular folks are titans, civic engagement—in all its expressions—is available to anyone.

But are you as "engaged" as you would be? You're not eighteen anymore. You can do more than strap yourself to a tree. You have wisdom, experience, and a vast network of connections. You know how to get things done. You have life experiences that have twined together like a formidable oak tree. You have the time and energy and ability to take your concerns to the next level; you can not only shine the spotlight on an issue but actually identify a solution and advocate for change. Don't just be a thorn in someone's side; offer ideas that help make things better. Be an active part of a thriving, self-correcting society. People like Marian Kramer set the bar very high. She's a lifetime activist with a clear vision on a large scale. But everyone can find their spot. You just have to look. And you have to act. As the Nike ad says, "Just Do It."

Finding Purpose in Pictures

A California orthodontist for eighteen years, Phil Borges had already begun to reshape his life by the time terrorists struck in New York City and Washington, D.C., on September 11, 2001. That moment, though, helped him clarify the new personal goals he had been mulling. Borges became convinced that if young people around the world were raised with greater awareness and understanding of foreign cultures they would have a better shot at achieving global harmony when their generation eventually inherits leadership of the world.

Having discovered a passion for travel and photography in middlescence, he decided to do his part by developing a cross-cultural program that helps kids in far-flung lands learn about one another through pictures. The nonprofit Bridges to Understanding (www.bridgesweb.org), which he founded in 2001, so far has connected four thousand kids through a simple exercise. A classroom in, say, Arizona or Florida gets paired with one in, say, Africa, South America, or Asia. Students on both sides explore a theme near to their heart—pollution or alcoholism, or child labor or orphanage life. They are given cameras and trained to tell their stories through photos, which they share via the Internet. "Storytelling is a transformative thing, not just for the people seeing the story but also for the people telling it," Borges says. "They learn something about themselves too."

Borges grew up in the projects in Oakland, California. His father, a truck driver, died of lung cancer when he was just seven. He's always had an entrepreneurial zeal. At nine years old Borges had his own newspaper route. He delivered the papers from a bicycle. Seeking to leverage that effort for bigger profits, he launched an illegal fireworks operation. At day's end he would fill his empty newspaper sacks with cherry bombs, roman candles, and firecrackers from dealers in San Francisco's Chinatown and haul them back to his neighborhood for resale.

Borges was in and out of trouble for much of his youth before going to work on a relative's farm. It was there, while milking cows and hauling hay, that for the first time in his life, he started to feel a sense of genuine accomplishment. "Instead of getting in trouble all the time I was getting praised for my hard work," he recalls. The farm experience turned Borges around. He began to work harder at school and eventually graduated from the University of California—Berkeley, with a degree in physiology and went on to become a dentist. He thrived as an orthodontist but soon came to believe that his dentist's life didn't have enough meaning for him. He was making good money, but what he really longed for was to make a difference. "I had this big practice," he recalls. "But I was going to the same office every day, doing the same work, and it was not stimulating."

That's when he discovered photography, and after just a few classes—at age forty-five—he decided to sell his dental practice and move to Seattle and become a professional photographer. In that role, he traveled widely to places like Afghanistan, Ethiopia, and Bangladesh. He loved meeting the children in such places and would take Polaroid snapshots and give them to the kids, many of whom had never before seen a photo of themselves. Borges was taken by how much all kids have in common, regardless of their culture or wealth.

But in his travels he also became aware of the extent to which much of the world resents the United States. While in Ecuador once, locals pointed out oil spills that occurred during oil drilling by U.S. firms and extensive deforestation as a result of efforts to fight trafficking in cocaine. "Tribes were being forced to move deeper and deeper into the woods to preserve their way of life because of our addictions," Borges says. "I thought if kids were telling this story I'm sure the press would pick up on it, and if I could hook up kids in the developing world with the kids in our world somehow it might help us all understand the impact of our choices."

Studies show just how insular kids in the United States can be—vast numbers of teens and young adults are unable to find the Pacific

Ocean on a map; the majority cannot find countries like India, Iraq, or Afghanistan. "My goal was to build empathy across cultures, build understanding between people of very different backgrounds," Borges says. "Then have them delve into global issues that must be solved across the continents, and turn them into effective global citizens."

In an early project, Borges had equipped gang members in Seattle with cameras and gotten them to produce striking photos of their daily life. The results were acclaimed in the *Seattle Times*, which ran some of the photos. That small success built confidence among the gang members and helped lift several of them into productive life. Borges, nicknamed "Click" by the Seattle youths, felt then that photography produced by kids might be the single best way to tell kids' stories and make them engaging to other kids. "I truly believe this work can make a very important contribution to a more peaceful and just world," Borges says. "It was a bitch to start, let me tell you that. It took a lot of my own money. If I knew how hard this was going to be I might not have ever started it. But now it's taking off and it's something I'm immensely proud of. I can see what I'm accomplishing."

Of late, we've been a star-obsessed society. But ordinary people like Borges can get things done through their quiet effort and resolve. Borges and the exploding number of other social entrepreneurs out there are the leading edge of the revolution that is taking shape all around you. These are the new activists; they are doing research, raising money and awareness, forming organizations, offering solutions, and rolling up their sleeves to work their ideas through to completion. At long last the media is beginning to take note of the Everymanthropy movement—ordinary Janes and Joes doing good deeds, giving, and creating solutions that serve humankind.

Thousands of foundations, nonprofits, think tanks, and media companies now formally recognize, publicize—and fund—this important movement. Civic Ventures (www.civicventures.org) offers grants of up to $100,000 annually for the winners of its Purpose Prize, who must be over sixty and doing something to make the world a better place. The Manhattan Institute (www.manhattan-institute.org) annually awards up to five prizes of $25,000 to social entrepreneurs. The Skoll Foundation (www.skollfoundation.org) offers similar awards and grants. CNN has a regular segment called "Heroes: Ordinary People, Extraordinary Impact."

No less a celebrity-centric publication than *People* has joined the Everymanthropy drumbeat too and may be setting the standard for coverage with its weekly column "Heroes Among Us." The magazine has highlighted the likes of Mark Maksimowicz, and Jeff and Vince Albanese, who founded Green Armada (www.greenarmada.org), a nonprofit whose sole purpose is to clean up the polluted waters near their childhood home in Tampa Bay; and Hugo and Alicia Keim, who have helped put more than five hundred young people with cerebral palsy and other physical impairments through college; and Larry Randall, who after Hurricane Katrina appointed himself coordinator of fund-raising for reconstruction on behalf of his tiny hometown of Pearlington, Mississippi (population: 1,700), which had no mayor or town council to assume leadership.

Not Your Father's/Mother's Activism

These examples do more than demonstrate the escalating level of press coverage devoted to ordinary people involved in a cause; they demonstrate the kind of energy and personal involvement that is taking the world by storm as people of all ages—but particularly those with extra free time in their forties and fifties and sixties—seek to infuse their life with meaning and contribution.

I'll never forget the side-splitting (at least I thought so) finale of *Seinfeld* in 1998, where Jerry, George, Elaine, and Kramer stood by and watched a man being robbed on the sidewalk. In the show, the town had just enacted a "good Samaritan" law, making it illegal to ignore someone in need. Ultimately, the TV gang was convicted of "criminal indifference" and packed off to jail, and one of the cleverest shows in history had run its course. But wait—that kind of thing really does happen. People really do stand by and ignore others despite their obvious need. Consistently failing to lend a hand to someone, anyone, in some small way during your life may not be criminal in the literal sense. But in an age when there is so much need and you have so much ability to help, it seems to me that indifference is at least morally against the law.

"Always do what is right," wrote Mark Twain. "It will gratify half of mankind and astound the other." Sadly, the Jerrys and Georges and Elaines and Kramers of the world remain abundant character types. Boomers, in particular, struggle beneath the weight of this self-centered image—not entirely fairly, as I've argued. But not without some justification either. As political activists, boomers' heyday has probably come and gone, argues social commentator David Gergen, who has served in the White House under Presidents Nixon, Ford, Reagan, and Clinton. "The brightest contribution they made to our politics came in the 1960s and 1970s when they were very young," he says. "But now when they are of mature age and you really expect them to make their massive contributions we're running short. We don't see the big breakthroughs that we need on health care or energy or climate change or a whole suite of issues."

Gergen isn't writing us off as a force for change. But he does believe that a lot of us aren't all that interested in stepping up right now. He hopes that will change as more folks reach sixty and beyond and have the time again to develop into a large movement. What worries him, though, is that we can't afford to wait. "The challenge is now," he says. "The next ten years are going to be very defining in terms of the twenty-first century and whether we can really bring ourselves together and deal with the big issues. So the big question about the baby boom generation is whether it will grow up in time."

That's your challenge and, of course, mine as well—to grow up in time. Younger generations may be well intentioned but they don't have the tools that you have. Some are speaking out with passion, like the pop star Pink whose release "Dear Mr. President" took issue with the United States' stand on everything from war and homelessness to gays and privacy rights. The new millennium band Bright Eyes found its voice in the critically acclaimed "When the President Talks to God" ("Does God suggest an oil hike, when the president talks to God?").

In Britain, the thirty-year-old actor Gael Garcia Bernal is certainly trying to be heard. He's at the vanguard of a British movement trying to get filmmakers to take on larger social issues—inspired, to a degree, by the success of Al Gore's powerful documentary on global warming, *An Inconvenient Truth*. Bernal wants Britain's charities to step to the plate and provide funding and research for more of such films to help spread their important messages. His current project is *Resist*, a film documentary on individual stories of rebellion, which is part of his plan to build an online community of activists interested in a wide range of social issues.

Bernal is building his credentials. He and his *Resist* backers were among filmmakers at the 2008 Britdoc film festival who took part in something called the Good Pitch, a presentation of social action documentaries (and a pitch for more funding) to leading charitable organizations, including the Sundance Institute, Christian Aid, and Amnesty International.

But it's hard to find the protest spirit among young artists on a wide scale. John Mayer says his generation is "Waiting on the World to Change." But who's going to change it? Younger generations? Probably not right away. They are still busy acquiring their basic life skills, and as Gergen points out we can't afford to wait around.

Maybe it's time to shake things up again.

It's not that boomers have a lock on caring, or understanding big issues or perceiving social flashpoints. But we are in a unique position. "There's never been a generation that reached this point in their lives, where they've had enough experience to know what they cared about, what they wanted, and enough time to do something with that experience," says Marc Freedman at Civic Ventures. Freedman believes boomers will measure up in the end and make the transition from success to significance in unforeseen ways. "Everybody is going to tell them what they think success is supposed to be in this stage of life," says Freedman. "But they are going to find their own path." I agree wholeheartedly and I believe that the time for this revolution is now.

Start Your Wave

An interesting thing happens when you decide to get involved. Your good act prompts others to act in a similar fashion, often in measures and ways that you can hardly fathom. Even the smallest of good acts is meaningful. They ripple across space and time, potentially creating a wave of action that greatly multiplies the impact of the original deed. This ripple effect has been given a name: "pay it forward," a notion that has been studied and documented.

While the phrase "pay it forward" is enjoying renewed prominence amid the giving revolution I've been describing, it actually has been around for many years. It surfaced in Robert Heinlein's 1951 novel *Be-*

tween Planets, and today there is even a Heinlein Society that preaches the ethic of good deeds for strangers. The concept of paying it forward, though, goes back even further and is evident in this letter written by Benjamin Franklin in 1784: "I send you herewith a Bill for Ten Louis d'ors [gold coins]. I do not pretend to give such a sum. I only lend it to you. When you shall return to your country with a good character, you cannot fail of getting into some business that will in time enable you to pay all your debts: In that case, when you meet with another honest man in similar distress, you must pay me by lending this sum to him; enjoining him to discharge the debt by a like operation when he shall be able and shall meet with such another opportunity. I hope it may thus go thro' many hands before it meets with a knave that will stop its progress."

Ben Franklin well understood the value of a good deed, how it can spread and gather steam and work magic well beyond the original act. So does the Dalai Lama, who wrote: "This is my simple religion. There is no need for temples; no need for complicated philosophy. Our own brain, our own heart is our temple; the philosophy is kindness."

Catherine Ryan Hyde clearly got it. She was inspired to write her novel *Pay It Forward* after a stranger with a blanket smothered her car's burning engine one night and left before she could thank him. Because of that unsolicited act of kindness she later made a point of stopping to help a stranded motorist, and told the woman she had helped not to thank her but to pay it forward. "I wanted to hold on to the idea that I could send one more person into the world owing a favor to a stranger," she says. "I spent the next twenty years wondering what kind of world it would be if an idea like that caught fire."

To a degree, Hyde's fantasy is becoming a reality. Her novel was turned into a movie in 2000 and starred Kevin Spacey and Helen Hunt as seriously flawed but genuinely decent people who find each other and fall in love—with considerable help from the Hunt character's child, Trevor. Spacey plays a seventh-grade schoolteacher who challenges his students on the first day of class to "think of an idea to change our world—and put it into action." Trevor devises a simple yet brilliant scheme: do something nice for a stranger—but it has to be big; "something they can't do for themselves"—and ask that person to repay the favor by paying it forward to three more strangers. As one character in the movie observed, "the numbers get big real fast."

Turning Calamity into a Lesson

Few people take the mission of changing the world by paying it forward more seriously than Darrell Scott, who also calls this kind of contribution chain-reaction kindness. After his seventeen-year-old daughter, Rachel Scott, was gunned down—the first of fifteen to die—in the Columbine High School massacre in Littleton, Colorado. In April 1999, Scott dedicated himself to speaking out on gun control and the causes of violence in schools. He ultimately founded Rachel's Challenge (www.rachelschallenge.com), an outreach program whose mission is to "motivate, educate and bring positive change to young people." The program aims to stem violence through education and "Friends of Rachel" clubs, which welcome into the mainstream any new or disaffected students—precisely the group most likely to end up lashing out and resorting to violence.

Rachel Scott was an extraordinary young girl; she left behind six diaries and several essays about her belief in God and how she wanted to change the world through small acts of kindness. Shortly before her death, she wrote an essay for school stating, "I have this theory that if one person can go out of their way to show compassion then it will start a chain reaction of the same." Upon her death, her family discovered the diaries and Darrell Scott has made spreading her message his life's work. The program now encompasses the entire Scott family, including Rachel's younger brother Craig, who was nearly shot that day as well. The Rachel's Challenge Foundation employs more than a dozen paid speakers to help spread the word, which is enthusiastically received by some 45,000 students a week. "Every time we speak we end up with six or seven more speaking requests," Scott says.

Scott regularly tours North America, speaking at churches, schools, and youth centers about Rachel's example, and he has coauthored three books about his daughter's life. His program has been employed in more than a thousand schools that hope to deliver a "chain reaction" of hope through school assemblies and workshops. "One of the things we train the kids to do is welcome other students, and we give them a very systematic way of doing that so that it's fun for everybody and no one has to end up being their best friend," Scott says. "We show them how it's done."

For example, at schools that have embraced his program the school supervisor may circulate the picture and bio of any new students to Friends of Rachel clubs made up of students in the school. Each member is then assigned a specific time to find the new student and approach them with a friendly "hello, how are you?" This happens repeatedly all day long. "The first day the new kid has five students walk up to him with a friendly welcome," Scott says. "He's been invited to lunch, and he's been told that another group will invite him to lunch tomorrow. This happens for five days, and at the end of it he's going to have twenty-five people who have introduced themselves to him from five different cliques. At that point the new student has probably found their place." The kids are encouraged to reach out to other students in similar ways—across cliques, ages, and cultures.

Speaking at the White House Conference on School Safety in October 2006, Craig Scott testified to the effectiveness of chain-reaction kindness: "We've seen bullying stopped; incidents where a student came up with hit lists or plans to shoot up his school and told either the speaker or a teacher about their plans, but had a change of heart. My sister is not the only one who believes in kindness, and she's not been the only one in her brave stance against the injustice, willing to stand up for the one who gets put down in school, to sit by the student that sits all alone at lunch, and to talk to or reach out to the one who is consistently ignored or made fun of. She literally has inspired millions of people to continue the chain reaction she started."

The seventeenth-century French philosopher Blaise Pascal observed that "kind words do not cost much; yet they accomplish much." Rachel's Challenge proves it. A simple string of welcoming invitations to a new or lonely student can prevent disaster—and perhaps, change the world.

But like so much of what I've suggested in this book, your good deeds may be as beneficial to you as they are to those around you. When you perform an act of kindness you feel good, and the kind act makes you feel even better. Doctors have found that when you act for the benefit of others the body releases endorphins, which results in a "kindness high" that has distinct physical and emotional benefits. As the Scottish novelist J. M. Barrie wrote: "Those who bring sunshine into the lives of others cannot keep it from themselves."

How the Ripple Spreads

The notion of simple goodness and how it inspires goodness in others crystallized for me one afternoon as I was meeting some of the kids and parents on my son's high school water polo team. Members of the team volunteered several hours each Sunday at a public pool to teach local special-needs children how to swim. I was impressed that a bunch of largely self-indulgent teen athletes would think enough to give their time each week this way, and proud of my son for being part of it. Please bear with me. This story isn't about Zak, or his teammates.

Zak and I were among the first to arrive at the pool to help set up. I was there mostly out of curiosity and had brought some work along; the kids did the heavy lifting. After everything was set, one of the kids tossed a ball in the pool, and Zak and his teammates jumped in; they began passing the ball around and laughing and splashing and having a good time. So it made for a stark contrast when, a few moments later, the children suffering from Down's syndrome began to show up. These kids were ages five to sixteen and had varying degrees of disability. My heart instantly went out to these kindhearted youngsters and their parents. Yet what I mostly thought about was how lucky Maddy and I were to have two healthy, able children and not to have this particular struggle in our lives.

As the kids and their parents gathered, one couple stood out. They were an attractive husband and wife, about my age, and they had with them not one, but two young children with the disability. I felt terrible and began wondering how this had happened. Did they have their first child late in life and get dealt this hand only to try again right away with the same result? How unfortunate they must feel. Well, as it turned out, the older of their two children was a legally blind, awkward boy who had been assigned to Zak. This boy was at first terrified of the water. But Zak cradled him in his arms and gently floated him around the pool until he felt safe. Eventually, the boy was confident enough to laugh and splash and thoroughly enjoy himself in the pool.

At the end of the session, I walked over and introduced myself to the parents of the fragile boy that Zak had been helping. They were pleasant and cheerful and thanked me for Zak's time—and I just couldn't help myself. I had to ask them about the incredible challenge it must be to raise two children with Down's syndrome. I was prepared to shower them with understanding and sympathy as they explained the hardship. But the wife responded first and totally disarmed me. "Not really," she said. "They're wonderful kids, and we're so happy that we adopted them."

Adopted them? Wait a minute. You signed up for this? That never occurred to me. I assumed they had been dealt a tough hand. But these parents had so much compassion and capacity for giving that their only two children were adopted, and both had Down's syndrome. This blew me away. Whatever was going on in my world—writing books, speaking, taking care of business—it was nothing. This couple was living life on a higher plain. They were clearly paying it forward in a most meaningful way. Their example brought out the best in my son, and it prompted me to think harder about my own priorities. I have to believe many other people that they come into contact with are just as impressed, and that their ripple is spreading far and wide. Who knows what greater good will come from this humble couple's generosity? Maybe a few more people will follow their lead and adopt a handicapped child. Maybe some scientist will be moved to reorient her research and discover a Down's syndrome breakthrough. Maybe someone will decide to become more compassionate and just be a better person, and then that person inspires another, and so on.

We live in a remarkable world at a remarkable time in history. Social and economic problems threaten to engulf us. Yet heroes really do come in all stripes and colors, and they are all around, often in silence and beneath the "celebrity" radar. But they are there, making a difference with unheralded grace and love—and improving the world through their example. You don't have to give away millions of dollars or devote every minute of your life to a grand cause. You just have to find your spot and be grateful for the opportunity to help in a way that brings you joy. There is a place and a calling for people who just want to lend a hand and spill the good vibes forward. Aesop captured this idea in his classic fable "The Lion and the Mouse":

A Lion was awakened from sleep by a Mouse running over his face. Rising up angrily, he caught him and was about to kill him, when the Mouse piteously entreated, saying: "If you would only spare my life, I would be sure to repay your kindness." The Lion laughed and let him go. It happened shortly after this that the Lion was caught by some hunters, who bound him by strong ropes to the ground. The Mouse, recognizing his roar, came and gnawed the rope with his teeth, and set him free, exclaiming: "You ridiculed the idea of my ever being able to help you, not expecting to receive from me any repayment of your favor; now you know that it is possible for even a Mouse to confer benefits on a Lion."

This is a tale of the unexpected ways that thoughtfulness and goodness ripple forward—and sometimes even back at you, as was the fortunate case for the lion. It works in real life too, not just in fables. In a study Robert Kurzban, of the University of Pennsylvania, and Daniel Houser, of George Mason University, showed that kindness does in fact breed more kindness. In a series of games that they devised, a stunning 73 percent of players exhibited increased generosity after seeing others perform a generous act.

Fables and games, of course, do not prove that people actually live their lives this way. But they do. In practical terms, the ripple effect may be most evident in the mentoring movement I described earlier. The

number of mentors has grown exponentially over the years, largely because those women and men who have been mentored almost always
report that the experience was positive, and the vast majority go on to
become mentors themselves. This creates a massive snowball effect where
a single person who serves as a mentor to one or two or two hundred
people might end up touching the lives of hundreds or even thousands of
people over several decades. Maybe you convince just one child to stay in
school, and they go on to excel and ultimately achieve great things in science or medicine, or charity or politics. The mentor who influenced that
child could reasonably stake a claim to having saved lives or improved
living conditions, possibly around the globe and possibly for generations
to come.

Think about Phil Borges again. He was in and out of trouble for much
of his childhood and early teens until he benefited from an informal
mentor relationship with relatives on the farm where he went to work.
Borges straightened out, and even though he subordinated his desire to
reach out to other troubled youths for his eighteen years as an orthodontist, the urge to help as he had been helped rebounded in his soul when
he turned forty-five. Since then he has had a positive impact on hundreds
of youths, including the Seattle gang members whom he brought into the
mainstream.

Think about Angela Wilborn and Michelle Mundy again. Wilborn
has never forgotten what it meant to have a mentor for most of her young
life. Now that she is graduating from college, she's looking for ways to
pay Mundy back—not by doing anything specific for her, but by paying it
forward. Wilborn's near-term goal is to found a Communities In Schools
mentoring program wherever she ends up settling. "I know so many
people who dropped out of school because they didn't have the motiva-
tion that my mentor provided for me," she says. "I know that I'd be good

at it, and I might even be able to have a bigger impact than a one-on-one relationship by organizing a whole program where there isn't one."

The ripple effect is also evident in the wonderful story of George Ginsberg, a man known as the "penny philanthropist" because he gave only in small denominations. People heard of him through word of mouth and eventually the media, and warmed to his genuineness and followed his lead by the thousands. This greatly multiplied the impact of his small donations. Ginsberg, who passed away recently at ninety-seven, would use a plain white envelope with "The Penny Philanthropy Fund" printed on the outside to hold his donations before he sent them. He recruited his three grandchildren and five great-grandchildren to help fill it. They would contribute the spare change they found on the sidewalk.

One of Ginsberg's favorite charities was the *New York Times* Neediest Cases Fund. He urged donors to send whatever they could. He might only send $5 but argued that if every reader gave $1 the fund would raise $5 million—a goal that he unofficially set for the annual drive one year. "Don't be ashamed to send it," he wrote in a letter. "Those dollars add up." The fund fell a little short of Ginsberg's goal that year. But his effort rippled across the country and stirred thousands to send in whatever they could—helping the drive to exceed the previous year's total. One of the many contributors who wrote to the *Times*, Judy Goldberg, had this to say: "Even though I am currently unemployed, I was touched by the story of Papa George." She sent $5.

Another powerful example of the ripple effect was beautifully chronicled by writer June Kronholz in the *Wall Street Journal*. She told the story of Edgar Lanpher, who died in 1961 and left three hundred shares of National Lead Company to Brown University with the suggestion that Brown use them to fund a scholarship. Brown sold the shares for just under $32,000. That sum was invested as part of the university's general fund, and over the years the income it generated has helped forty-two students through school, including scientists, doctors, lawyers, and teachers—a group of professions that are very involved in giving back.

Some of them, recalling how their financial aid package helped set them up in life, have since found ways to give back even beyond their professional capacity—like David Katz, who left Brown in 1967 and ultimately became interested in contraception and reproductive biology and moved to the University of California at Davis to head its biomedical engineering program. "I thought this engineering could have more meaning," he told Kronholz. The Davis lab made several important discoveries that led him to an interest in sexually transmitted diseases, where he has made more breakthroughs. He is now a regular contributor to Brown's scholarship fund—but says his real give back is in training technicians at reproductive health clinics throughout Africa.

They say if you take care of the little things the big things will take care of themselves, and I believe that is often the case. But you be the judge. Does a simple act of kindness, a small donation, or moment of friendly advice and direction, really matter in a world with massive and seemingly intractable problems? I say it does matter. It must matter. While I'm electrified by big events and magnanimous actions, I also believe in the power of one; the potential impact of micro-loans and small deeds and their ripple effect. I believe in simple good deeds lifting people, who in turn lift others. I believe in small donations of money or kindness rippling across time and building enough momentum to change life for the better for many people.

Giving and good deeds beget more giving and good deeds. Spreading goodness by example is an effective tool. When you show consideration to others, they notice it and are more inclined to emulate the behavior.

A little guidance to someone in need may set that person on the path to great achievement and enable him or her to help many others.

"If you can't feed a hundred people, then just feed one," said Mother Teresa. This is the essence of the significance revolution I've described: you don't have to be rich, famous, brilliant, or influential; you just have to care, and want to contribute something to make life's final key transition—the one that will take you from success to significance, and to your ultimate fulfillment as a thinking, caring, engaged, and contributing member of the human race. This is your new challenge—to find purpose by giving of yourself and serving others in a way that excites you and bestows benefits on those around you.

Let's agree to do this together, and let's agree to start now.

WITH PURPOSE
ONLINE RESOURCE SUGGESTIONS

Here are some Web sites that were indispensable in researching and writing this book, and which you may find useful in your search for a higher purpose. I've organized the Web sites into broad categories along the same lines as the chapters in the book and list each of them only once. But many of these Web sites apply across several categories. I encourage you to browse.

GENERAL SITES TO EXPLORE TO UNDERSTAND NONPROFITS AND WAYS TO CONTRIBUTE

www.philanthropy.com

www.independentsector.org

www.philanthropyuk.org

www.bridgestar.org

www.guidestar.org

www.nationalservice.org

www.nptimes.com

www.ncna.org

www.taprootfoundation.org

www.pointsoflight.org

www.teachforamerica.org

www.usafreedomcorps.gov

www.charitychannel.com

www.escus.org

www.salvationarmyusa.org

www.unicef.org

www.globalgiving.org

www.worldvision.org

www.secondharvest.org

www.manhattan-institute.org

www.irs.gov/app/pub–78

www.ilibrary.org/cgi-bin/ilib_
     authorize.pl

www.onphilantrophy.com

www.serviceleader.org

HELPFUL SITES FOR BASIC SERVICE OPTIONS

www.redcross.org

www.citizencorps.gov

www.un.org

www.cartercenter.org

www.volunteermatch.org

www.primetimeforschools.com

www.worldvolunteerweb.org

www.national.unitedway.org

www.cityyear.org

www.wish.org

www.compact.org

www.cnvs.org

www.voa.org

www.onlinevolunteering.org

www.boardmatch.org

www.charityguide.org

Helpful sites for crafting your own experience

www.ashoka.org

www.purposeprize.org

www.skollfoundation.org

www.schwabfound.org

www.fuqua.duke.edu/centers/case

www.gsb.stanford.edu/csi

www.se-alliance.org

www.kaufman.org

www.design21sdn.com

www.ppv.org

www.yearup.org

www.volunteer.gov

www.foundationcenter.org

Helpful sites for vacateers

www.dosomething.org

www.projects-abroad.com

www.voluntourism.org

www.voluntours.org

www.worldvolunteerweb.org

www.grouptripadvisor.com

www.goworldtravel.com

www.habitat.org

www.amizade.org

www.globalservicecorps.org

www.peacecorp.gov

www.sci-ivs.org

www.volunteersforprosperity.gov

Helpful sites for mentors

www.bbbs.org

www.hsph.harvard.edu/chc/
  mentoring

www.cisnet.org

www.nationalservice.org

www.menttium.com

www.score.org

www.americaspromise.org

www.savethechildren.org

www.mentoring.org

www.ja.org

www.mentors.ca

www.peermentoring.com

www.peer.ca

www.coachu.com

www.choice-online.com

www.bgca.org

www.seniorcorps.org

www.scouting.org

www.girlscouts.org

www.girlsinc.org

www.nbcdi.org

www.kapow.com

www.ymca.net

www.advancementoring.com

www.mentornet.net

www.mentoryouth.com

Helpful sites for finding meaningful work

www.civicventures.org

www.bls.gov/oco

www.careervoyages.gov

www.mediate.com

www.careerkey.org

www.mynextphase.com

www.self-directed-search.com

www.2young2retire.com

www.caremanager.org

www.coachfederation.org

www.experiencecorps.org

www.cssny.org

www.celebrantusa.com

www.cgcareers.org

www.nonprofitjobs.org

www.idealist.org

www.job-search.aarp.monster.com

www.deepsweep.com

www.execsearches.com

www.independentsector.org/
   members/job_postings.htm

www.opportunitynocs.org

www.nonprofitoyster.com

www.ecojobs.com

www.nonprofitcareer.com

www.dotorgjobs.com

www.interaction.org/jobs

Helpful sites for activists

www.moveon.org

www.AARP.org

www.celfoundation.org

www.rootcause.org

www.greenpeace.org

www.acorn.org

www.one.org

www.americorps.org

www.americaforward.org

www.blueocean.org

www.oceana.org.

www.erasemyfootprint.com

www.bonnieclac.org

www.doctorswithoutborders.org

www.doctodock.com

www.abanet.org/secondseason

www.bridgesweb.org

www.greenarmada.org

www.edf.org

www.wateraid.org

www.poverty.com

www.amnestyusa.org

www.care.org

www.oxfamamerica.org

Helpful sites for philanthropreneurs

www.kiva.org

www.microplace.com

www.microlending.ca

www.givingcircles.org

www.givingforum.org

www.boldergiving.org

www.diningforwomen.org

www.p2pnobank.com

www.kwd100projectsforpeace.org

www.charitywatch.org

www.charitynavigator.org

www.socialinvest.org

www.socialfunds.com

www.Capricornllc.com

www.calvert.com

www.paxworld.com

www.domini.com

www.Sierraclubfunds.com

www.Parnassus.com

www.Zopa.com

www.Prosper.com

www.partywithpurpose.org

www.morningstar.com

www.charity.org

www.usnews.com/usnews/biztech/
charities/char_home.htm

www.justgive.org

www.givespot.com

www.charitywire.com

www.charitablegift.org

www.philanthropyroundtable.org

www.charity-charities.org

www.schwabcharitable.org

www.nptrust.org

www.vanguardcharitable.org

www.ncfp.org

www.morethanmoney.org

www.givedaily.org

www.donationrewards.com

www.programforgiving.org

www.givingboard.org

www.networkforgood.org

Helpful sites for continued personal growth

www.webspace.ship.edu/cgboer/
   maslow

www.learningtoforgive.com/index

www.gu.org

www.hollandcodes.com

www.payitforwardfoundation.org

www.strengthsfinder.com

www.caringinstitute.org

www.rachelschallenge.com

www.actsofkindness.org

www.chainreaction.be

www.personalgrowthplanet.com

www.selfgrowth.com

www.Esalen.org

INDEX

G one are the days when retirement meant a few years of
golf and tropical holidays
before a slow slip into old age. Today's
retirees have the gift of decades of physical
and mental health ahead of them—and the
responsibility of deciding how to spend
that gift. Should you enjoy those years qui-
etly, savoring your accomplishments? Or
should you instead focus your attentions
on creating a different kind of legacy, one
of significance, not just success?

With Purpose answers those questions by
suggesting a new life model—instead of
"learn, earn, retire," why not instead embrace
a practice of "learn, earn, return"? Why not
devote some of the best years of your life,
years blessed with the wisdom of decades of
experience, to giving back to the community? *With Purpose* will show you that taking
action and improving the world around
you—in big or small ways—is achievable,
no matter whether you have only your time
or thousands of dollars to give.

Both practical and inspiring, *With Purpose* is
filled with stories of people who have chosen
to make a difference and with action plans
for how you can make a difference, too.